Henry Edward Manning

England and Christendom

Henry Edward Manning

England and Christendom

ISBN/EAN: 9783337260644

Printed in Europe, USA, Canada, Australia, Japan

Cover: Foto ©ninafisch / pixelio.de

More available books at **www.hansebooks.com**

ENGLAND AND CHRISTENDOM.

BY

HENRY EDWARD,

ARCHBISHOP OF WESTMINSTER.

LONDON:
LONGMANS, GREEN, AND CO.
1867.

CONTENTS.

	PAGE
INTRODUCTION	vii
THE CROWN IN COUNCIL ON THE ESSAYS AND REVIEWS	3
THE CONVOCATION AND THE CROWN IN COUNCIL	33
THE WORKINGS OF THE HOLY SPIRIT IN THE CHURCH OF ENGLAND	81
THE REUNION OF CHRISTENDOM	137
APPENDIX	227

ENGLAND AND CHRISTENDOM.

INTRODUCTION.

THE TITLE 'England and Christendom' expresses in two words all that is dearest to us upon earth. In the natural order, England has for all its sons a sweetness and a fascination both in its history and in its presence, which surpasses all other affections.

Cicero says: ' Omnes omnium caritates patria una complectitur.' The intense and pathetic love of the Irish for Ireland will ever plead for the love of an Englishman for England. Too true it is that an Irishman loves Ireland not only with the natural love of a son to a mother. The sorrows, wrongs, afflictions, the patience, dignity, and martyrdom of Ireland for the Faith, all mingle with his patriotism to purify and elevate it to the supernatural order. With Englishmen, also, it is the love of sons, which cannot be turned away even by persecution and wrong:—

> A mother is a mother still,
> The holiest thing alive.

And such is my feeling towards England: but I trust without a shade of insular self-exaltation or critical depreciation of other countries. All have their good and their evil. We have faults enough. But the love of my own mother does not nurture or sustain itself upon dislike or detraction of the mothers of other men. It is an original, spontaneous, self-sustaining affection of our nature; and it is perfect in proportion as it is pure of all inferior and foreign motives. A mother would be little consoled by a love which is kept alive by aversion from others. The love of country is a part of charity. It is natural affection and natural benevolence trained in the home of our kindred, and extended as we grow up into maturity to the race and society of which we are members. As such, England of the past, while yet in the unity of the Faith, had a beauty and a sweetness which command a singular love. And England in its separation and isolation, with all its spiritual sins and social disorders, is still an object of a powerful constraining affection, the highest and deepest of the natural order, rendered personal and intense by the intermingling of the love of friends and of kinsmen. In reading over, therefore, the following pages for republication, I have carefully watched for any expression which is wounding or unkind. I never consciously wrote one such word. I have not, to my knowledge, left in this volume one such word to stand. I cannot soften facts, nor take the edge off the truth. Facts and truths are our masters, not our servants. In the first and second Letters a great and unchanged affection for the friend I was writing to, made every unkind feeling impossible. The third Letter will speak for itself. I have never heard it found fault with for want of kindness. Indeed, I have seen it contrasted with the fourth to condemn this last as changed in tone. But such critics forget that the last was not addressed to the same person; and, I may add, that in the interval, I had learned what before I had never allowed myself to think possible. This laid upon me higher duties, into which personal feelings have no right to intrude. Still, charity must not be wounded even in giving judgment; and I am unconscious of having wounded it.

But it will be said, 'Of what worth are expressions of personal kindness when you write hard things of that which I ought to love better than myself?' I would answer, Charity is always worthy of charity in return; and he who is charitably admonished betrays the absence of charity if he does not respond charitably; much more if he shows the coldness of offence or the estrangement of an averted kindness. 'I am angry with reason', was the excuse of a Prophet. But it was not a good one; and it was not accepted.

Nevertheless, I am afraid that much in the following pages will give pain to those whom I would not willingly wound by a word. But truth ought to be dearer to us than friends, and Christendom than England. If the love of the natural order prevail over the love of the supernatural, we shall sin against God. I acknowledge that the unity and divine certainty of the Faith, the peace and order of the universal Church, are dearer to me than England with all its homely sweetness and beauty, and all its lingering and broken lights of Christianity. Life is fast fleeting. If in the little that remains, by anything I could do or suffer, I could help, in the least and lightest measure, to bring England and Christendom once more a shade nearer in the unity of truth and peace, I should accept it as a grace and a consolation from the love of our Divine Lord. It is indeed true, that the highest authority on earth has been compelled to check all hope of reunion between the Anglican and the Catholic Church, founded on mutual concessions, reciprocal interpretations, much more, on compromises, or concordats. To do so would be to bind up a broken limb without setting it, or to tie a graft against the bark of a tree, instead of inserting it into the symmetry and the sap of its vital structure. For the sake of truth, and for the salvation of souls, and in obedience to the divine authority of the Church, and in conformity to the light of the Spirit of Truth, who guides its judgments, we are compelled to decline all overtures as of contracting parties. The commission of the Church is to 'make disciples of all nations.' A disciple recognises and submits to his teacher. The disciple who argues with his teacher is a judge, not a learner. To treat with the Church of God is to deny its Divine authority: but its Divine authority is a primary article of Revelation, and runs through every other article of Faith. If a man believe the whole Faith and yet offend in this one point, he is incapable of admission to the unity of the Church. He who denies one article of Faith, even the least and remotest from the higher, denies the Divine authority of all articles of Faith. Even if he do this through invincible ignorance, he is in material heresy. If he do it, *sciens et pru-*

dens, knowingly and deliberately, he is in formal heresy. For instance, to deny the eternity of punishment is also to deny, as an article of Faith, the eternity of bliss; for both rest on the same Revelation and are delivered by the same Divine voice. Such a denial rejects the Divine authority, by refusing to believe its word; and he who does so in this has no warrant to rest on that Divine authority even in other articles of Faith, which he may still believe. He cannot submit to it in one thing and resist it in another, without resisting it as such. If he will not believe the eternity of punishment, even upon Divine authority, it is evident that it is upon his own opinion of intrinsic credibility, and not upon Divine authority, that he believes the eternity of bliss. If this be true in respect to the remoter articles of Faith, how much more is it true in the highest: most of all in the Divine authority of the Church as our Teacher, which runs through every article, as the Divine security and Divine certainty of the whole Revelation? It is not, therefore, we who close the door. It is 'He that hath the key of David: He that openeth and no man shutteth; shutteth and no man openeth.'* It is like the power of binding and loosing

---

* Apoc., iii. 7.

in which we have no discretion beyond the law we administer. The *Clavis scientiæ* is as peremptory in its Divine procedure as the *Clavis jurisdictionis*. If we were illicitly to open on earth, He would shut in Heaven. We should only betray the truth, and deceive souls to their eternal loss.

This then must be, and I am confident to all calm men will be, the justification of the firm and precise language in which the Catholic Church refuses all overtures and negociations which exclude as their first article the recognition of its perpetual Divine authority; or, in more explicit terms, the exclusive infallibility of the Catholic and Roman Church and its correlative duty, namely, the obligation of every soul to submit to it in all matters of Faith as a condition necessary to eternal life.

The four Letters contained in this volume were written at different times; but they treat from first to last of one subject, and state, in outline at least, the relations of England and Christendom. The first was written at the request of a friend, who foresaw that the consequences of the Judgment of the Crown on the 'Essays and Reviews' must be far-reaching, though he did not foresee all that the last two years have so rapidly brought to a head. The second was written when the Anglican Convocation, in doing its utmost against that Judgment, all the more visibly revealed its incompetence either to resist the Civil Power in matters of Religion, or to define its own doctrines. The third was drawn from me by the frequent mention of my name by Dr. Pusey in a printed pamphlet. He has since stated that his 'Eirenicon' was written at the instance of the late Mr. Keble, in answer to that Letter; in which I affirmed that the Anglican Church appeals from the living voice of the Church at this hour, thereby denying its Divine authority. Dr. Pusey in the 'Eirenicon' does so, thereby confirming the argument of my Letter. The fourth Letter was required of me by public duty, and will explain itself.

I will now add some further reflections on the general subject of England and Christendom.

The first thirty years of the nineteenth century were marked by political and military events which fix an epoch in history. The ascendency of the first French Revolution, the first Empire and its wars, the persecutions and restoration of the Sovereign Pontiff, the reconstruction of Europe on the basis of 1815, which has lasted for a generation of men—all these are events of a vast and exceptional greatness. And yet, it must be affirmed, that the last thirty years, from 1830 to the present time, constitute a still more momentous and exceptional period. The European reaction towards the Catholic Church ; the ascendency of the principles of 1789 in France, and, by sympathy, in all Europe; the emancipation of Catholics; the dis-establishing, short of impoverishing, of the Anglican system; the reorganisation of the Catholic Church and its wonderful expansion in England ; the conflict of the Italian Revolution with the Holy See ; the profound intellectual change which has penetrated throughout England, dissolving traditional Protestantism by Rationalism on one hand, and by an approximation to a higher belief on the other— all these things, to pass over political and continental events, make the last thirty years the most prolific of change, and the most powerful in their action on the future, of any period since the convulsions of the so-called Reformation. I cannot, therefore, reprint these pages without a few more words. The last three years, since the first of the Letters were published, are crowded with events. The Religious changes in England are moving with an accumulating ratio of speed. And this, too, not only in their downward, but also in its upward tendencies. The only system which is stationary is the Catholic Church. All around it seems to be in rapid and eccentric motion, like the meteors of last November.

In the time of Bossuet, the variations of Protestantism were felt to be proofs of its human origin. Now, its perpetual changes, and spontaneous generation of new diversities, are affirmed to be signs of life. About twenty years ago, a thoughtful and respectable book was published under the title of 'A Retrospect of the Religious Life of England.' It is not deep nor exact, but it is in the main a correct outline of what has passed in England since the Reformation. The author states truly enough that, in the Religious life of England there are three principles: Tradition, embodied in the Hierarchical Anglicanism; Scripture in the Puritan school both within and without the Established Church; and Free Inquiry, which was vindicated chiefly by the Latitudinarian school of the Revolution of 1688. Now it is certain, that all these three co-existed in the Anglican Reformation from the beginning. The Traditional school was in the ascendent from Elizabeth to William III., that is, from 1560 to 1688. The Scriptural, which had been growing up under the ascendency of the Traditional period, gained the supremacy when the Hierarchical and Traditional spirit were cast out with the Non jurors in 1688. But even in the moment when the Scriptural school was dominant, the Latitudinarian or Rationalistic method was growing up to overthrow it, as it had before overthrown the school of Tradition. The Scriptural school may be said to have existed from 1688 to 1830. From that date the Latitudinarian or Rationalistic school, which had long been gaining consistency and strength, has evidently arisen in the order of legitimate procession or production, and gives every sign and promise of a complete final ascendency. The writer above quoted imagines that these three schools represent the three Patriarchal Sees—Rome, and its traditional stiffness; Antioch and its Scriptural exegesis; Alexandria, and its philosophy. If so, I am afraid that, so far as England is concerned, these three have long ceased to balance and to compensate for each other's action. The English Antioch has devoured Rome, and Alexandria is devouring both. *

These three theological *loci*, Tradition, Scripture, and Reason, are to be found nowhere in full application and in full harmony except under the supreme guidance of the living mind and living voice of the Catholic Church. They co-exist in it at this hour, as every student of S. Thomas knows, in every article of his *Summa*. They co-existed in England before the schism of the sixteenth century. But when the

* Tayler's Retrospect of the Religious Life of England, pp. 469-472.

Divine bond of unity and authority was broken, they parted asunder into three conflicting tendencies of thought, the sources of perpetual controversy. And these three methods of Religious thought mark the three progressive phases of decline from Faith to unbelief, through which the intelligence of England is passing.

In this the Greek Church presents a contrast. It has been for more than a thousand years in collision with the Catholic Church; and yet it has retained, with a precise and pertinacious fidelity, all its doctrinal traditions: excepting only those in which it is in collision with the Holy See. Not so the Anglican. For three hundred years it has been in collision with the Catholic Church; and every century, every generation, almost every decade of years, has marked some greater departure from its original doctrines. The chief cause of this is obviously in the fact, that the Greek Church believes its tradition to be Divine and, therefore, immutable, in virtue of our Lord's promises; namely, the perpetual assistance of the Spirit of Truth, and His own Presence all days, even to the consummation of the world. The human Reason is thereby subjected to the law of Faith as to a Divine authority. In the Anglican Church, even from the outset, the Reason revolted, and subjected both

Scripture and Tradition to its own criticism. The leprosy came up upon the wall, and ate into the stones and timbers of the house.

In its three hundred years of conflict with the Catholic Church, England has had two chief and decisive collisions: and all signs portend that it may yet have a third. The first great collision was from 1538 to 1562; that is, from Edward VI. to Elizabeth. The Civil Power was victorious, and the Hierarchical Anglicanism of Hooker, Bilson, Andrewes, and afterwards of Laud and Hammond, were the ultimate result. This was the first declension of England from the Catholic faith and unity. Much was retained in name and in semblance. A belief in a Hierarchy, priesthood, sacraments, survived in the minds of men, and ran on as a living tradition, interpreting the mutilated Prayer-book, with its discordant Rubrics and the vagueness of the Thirty-nine Articles. The unwritten tradition and floating Christianity of a people once Catholic, survived for generations, as vital warmth lingers after a mortal wound, even after death itself. It would not be easily believed at this day that the Pope had twice offered a cardinal's hat to the late Archbishop of Canterbury. Yet, absurd and impossible as the tale was, it was believed in Archbishop Laud's time, to his peril and cost. The two Churches, so to speak, must have been inconceivably nearer to each other when, as Heylin tells us, the churches retained the greatest part of their ancient furniture, and when the Province of Canterbury passed such a body of Canons as those of 1603. A great part of the aristocracy and richer commonalty were still Catholics. Only fifty years before, the Catholic worship was universal in England: and England was in communion with Christendom. Let us suppose that England had been Catholic in our boyhood—we should hardly have lost the instincts of our homes and education. Nevertheless, the recoil was violent and sudden. The Parliamentary or Puritan party, reinforced and governed by the fanatical spirit of Scotland, carried all before it. The Anglican Church underwent a second reformation, which swept away the lingering traditions of Ritual and Ceremonial, and extinguished the popular usages and customs of piety which had been, till then, sustained by them. After the twelve years of the Commonwealth the Anglican Church was raised again, like a ship which has been for a time under water. All but its lines were washed away. The Church under Charles II. was as unlike Heylin's description of the Church under Charles I. as that was from the Church in the first years of Elizabeth. During the whole of the seventeenth century the hierarchical and ceremonial character of the Church, with the doctrines and habits of mind which go with it, was steadily on the decline. The relics of the old Religion were dying out, and the sympathy of the Anglican system with its own past, was becoming less and less.

Then came the second great collision with the Catholic Church under James II. and William III. Throughout the disastrous reign of James II. the Holy See was instant and urgent in counselling the king to refrain from violating the laws and instincts of the country by stretches of prerogative and of absolute power. The Letters of Cybo, the Cardinal-Secretary, to persons at the Court of St. James's, prove that the Holy See was in no way partaker of the acts of the king. The end might have been predicted. All that was bad, and much that was good, in the public opinion and feeling of the country rose against a ruler in whom despotism and Catholicism were supposed to be impersonated, and Catholicism to be the counsellor and instigator of despotism. The alleged Spanish policy of Mary and French policy of James, have indelibly impressed the people of England with the false belief that the Catholic Church is the author of persecution and absolutism. The Revolution of 1688 was made upon this theory, and a century of penal laws in England and Ireland, —as cruel and degrading as the world has ever seen—has been the result. So much for the political and external collision. During the whole reign of James, a bitter controversy was waged against the Catholic doctrines. Gibson's 'Tracts,' in three folio volumes, are the *primitiæ* of the Protestant labour. Anything more unfair, irrelevant, arbitrary, and inconclusive cannot be conceived. But the Catholics were few and ill-provided. The Anglicans had the whole world with them, and commanded every material advantage. All they said or wrote was listened to, read, and believed. What the Catholics said or wrote nobody would hear, read, or believe. It was then as it was fifteen years ago, when the Papal aggression madness drove Englishmen out of their common sense. What lately was a paroxysm then was chronic.

The result of the collision of 1688 was a recoil— political, social and intellectual—from the Catholic Faith and Church, which carried the public opinion and public policy of England into latitudinarian Protestantism. As compared with 1588, the Church of England and the people of England had descended by many degrees from the hierarchical Protestantism of Elizabeth, and had departed by a far wider interval from the Catholic Church. It is certain, as I have said, that the school of Tradition was finally overthrown by the school of Private Judgment. It lingered on in a few writers, and for the most part it went out with the Non-jurors, and with them it died.

A writer in the 'Essays and Reviews' has justly fixed this date of 1688 as the beginning of a new period. In the Essay on the 'Tendencies of Religious Thought in England,' the author, speaking of the agencies which modified Religious thought in the eighteenth century, says: ' Of these agencies there are three: 1, the formation and gradual growth of . . . Toleration ; 2, the great rekindling of the Religious consciousness of the people, which became . . Methodism and . . the Evangelical movement ; 3, the growth and gradual diffusion through all Religious thinking of the supremacy of Reason. This, which is rather a principle, or a mode of thinking, than a doctrine, may be properly enough called *Rationalism*.' 'Rationalism was not an anti-Christian sect outside the Church, making war against Religion. It was a habit of thought ruling all minds. The Churchman differed from the Socinian, and the Socinian from the Deist as to the number of articles in his creed ; but all alike consented to test their belief by the rational evidence for it.' . . ' The title of Locke's treatise, " The Reasonableness of Christianity," may be said to have been the solitary thesis of Christian theology in England for great part of a century.' He then adds, 'We might, for the sake of a convenient landmark, say that it (this system) came in with the Revolution of 1688, and began to decline in vigour with the reaction against the Reform movement about 1830. Locke's "Reasonableness of Christianity" would then open, and the commencement of the "Tracts for the Times" mark the fall of Rationalism.'* The writer then goes on to say, 'This whole rationalist age must be again subdivided into two periods... These periods are of nearly equal length, and we may conveniently take the middle of the century (1750) as one terminus of division.... In the first period the main endeavour was to show that there was nothing in the contents of the Revelation which was not agreeable to Reason. In the second, from 1750 onwards, the controversy was narrowed to what are usually called the "Evidences."'† This account seems to me to be substantially correct; and it is full of admonitions and of conclusions. The writer adds very truly, 'When an age is found occupied in proving its creed, this is but a token that the age has ceased to have a proper

---

* Essays and Reviews, pp. 256–259.   † *Ibid.*, p. 260.

belief in it.'* The English people had a belief in their creed till the rebellion of the sixteenth century against the divine voice of the Church, robbed them of the rule and certainty of Faith. Through the seventeenth century they believed still so much of Christian doctrine as survived the great disorders of Edward and Elizabeth, and they believed it on a supposed tradition of authority. The collision of 1688 swept away this semblance of Tradition. In the presence of the Catholic Church there can be no alternative but submission or Rationalism. The Anglicans of 1688, in refusing submission to the divine Tradition, swept away Tradition altogether from their own system, and accepted in full the only alternative, namely, Christianity tested by Reason. Such, under all its phases and disguises, has Anglicanism always been. But it did not so declare itself until the collision of 1688 compelled it. The controversy with the Catholic Church then ceased. Penal laws were better than arguments. But no sooner was controversy silent *ad extra* than it sprang up *ab intra*. Arianism, Socinianism, Scepticism, Deism, and Atheism had formed themselves in the Anglican system; and from thenceforward for a century Anglican and Protestant writers were labouring to keep down the

* Essays and Reviews, p. 264.

poisons they had sown with both hands. 'Stillingfleet, who died . . . in the last year (1699) of the seventeenth century, marks the transition from the old to the new argument. In the six folios of Stillingfleet's works may be found the latest echoes of the Romanist controversy, and the first declaration of war against Locke.'* The next fifty years were spent in a controversy against those who denied the existence of God, of all Revelation, all supernatural truth; or, admitting Revelation, who denied the Godhead of our Lord, His coequality with the Father, the doctrine of the Holy Trinity, the inspiration of Scripture, the authenticity of the Sacred Books. The last fifty years of the seventeenth century were spent in controversy with the embers of these heresies, and with those who denied the Sacrifice and Redemption of Calvary, the operations of the Holy Spirit, the necessity of Grace—in a word, the whole interior work of God in the soul. Such was the century which sprang from the second great conflict of England with the Catholic Church ; and, though it lies beyond my present purpose, I cannot refrain from quoting from the same author—certainly an impartial witness for my purpose—a picture of the morals of the same

* Essays and Reviews, p. 266.

hundred years: 'Were the "corruption of manners" merely the complaint of one party or set of writers, a cry of factious Puritanism, or of men who were at war with society, like the Non-juring clergy, or of a few isolated individuals of superior piety, like William Law, it would be easily explicable. The "world" at all times, and in all countries, can be described with truth as "lying in wickedness," and the rebuke of the preacher of righteousness is needed in every age. There cannot be a darker picture than that drawn by the Fathers of the third century of the morals of the Christians in their time (see passages in Jewel's "Apology"). The rigorous moralist, heathen or Christian, can always point in sharp contrast the vices and the belief of mankind. But, after making every allowance for the exaggeration of religious rhetoric, and the querulousness of defeated parties, there seems to remain *some* real evidence for ascribing to that age a more than usual moral licence and contempt of external restraints. It is the concurrent testimony of men of all parties, it is the general strain of the most sensible and worldly divines, prosperous men who lived with this very world they censure, men whose code of morals was not large, nor their standard exacting. To attempt the inquiry what specific evils were meant by the general expressions " decay of religion " and " corruption of manners,"—the stereotype phrases of the time—is not within the limits of this paper. No historian, as far as I am aware, has attempted this examination: all have been content to render, without valuation, the charges as they find them. I shall content myself with producing here one statement of contemporary opinion on this point; for which purpose I select a layman, David Hartley (" Observations on Man," vol. ii. p. 441) :—

" There are six things which seem more especially to threaten ruin and dissolution to the present States of Christendom.

" 1. The great growth of Atheism and Infidelity, particularly amongst the governing parts of those States.

" 2. The open and abandoned lewdness to which great numbers of both sexes, especially in the high ranks of life, have given themselves up.

" 3. The sordid and avowed self-interest, which is almost the sole motive of action in those who are concerned in the administration of public affairs.

" 4. The licentiousness and contempt of every kind of authority, divine or human, which is so notorious in inferiors of all ranks.

" 5. The great worldly-mindedness of the clergy,

and their gross neglect in the discharge of their proper functions.

"6th. The carelessness and infatuation of parents and magistrates with respect to the education of youth, and the consequent early corruption of the rising generation.

"All these things have evident mutual connexions and influences; and, as they all seem likely to increase from time to time, so it can scarce be doubted by a considerate man, whether he be a religious one or no, but that they will, sooner or later, bring on a total dissolution of all the forms of government that subsist at present in the Christian countries of Europe."' *

Thus much I have quoted in proof of what has been affirmed—namely, that the second collision of England with the Catholic Church in 1688, produced a far more violent recoil, and a far wider departure from Faith, than the first in 1562; and I do so for the purpose of showing that the tendencies of Faith and Unbelief at this time give reason to fear that another collision may come hereafter, of which the result would be a still greater recoil from Faith and a wider departure from Christianity. This may sound strange and irreconcilable with the hopes

* Essays and Reviews, pp. 321–323.

which Catholics entertain, and with the prayers they daily offer at the Throne of Grace, for the conversion of England. But they who hope most may have their eyes open to danger; and for the very hope's sake may be the more explicit in pointing out where dangers may arise, and how they may be averted.

Now, it is certain, as has been shown, that from 1550 to 1750, there was a perpetual decline of Faith in England. The Christian doctrines which survived the Reformation faded, one by one, out of the mind of the multitude. They had not only been mutilated by change, but disbanded by the rejection of the divine principle of Faith. By action and re-action of Tradition and Scripture, Anglicanism and Puritanism, Secularity and Fanaticism, laxity and rigour, hot fits and cold, like the last stages of fever, the religious life of Englishmen was dying out. Unbelief and immorality had their climax about the middle of the last century.

But it is also certain, that from that time until now there has been a gradual and steady re-ascending towards Christian Faith. Men returned to the belief that Christianity is reasonable; then, that it is true; then, that the Holy Trinity and the Incarnation are Christian doctrines; then, to belief in the operations of Grace, of the Redemption by atonement and sacrifice; then, of the institution, grace, and obligation of Sacraments. This brings us to about the year 1830, the close of the Rationalistic period, according to the author quoted—the opening of it, in its last and worst form, as I fear we must rather believe. But of this hereafter.

It is certain that the great continental events of the thirty years from 1800 to 1830 had stimulated the political movements in England and Ireland, and brought about the emancipation of Catholics; and that this had broken down the barriers of exclusion which kept Catholics out of contact with the intelligence of England, and had destroyed the artificial and delusive foundation on which Anglicanism believed itself immoveably to rest. The emancipation of Catholics brought the Catholic Church, for a third time, face to face with the dominant Anglicanism of England and Ireland. Immediately two counter-tendencies were thrown out in opposition, the hierarchical Anglicanism of the seventeenth century and the rationalistic Protestantism of the eighteenth. The former showed itself in the 'Tracts for the Times,' and in the wide Anglican movement throughout the country, which had for its object to find a basis for the Church of England tenable alike against Romanism and Protestantism, and dependent neither upon communion with Christendom nor upon Civil Power. The latter took the form of Exeter Hall—partly Calvinistic, partly Lutheran, with a large infusion of the Apocalypse. The sincere and excellent men who represented this school, entirely believed themselves to be the direct opponents of Rationalism. They honestly feared and abhorred it as an impiety towards the Word of God; little knowing, from want of analysing their own rule of Faith, that it was also essentially rationalistic. What has been the course and fate of these good men I know not. They seem to have melted away on every side. They do not appear to have replenished their number, nor to have held their ground, nor to have any succession. The so-called Evangelical school appears to have been a form of personal piety which could not perpetuate itself. It contained a multitude of the highest and noblest English natures, of whom invincible ignorance of the Catholic Church may be predicated with full confidence. The 'Bible' and the 'Following of Christ' were their text-books; and their lives were singularly conformed to the Catholic type of humility, patience, piety, submission, self-denial, and communion with God. Baptism had made them children of God and of His

Church; conscious desire to believe all He had revealed, to obey all He had commanded, and to suffer all He might require, and unconsciousness of a thought in wilful deviation from His Truth, or of an intention at variance with His Will sustained them in their innocence, or raised them again by repentance to union with their Father in Heaven. But this race was not fit for the rough days which were coming upon us.

In the last thirty years a vigorous and masculine movement took possession of the intellects and the wills of great numbers in the Anglican Church. New truths arose upon them—the Succession of the Apostles, the Divine foundation, order, and perpetuity of the Church, the unwritten Word of God, the authority of universal Tradition, the character of Priesthood, the power of Sacrifice and of the Keys, the Church Militant, Purifying and Triumphant, the law of unity, the claim of authority,—all these began, one by one, to dawn upon the clergy and the laity of the Church of England. They then moved onwards and upwards towards a higher system, and nearer towards the Catholic Church, without so much as a desire or thought of entering it. In others these truths suddenly, and with an intensity of light, culminated in the indissoluble Unity and perpetual Infallibility of the one only Church, or rather in the presence and office of the Holy Ghost—the author of all Unity and Truth. One by one, such minds submitted to the only Church from which their forefathers had rent them, as Adam separated us all from God. And yet, it was not the preaching, nor direct action of the Catholic Church, which produced these convictions. They never set foot in a Catholic church, or saw the face of a Catholic priest. It seemed to come upon them in their thoughts and prayers,—like as the ear anticipates the next chords in a melody from the notes which already fill the sense. Be it as it may, they found their way, one by one, into the noontide— up into the Guest Chamber, where the lights of Pentecost are still luminous and changeless. What was before an act of Reason, became a habit of Faith; what was an argument of the intellect, became a consciousness of the soul. When men asked them, 'How was it?' all they could say was, 'Whereas I was blind, now I see.' And when friends reproached them and ascribed their Faith to unknown agencies of evil, all they could say was, 'Herein is a wonderful thing, that you know not from whence He is, and He hath opened my eyes.'* The consciousness that what they believed is the Faith of all the world, supported them

* St. John, ix. 25-30.

in their isolation. The unity and universality of Christendom were the countersign and the counterpart of their lonely faith.

In this way, from 1830 to 1850, the Catholic Church in England spread and penetrated. In that year came an event which marks an epoch. One hundred years after the turn in the tide from Unbelief to Faith, the Church in England was restored to its perfect organization. From that date a new period of power and expansion opened. The Church had for twenty years acted here and there by its individual members upon individual minds. From that time it began to act as a body by its corporate presence and influence upon public opinion and upon every class of the English people. It is not my intention here to draw this out further than for the purpose of noting, that never since Edward VI. has the Catholic Church entered so visibly and audibly into the eyes and ears of the English people as at this moment. By its hierarchy and priesthood, by its convents and colleges, by its churches and schools, by its unnumbered institutes and activities of charity and mercy, by its divine worship and perpetual round of feasts and solemnities, by preaching and by devotion, by its rising literature in many kinds, by its entrance into every class and profession, by the multitude of those, who all over England, turn back to it as the sanctuary of Truth and the only way of Salvation; by all these manifestations the Catholic Church at this hour is in contact with the intelligence and the consciousness of the people of England, so as it has never been since the last 'Requiem' was sung in Westminster Abbey.

While this has been passing in the Catholic Church in England, a marvellous revival has taken place in the religious feeling of the English people. The movements which were called Methodistical and Evangelical, have borne their fruit. Sensual immorality and spiritual death reigned widely over society in England when they arose. It is undeniable that the zeal and piety of these two movements brought multitudes back to the consciousness that they had souls to save, and that unless they turned from sin to God they would perish eternally. The hatred and ridicule with which both Methodists and Evangelicals were treated, is proof enough of the irreligious state of society. They were hated and ridiculed—not so much for their faults and weaknesses, though they had both, but for their piety. What was bad or foolish in them sometimes excited social persecution: but what was good and wise in them almost always did so. Such was their state at the beginning of this century. In thirty years they had won their position, and so far changed the aspect of society that they were, perhaps, only too much followed and respected: and that to their own hurt. So great was this change that a person who went to India in the early days of the Evangelical movement, and returned near its close, said, 'When I left England, here and there an individual was mad: now the whole world is mad.' To this deeper personal religion, founded on interior convictions and affections, and sustaining itself chiefly upon the writings of Puritans and the devotional use of the Holy Scripture, may be ascribed the change which has come over the Church of England. It affected men of the most remote and even opposite opinions. Even the old Church-and-State, or Establishment school, warmed and moved more actively. There can be no doubt that the ardour and energy of the Church Missionary Society spurred the Society for the Propagation of the Gospel into the activity and organization which issued in the multiplication of Colonial bishoprics. But there was needed a *tertium quid*, in which whatsoever was living and true of these two movements might unite and, by a composition of forces, take a new direction. This arose in the Oxford movement, which readily sympathised with the interior personal religion of the Evangelicals, distinct from their heterodoxies, and with the hierarchical and sacramental principles of the High Church, distinct from their Erastianism. The Oxford men hated both the Puritan theology and the secularity of the Establishment. By the Oxford men and the Oxford movement, I do not mean the men or the movement within the University or the city alone. This was, indeed, the focus of its activity, and the inner circle of its momentum. But the influence which went out from it spread all over the country. It penetrated into every diocese, and almost into every parish. The Oxford graduates among the country clergy had a nearer contact and a readier affinity to their own University; yet it spread among the Cambridge men also. There can be no doubt that the majority of the Anglican clergy were predisposed to receive the principles and spirit of the Oxford movement during the first ten years of its progress; that is, from 1833 to 1843. After that date the rapid advance of certain minds in Oxford towards the Catholic Church, separated them from the body of the clergy. The leaders went forward alone, and were lost sight of, one by one. But the movement did not cease. A great body of the clergy have, from that day to this, slowly but steadily advanced towards a juster and fuller perception of truths and principles of which the Reformation has deprived them. This onward movement has been guided, indeed, by the books and influences which issued chiefly from Oxford; but its steady and continued advance is to be ascribed to another cause. The emancipation of Catholics and Dissenters, and the admission of both into the social and public life of England, is morally the dis-establishment of the Church of England. It retains its wealth and titles; but its exclusive ascendency is gone. It is only one of many religious bodies,—the richest and most political, but not the oldest, nor the most powerful in its action upon the intellects and hearts of men. Nevertheless, this moral dis-establishment of the Anglican system has wrought upon it a great change for the better. It has elicited the zeal, activity, enterprise, inventiveness, generosity, which is in the nature of Englishmen and Englishwomen; and the Anglican Church of to-day is no more like the Establishment of 1830, than the Anglicanism of 1890 will be like the Anglican system of to-day. The metamorphoses have fallen again upon men. Thirty years ago, except in the towns of England, hardly a Church of the Establishment was open on Good Friday. Ascension Day, Saints' days, Ash Wednesday, were remembered by lawyers' clerks and school-boys because of holidays and the annual salt fish; but throughout England they were forgotten. In country churches the Sacrament was administered once a quarter, or three times a year. In church men stood, women sat,—few knelt. The clerk answered for the people. The rich attended church to set example. The poor slept or stayed away. Excepting only the parishes of the so-called Evangelicals, and a certain number of men whose natural energy and simplicity lifted them above their system, such, thirty years ago, was the state of country parishes, that is, of England at large. At that time also parish schools were rare; those that existed were not efficient. The advocates of popular Education were ridiculed as theorists and mistrusted as dangerous. Truth and justice towards the Anglican system, and a grateful recognition of the working of the Spirit of Grace, demand a full acknowledgment of the change which has passed upon it.

First, came a restoration of Divine worship on Festivals and Saints' days, extending sometimes even to daily service morning and evening; and that in the remotest country churches.

Secondly, a restoration of frequent Communion; what was before once a quarter became once a month, once a week, and now, in some places, is every day.

Thirdly, arose one of the noblest and most beneficent works of the Anglican clergy, the Education movement, which sprang up in 1837, and has continued to this day.

Fourthly, came the Colonial bishoprics, which have called forth great energy and devotion, and by reaction have powerfully affected the Anglican clergy at home.

Fifthly, sprang up a sense of the need of theological training for clergymen, which, through much opposition and evil report, succeeded at last in forming one or two Diocesan Colleges, and in moving the Universities to a tardy and insufficient endeavour to provide for this obvious need.

Sixthly, a restoration of sacred and religious literature; first Anglican, then patristic, next mediæval and scholastic; and finally, Catholic; which has penetrated and elevated the Anglican system, both clergy and laity, with a higher knowledge, and with perceptions, aspirations, and sympathies which were extinct in the last century in England, and have their true home only in the ever-living and changeless Church of God. The doctrines taught and believed, the devotions and practices of piety now in use among Anglicans, show that the mind and spirit of the Church has breathed itself into multitudes who are still detained in the Anglican system. Over every instinct that opens in it, every pulse that beats in it, every aspiration which rises in it, every line of conformity to the Catholic Church which is retraced upon it, I rejoice with all my heart.

Lastly, there has sprung up in the Anglican Church a consciousness that Protestantism cannot be the essence of its nature, but a mere attitude of supposed and transient necessity. It has become now the acknowledgment of calm and good men among them, that unless the Church of England be Catholic it is nothing; and that unless it be in substantial agreement of Faith with the Christian world, it cannot be Catholic. This is to be found pervading the higher minds and natures of the Anglican clergy. In all this there is no disloyalty to their position, no unnatural appropriation of Roman doctrines, no unauthorized adoption of the Roman ritual. Of these two last phenomena I will speak hereafter.

So far as I have described the steady ascending of the mind and spirit of the Church of England, it has my hearty and hopeful sympathy. I pray that showers of blessings may fall, with the early and the latter rain, upon 'the land that was desolate,' and that the wilderness may 'flourish like the lily.'

Every fresh light which springs up, every gleam of the true Faith which spreads over England, is a cause of thankfulness to the Father of lights from whom alone it comes. As I have said, in the third of the Letters here reprinted, it is a dictate of Faith to believe that the Spirit of God is working mightily, sweetly, and wisely in all who are faithful to His grace. The Catholic Church bears the heart of Him 'who will not break the bruised reed, nor quench the smoking flax.' No one who has a love for souls can look upon this rising of the Spirit of life in the Anglican system without a tender and loving care. I pray God, day by day, to perfect the work which He has begun, and never to stay His hand until He has reunited England to Christendom. Every scattered and isolated truth in the Anglican system is a germ of Faith; every measure of grace is an earnest of more. In proportion as men know and love God they are nearer to the Council of Trent, and to the Vicar of the Incarnate Word. Twenty years ago I wrote the words which follow. Every year has made me hold them more maturely, and to love the truths expressed in them with a fuller and firmer adhesion of my whole heart and reason: 'Any light is better than darkness, any food than famine: even crumbs of the "bread which came down from heaven," than the husks of this fallen earth.'

'Thus far we have taken it on the lowest ground, supposing that the least measure of truth is preached. Yet, even in this least measure there is cause for joy; for thereby the love of God in Christ is declared. And at this we may rejoice, leaving to Him to measure and to gather in what fruit He will.

'If this be true of the least measure of Christian truth, how much must the force of the argument rise with every increase in that measure? As knowledge rises towards the perfect Faith, every such advance is so much more of union between the spirit of man and the character and will of God. I am now speaking of knowledge only as a means of illumination and obedience; not as imposing the responsibility of attaining the perfect truth. It is enough, for the present, to consider truth as being in itself, and by the virtue of its own nature, a means of conversion to God. Every light which reveals God's love leads on towards conversion. How much more, then, will this appear as we advance into the fuller teaching of Christian doctrine among the less erroneous of sectarian bodies, or in the Nestorian and Eutychian Churches of the East. Among these are taught and believed the love and Passion of our

Lord, the presence and gifts of the Spirit, the mystery of the ever-blessed Trinity. Imperfect and darkened as all these doctrines must be when rent from the unity and charity of the Church, yet they do so far bring the spiritual nature of man under the dominion of truth and the powers of the world to come. Taken at the lowest, this must surely be joy to all who desire to see God enthroned in His own world. If only it be that pagan rites and philosophical schools have consumed away, or have been transformed into Christian sects and Christian philosophies—that is, even if there were no Faith, but only Reason; no spirit of sanctity, but only a higher moral law; even so it would be a blessed and joyful sight, a bright softened twilight issuing from the illumination of the Church, and a ripening, it may be, of mankind for the reception of the full powers of Faith. Let us not, like Free-thinkers, stumble at the mystery that the Church is not universal. All God's dealings are progressive; and all progressive dispensations have to our eyes an imperfect outline and discordant preludes, and a circumference or halo of indistinct, and, as it were, of morning or evening light. Such is the Christianity which surrounds the Church.' *

* Sermons, vol. iv. pp. 67–69. 'Christ preached every way a cause of joy.'

To what, then, is this resurrection of the Anglican system tending ? Is it to a third collision with the Catholic Church, and to a farther recoil and departure than in 1588 or 1688 ?

There are many indications on both sides, some of which menace a more terrible collision and a wider deviation from Christian Faith, and some which portend a happier future. I will endeavour to enumerate at least the chief on either side.

The author of the Essay on the 'Tendencies of Religious Thought in England,' gives as his opinion, that the period of Rationalism closed with 1830. I believe the direct reverse to be true. The inchoate or partial Rationalism of private judgment criticising and measuring Christianity by its reasonableness, came to an end when the reaction towards authority and Divine certainty commenced: but the period of complete and consistent Rationalism, formally opened by a new reaction against this revived claim of authority, commenced about five or six years later. The Essay above quoted proves beyond a doubt that, from the time of Locke down to the time of Whately, the reasonableness of Christianity, that is, the credibility of its doctrines tested by the Reason, was the dominant theology of Anglicans. This, as I have affirmed in the second Letter to an Anglican friend, is essential though undeveloped and unconscious Rationalism. But it is the basis of the whole Anglican system.

The Rationalism of the last thirty years, however, is far more formal and complete. It is the Rationalism of Germany, in which all truth is supposed to be contained within the limits of the Reason, and no supernatural Revelation to be necessary. The developed consciousness of the Reason yields all truth to man.

The Rationalism of Whately, Hinds, and Hampden, was of the earlier period; and although the last seems to have borrowed from M. Guizot, it was English and indigenous. The Rationalism of Arnold and his followers is German, and is having now its legitimate development. It is remarkable that the first formal action and manifestation of this school took place when, under the pressure of the rising Oxford movement, the Heads of Houses censured Dr. Hampden for his Bampton Lectures. From that day a collision with, and a reaction from, the Oxford movement sprang up, the issue of which is yet far off. I remember on that day, after giving my vote against Dr. Hampden, standing in the theatre, behind the Vice Chancellor's chair, with a very dear friend, to whose earnest Christian piety I owed much. He had then already begun to deviate in the line of the

German philosophy, and consistently on that day he had voted in favour of Dr. Hampden. As we were standing together, Dr. Newman voted and passed us. My friend said, 'Before long we shall be summoned here to vote against Neander.' His prophecy was truer and fuller than he then knew. From that time the school of Dr. Arnold took form and multiplied, chiefly encouraged by Chevalier Bunsen and his friends. The contact with Germany decided its character. The volume called 'Essays and Reviews,' and the works of Dr. Colenso, are a legitimate product of this consistent Rationalism: and there can be little doubt that this disbelief and exclusion of the supernatural in religion represents the mind and tendency of the majority of English laymen. There is every reason to believe that this form of unbelief will spread more and more widely. The material habits of English society make it especially susceptible of a Christianity without mysteries, and a Faith which is only coextensive with Naturalism. It is obvious that this is the antagonist of supernatural Faith, and therefore, in a special way and degree, of the Catholic Church. There can be no doubt that the whole attack of Rationalism will hereafter be concentrated upon it. All that is intermediate will either be absorbed by latitudinarian Rationalism, or will make terms with it, and will unite with it against the claim of a Divine authority in matters of Faith.

The author of the Essay already quoted says this in substance in the following passage:—' In the Catholic theory the feebleness of Reason is met halfway and made good by the authority of the Church. When the Protestants threw off this authority, they did not assign to Reason what they took from the Church, but to the Scripture. Calvin did not shrink from saying, that Scripture "shone sufficiently by its own light." . . . Time, learned controversy, and abatement of zeal, drew the Protestants generally from the hardy but irrational assertion of Calvin. . Church authority was essayed by the Laudian divines, but was soon found untenable; for on that footing it was found impossible to justify the Reformation and the breach with Rome. . . . There remained to be tried Common Reason, carefully distinguished from recondite learning, and not based on metaphysical assumption. To apply this instrument to the contents of Revelation, was the occupation of the early half of the eighteenth century: with what success has been seen.

' Such appears to be the past history of the theory of belief in the Church of England. Whoever would take the religious literature of the present day as a whole, and endeavour to make out clearly on what basis Revelation is supposed by it to rest, whether on authority, on the inward light, on Reason, on self-evidencing Scripture, or on the combination of these four, or some of them, and in what proportion—would probably find that he had undertaken a perplexing but not altogether a profitless inquiry.'*

Such is his summing up of the actual state and tendency of belief in the Church of England. He seems to recognise that the relation assigned to Reason and Revelation in the Catholic theology is at least coherent, and that the rejection of it by the Reformation has launched the intelligence of England upon a flood in which there is neither anchorage nor haven. He distinctly shows that neither the authority of Anglicanism, nor the Calvinistic clearness of Scripture, nor the inward light of Pietism, nor the criterion of Reason of the last century, either severally or all together, will provide a basis of certainty which excludes doubt. I have pointed out in the second of these Letters that all these processes have but one principle, and are all resolvable at last into simple Rationalism. The Anglican claim of authority is no more than the collective private judgment of a number of individuals, be it few or many, projected

---

* Tendencies of Religious Thought in England, pp. 328–329.

before the minds of those who are either willing to submit to them, or are led by the illusion that such an authority is a principle of certainty. The vote of a majority in Parliament may make law, but it cannot make Truth. The vote of a majority in Convocation is equally uncertain and disputable, because equally human. It may make terms of communion, not doctrines of Faith. The authority by which, as this author says, the Catholic theology meets 'the feebleness of Reason,' is the authority of a Divine Person, perpetuating by His Presence and His assistance the light of the original Revelation, and the enunciation of the same objects and definitions of Faith. Let men say that this theory is incredible, or false, if they will; only do not let them confound it with the theories of Anglican authority, as if it were the same in kind, and differing only in degree, that is, in antiquity and in extent. It is generically different, and irreconcilably at variance with it.

The Anglican system,—including its most advanced developments of Anglo-Catholicism, Unionism, Ritualism,—rests upon one and the same basis; and the period which commenced with 1830 and the 'Tracts for the Times, diverse as its phenomena may be, is nevertheless in principle, in procedure, and in result, as purely and simply rationalistic as the period from 1688 down to that date. As the school of authority developed on the one side, the pure and formal Rationalism developed on the other ; and now for the first time since the sixteenth century is the Protestant and Anglican Reformation brought adequately in contact with the Divine authority of the Catholic Church. The contests among Protestants and Anglicans in these three hundred years, have been contests between men differing in conclusions, but agreeing in principle. The criterion of the Reason lay at the root of all, whether their appeal was to Scripture, or to antiquity, or to intrinsic reasonableness, or to extrinsic evidence, the Reason remained sole and supreme as the ultimate tribunal and judge. There was no higher presence, no higher person, to whom the Reason should submit, of whom the Reason should learn. Such the Catholic Church affirms itself to be by Divine institution. Deny it who will, but do not confound its authority with that of the Provinces of Canterbury and York, as if it were the same in kind. The belief, full of fear and sorrow, which is forced upon me by the events of the last year, is this: that every 'Eirenicon' against the Catholic Church is a fresh reinforcement to the Rationalism of England. The object of the book was to justify the Church of England, and to hinder people from going over to the Catholic Church. The experience, indeed, of the last year proves, that where it keeps back one it sends on three. But the keeping back or the sending onward of individual minds, is the accidental effect of particular passages of the book. Its essence and principle, and therefore its main effect, is to stimulate and encourage the critical spirit. It is identical in principle with the theology of the eighteenth century; and its chief ultimate result will be to undermine the Anglican Church.

I cannot better illustrate the tendency of this period of the Anglican system towards a latitudinarian vagueness, which is essential Rationalism, than in the words of Bishop Tait, in his late Charge to the clergy of his diocese. Before I do so, I must bear witness to the sincerity and reality which are manifest in it. He writes with the feelings and prejudices which are inseparable from his position. But even his opposition to the Catholic Church is manly, impersonal, and temperate; presenting a marked and honourable contrast in these respects to the tone and manner of others, over whom kindly memories would make me wish to pass in silence. He affords most direct and copious evidence, that the events of the last ten years have given to the Rationalistic tendency a development and a momentum which it has never received till now.

The mutations of the Anglican theology in the last three centuries can hardly be more truly and briefly summed up than in the following words: 'How often has it been noted that the Church in whose primatial chair have sat Abbot, Laud, Tillotson, Howley, Sumner, has never committed itself to the dogmatism of one school of thought.'* The force of this passage is to be found not only in the diversities of these five theologies, but in that which had been here affirmed throughout, their essential unity of principle; that is, private judgment, or, as it has been here described, 'the supremacy of Reason.' Laud was as purely critical in his authority of Tradition as Tillotson in his reasonableness of Christianity, or Sumner in his supremacy of Scripture. The ultimate judge and interpreter with all three, is the individual Reason.

Bishop Tait describes the basis of the Anglican Church to be a common belief in the essentials of the Christian Faith; and these are plainly stated in the 'formularies' as in the 'Bible.' †

'Is it true,' he asks, 'that there are men who even desire to act as Christ's ministers amongst us,

* Charge, p. 7. † Ibid.

without believing in the Resurrection of Jesus Christ? I can hardly credit the assertion.' . . . . . 'For those who do not believe in the Resurrection of Christ, we have no place; as we have none for those who do not believe in Christ's Divinity, nor in the Divinity of the Third Person of the Blessed Trinity. The essentials of the Christian Faith are incorporated in our formularies from the Bible and the Apostles' Creed—explained and enlarged on, but not added to: the liberty of thought which is consistent with loyalty to our Church is, therefore, hedged in by these essentials.' * How closely, we shall see. On the side of the Catholic Church the hedge might be thought stiff enough, but that the whole Unionist body have driven through it. 'The Bishop of Rome hath no jurisdiction in this Realm of England.' 'The sacrifices of masses, &c., are blasphemous fables and dangerous deceits.' 'The body of Christ is given, taken, and received in the Lord's Supper only, &c., &c.' The sufficiency of these fences is then shown by a description of Ritualism. 'There are churches amongst us in which the ornaments about the Communion Table, and the dress, and attitudes, and whole manner of the officiating clergy, render it difficult for a

* Charge, p. 8.

stranger when he enters to know whether he is in a Roman Catholic or a Church of England place of worship.' 'When this is the case, the actors in these scenes are, no doubt conscientiously, preaching by their worship a doctrine which is very dear to them; but let them remember it is not the doctrine of the Church of which they are ministers.' * 'To judge, indeed, by certain unauthorised catechisms and manuals of devotion, which some of the supporters of this Ritualism have already put forth, I fear they have not succeeded in this attempt to divorce Ritual ceremonial from deadly Roman errors.'† Such is the hedge of essentials on the side of the Catholic Faith.

Now on the other. Dr. Tait has given a luminous and complete illustration of the definite circle which protects the essentials of the Anglican Religion, and of the Christian liberty allowed to the members of the Anglican Church, by an elaborate defence of the Judgment of the Crown in Council on the 'Essays and Reviews,' and of the Appellate jurisdiction of the Crown in matters of Religion.

On the side, therefore, towards Rationalism, we have the landmarks set up so far afield as to include the 'Essays and Reviews.' At pages 19, 20 of this

* Charge. pp. 10, 11. † Ibid. p. 17.

volume I have given the enumeration published by
the Convocation of Canterbury of the errors which
the Crown dismissed with impunity. They reach
from the Incarnation and Redemption to the Resurrection and Eternal Punishment. But I will now
dwell on one alone, because it constitutes the first
decisive and legal victory of the Rationalistic over
the Scriptural school, and the opening of a new
period in the Anglican Religion—I mean the denial
of the Inspiration of a large part of Holy Scripture.
The Judgment of Dr. Lushington, to the effect that
it is lawful to clergymen of the Church of England
to reject portions of any Book in Scripture as not inspired, so long as they do not reject any entire Book,
is the authoritative enunciation of the liberty which
Dr. Colenso has been the first to use. There can be
no doubt that, if Dr. Colenso has used this liberty
somewhat immoderately, he has offended only in
degree, not in principle. I need not dwell on this
further than to observe, that it ruins the whole base
of the Anglican Reformation. It subjects even the
Scripture to the supremacy of Reason. Now, Dr.
Tait declares, that he does not agree with Dr. Colenso,
and, without doubt, he does not agree altogether with
the 'Essays and Reviews.' But he justifies and
vindicates the whole principle upon which Dr. Colenso

and the Essayists alike rest. He concurred in dismissing the Article of Charge, on the ground that the extracts on which it was founded were not inconsistent with the 'formularies' of the Church of England. From this the two Archbishops dissented. What Mr. Wilson has said and done, all clergy of the Church of England may say and do in respect to Inspiration, which he declares cannot be 'predicated of every statement and representation contained in any part of the Old and New Testament.'

And further: Bishop Tait not only justifies the procedure and sentence of the Privy Council, but in his Charge he elaborately justifies the tribunal itself. He says, The Church of England judges by the Church Courts, the Consistorial Court of the Bishops, and, above them, the Provincial Court of the Metropolitan: and as she recognises no Patriarch to control the independent judicature of each of her four Archbishops, she says; 'the last appeal from these must be made to a Court within the Realm, and with power in all provinces of the Realm, held in the Queen's name, but still a Court judging by the law Ecclesiastical—a Court, indeed, which shall symbolize and represent the union between Church and State.' *

* Charge, p. 28.

' A Court of Appeal, similar to this in all essentials, has been maintained ever since the settlement of the Reformation, when the usurped power of the so-called Universal Patriarch was repudiated as encroaching on the independence of a National Church.'*

He also says, ' The Final Court ... cannot be held in the name of any Ecclesiastical authority, since it is an appeal from one or other of the Metropolitans.' ' To whom is there to be an appeal ? At the Reformation it was held that the appeal should be to the Sovereign, as, indeed, had often been contended before.' †

On this I have only to remark, as I have in the second letter here reprinted, that this tribunal fitly represents the Anglican Reformation, which consists in isolation from Christendom, the supremacy of the Civil Power, and the supremacy of the Reason to the exclusion of supernatural character and guidance in the tribunal, procedure, and judge. Dr. Tait says that this appeal had been often contended for before the Reformation. If so, it had never been allowed. But it had never even been claimed. An appeal in any matter involving the admissibleness of doctrine, or the interpretation of the doctrinal ' formularies ' had

* Charge, p. 30.   † *Ibid.*, pp. 43, 45, 46.

never been so much as ventured upon. Lord Coke, indeed, in the well-known Cawdrey case, endeavoured to produce some fifteen or twenty examples of high Ecclesiastical jurisdiction in the Crown. But not one exists in which a judgment of the admissibleness of doctrine, or the interpretation of formularies, is to be found. The supremacy before the Reformation was strictly in the temporal and civil aspects of Ecclesiastical causes. Into the merits of a spiritual or doctrinal question it never ventured to intrude. The law of Christendom guarded the Faith. Never till 'National Churches' arose was the claim so much as pretended.* 'A National Church,' as Bishop Tait well says, 'cannot have an ultimate Ecclesiastical Court.' It must be Civil. But the Catholic Church cannot have an ultimate Civil Tribunal. It must be Ecclesiastical in all matters of the Divine Faith and law. To deny this is to deny the Divine office of the Church. It is of no avail to say that these appeals are not for the definition of doctrine, nor for the declaration of Truth, but are only judicial causes as to the legality of doctrines and the conformity of the teaching of the clergy with the formularies of the Church.

* Stillingfleet's Ecclesiastical Cases, vol. ii. p. 86. The Appellate Jurisdiction of the Crown in matters Spiritual,—*A Letter to the Bishop of Chichester by H. E. Manning.* Murray, 1850.

Even so, they involve an interpretation of those formularies, and a judgment on the sense of theological works. What more does the Holy See do in interpreting the Council of Trent, or in condemning heretical propositions? To determine the sense of the 'Essays and Reviews' is a process like that of determining the sense of the books of Jansenius. It is an exercise of the discernment of dogmatic facts, and this the Catholic Church holds to be a part of its Divine office. This power the Law of England, at the Reformation, vested in the Crown; and the Crown exercised it in pronouncing the sense of Mr. Wilson's writings not to be contrary to the formularies of the Church of England.

It is not wonderful then that, as Dr. Tait says, only three cases are to be found on record of any one accused of false doctrine being condemned by the Ecclesiastical Courts. And these instances are full of instruction. They are as follows: First, 'that of Mr. Stone, under Bishop Porteous, for denying the Divinity of Christ; Mr. Oakeley, under Bishop Blomfield, for claiming to hold all Roman doctrine— both in the Consistorial Court of London; and that of Mr. Heath, before the Privy Council.' And yet it is undeniable that Arianism, Semi-arianism, Sabellianism, Unitarianism, Pelagianism, with every kind of Sacramentarian heterodoxy, have been held and taught by clergymen of the Church of England, openly and with impunity. A solitary Socinian, an eccentric clergyman, and one of the most exemplary, cultivated, and devoted sons of the Anglican Church— now a venerable Catholic priest—these stand on record as the 'Triste bidental' of Ecclesiastical condemnation. Whole schools of erroneous doctrine, from semi-Catholicism to Rationalism, increase and multiply under the eye of authority, and only here and there a solitary individual is censured; and this state of confusion or of conflict is regarded as a normal condition. 'Two brother professors, greatly esteemed and distinguished, are the leaders of these schools. Neither of these men, I venture to think, could our Church have retained in its communion if its judicature had been conducted on other principles than those I have described.' 'For myself, I will not hesitate to say that, on the whole, I think it well we have retained them, and that I trust the great power they possess *to spread amongst us what I feel to be erroneous doctrine*, may be counteracted by other influences, and even by the practical lesson of their own lives.' *

This is an acknowledgment—

* Charge, pp. 48, 49.

1. That the Anglican formularies do not represent nor guide the minds of the Anglican clergy.

2. That they are violated by them, both on the side of Ritualism and of Rome, to such an extent that but for the difficulty of obtaining any condemnation for any error of doctrine, Dr. Pusey and Dr. Jowett would have been put out at the opposite sides of the Church.

3. That the formularies of the Church of England are so vague and ambiguous as to allow the coexistence of these contradictory schools.

I will not stay to ask how such a body is 'the pillar and ground of the Truth;' or 'the witness and keeper of Holy Writ;' or the guardian of 'the Faith once delivered to the Saints;' or the teacher of the 'Truth as it is in Jesus;' or how it can be said of its voice 'he that heareth you heareth Me;' or how it can be held to be 'a straight way, so that fools shall not err therein.' To Catholics all this is simply fearful. It shocks the first instinct of Faith, and of fidelity.

But I pass all this by. I would only ask, how is it to be reconciled with the principles laid down in the Charge?

The procedure of the Privy Council is described as follows:—'The Judges ... have practically acted on the principle that they must be guided entirely by the *written* law of the Church, *known* and *understood* and *acquiesced* in by *all* who are subject to their authority.'* But, it is precisely this written rule which is not 'understood' nor 'acquiesced in'—I was almost going to say, by any in the same sense. The sense of this written rule by the Privy Council is only one more sense among many. Dr. Pusey has his own; Dr. Jowett has another; the Privy Council has a third. Can this mislead any consecutive intellect? 'We have,' he says, in another place, 'that sort of unity in essentials which Christ intended should characterize His Church, and we desire none other.' † But what are the essentials in common with Dr. Pusey and Dr. Jowett, or with either of them, and the Privy Council? Is the Inspiration of Scripture an essential on one side—or the Real Presence on the other? With which does the Privy Council hold? With neither, or with both? I had thought that the word 'essentials' had long ago departed with 'fundamentals,' into the Limbus of infantine theology.

To return, then, to where we set out. The hedge of the Anglican formularies is sharp and close, indeed, towards the only definite Truth in the world, the

* Charge, p. 46.   † *Ibid.*, p. 10.

Holy Catholic Faith; but it is thin and open in its whole circuit towards the wilderness of obscurity and Rationalism. The circle of essentials has so short a radius, that it is difficult to enclose in it any perfect Christian truth. The Charge says, ' For those who do not believe in the Resurrection of Christ we have no place, as we have none for those who do not believe in Christ's Divinity, nor in the Divinity of the Third Person of the Blessed Trinity.' And yet, the Convocation of the Province of Canterbury charges the 'Essays and Reviews' with denying the Incarnation of our Lord, Salvation through His blood, and the Personality of the Spirit.* All this is not the λογικὴ λατρεία, the *rationabile obsequium* of St. Paul: it is the supremacy of Reason, or Rationalism incipient or complete, as the case may be, in the individual; but dominant, essential, and all-pervading in the nature of the Anglican system.

I am bound, in justice to Dr. Tait, whose tone throughout the Charge is manly, kindly, and earnest, to declare that his account of the Anglican system appears to me to be just and true. It is undeniable that the Anglican Church, since 1688, has permitted the latitude he claims. He is a fair and consistent type of the Church of England theologian, dating

* Letter, p. 20.

from the last great collision with the Catholic Church. The liberty he claims undoubtedly exists. In his own theology he uses it with great moderation. But the permission of such a liberty in matters of Revelation is fatal to Faith. It can exist only where Reason is supreme; that is, where Rationalism is the source or criterion of religious belief. But this is destructive to the system which admits it: and its full development into the rejection of all supernatural Revelation, though retarded long, is inevitable at last.

In what I have written there is not, I trust, a word to give needless pain or personal offence to Dr. Tait, for whose sincerity and goodness I have a true respect.

Such, then, is the manifest tendency of the Anglican religion at this moment. And this tendency is not counterbalanced by the so-called Anglo-Catholic movement. The broad stream of religious opinion in the laity of the Church of England is towards the system described in the Charge. The upward movement, as I have said in pages 148, 149 of this volume, is a narrow current in the main tide. The natural stream of the English mind is advancing towards the loss of Faith. A supernatural movement against the tide is ascending towards the Truth. But public opinion is adverse to it, and to the Catholic Church

JOURNALISM ADVERSE TO FAITH. lxvii

to which it appears to be approaching. This gives no good omen for the future.

Nor again does the domination of journalism which reigns over us. Of all the newspapers which, week by week, or day by day, colour and direct the public opinion of England, hardly half-a-dozen are Catholic. The influence of the whole tide of anonymous writers all over England, and in all its towns, is hostile to the Church, to its Head, and to its Faith. And not only so; it is in a great part hostile, I might say, to Christianity. For the papers which defend it are few, or feeble, and little read. The great majority write as if Christianity had no claims upon the world, upon society, or upon any one unless he choose by the indulgence of a private consent to enter into terms with it. The all but universal effect of our daily newspapers is to wipe religion out of the minds of men. Even if religion be not directly attacked, the principles assumed and insinuated are incompatible with Faith. And yet, great numbers of Englishmen read little else, and are either consciously or unconsciously led and fashioned by the confident and peremptory tone of writers who are imposing because they are anonymous. Add to this, that the concealment of anonymous writing gives facility to very special forms of deception. There is every reason to believe that the articles of some of the leading newspapers on the subject of Italy, Rome, and the Pope, are habitually written by infidel Italian Revolutionists, members of the Secret Societies. Englishmen would turn from such writers with aversion, if they knew their names. But, under the mask of concealment, they pour out lies like water, and we drink down poison with perfect credulity. So again, the Articles on the Anglican Church are said to come from a Scotch Presbyterian of the sister Establishment. That the effect of the whole newspaper Press, with few exceptions, is to wear and to waste down all distinctive principle, all precise doctrine, to the level of latitudinarian Protestantism and sensuous Rationalism, is as certain as that the St. Lawrence carries the *detritus* of its banks into the sea. They who can remember what was the public opinion of England thirty years ago in respect to Christianity, and know what it is now, will perceive that a flood has gone over it. By common consent Christianity is banished from public life. It is a matter for individuals, not for society. Society is without Faith. But it was society without Faith which, in the beginning, pursued the Church with ten persecutions, and in 1848 threatened to overturn the Christian civilization of Europe. This bodes no reconciliation between the public opinion of England and the Catholic Church.

Add to this, again, the action of the Press in all its manifold forms, from volumes to fly-leaves. It is not too much to say that not a thousandth part is Catholic, and that a proportion, how large I am afraid of conjecturing, is positively anti-Christian. Either, like Mithridates, men can swallow poison and thrive upon it, or the people of England are being poisoned day by day. The hideous caricatures of the Catholic Church and of the Catholic Faith, and, what is more, of the words, acts, and lives of Catholics, which are palmed upon England in histories and in fictions, seem a kind of judicial delusion. There are many who hate the Catholic Church, and love to hear evil of it. They seem to be given over to believe whatsoever their hostility to the Church inclines them to desire, and this, like Original Sin, reigns over them also who have not sinned as their forefathers. Every generation is born into this delusion: and there is reason to fear, that in certain classes at least, this animosity against the Catholic Church is on the increase rather than the decline.

And further: for the last thirty years the political society of all European countries, and especially of England, has been putting off religion in its public character and action. When the Empire became Christian, the Catholic Church consecrated the Civil Powers of the world. The Reformation divorced them from the Church. For the last thirty years religion has been excluded from Government and Legislation. The political society of England has no religion. The Established Church is powerless over the course of public law. Its contact with the Crown and with the House of Lords makes Anglicanism secular, but does not make the Legislature Anglican. The whole weight of modern legislation excludes religion from public influence. The organized life of England, as it is compacted together by its Legislature, Government, and public laws, is anticatholic. It can easily be foreseen which side it would take in the event of any collision with the Catholic Church, by the line it did actually take in the so-called Papal aggression.

Finally, for the last three hundred years, and especially in the last hundred, since the rise of the British Empire, and above all in the last thirty years, since the application of steam called into existence the world which the civil engineers have created, the English people have been becoming, more and more, material in their lives and hearts. The magnitude of the old Empire of Rome may be measured by its amphitheatres and its aqueducts: that of the British Empire by its viaducts and railroads. In material and mechanical development the world has seen nothing greater. But its people are becoming mechanical and material like itself. Nobody who has conversed with foreign, especially with Catholic nations, and above all with the Italian and the Irish people, can fail to feel how inert and tardy is the intelligence of the English compared with the vividness and intuitive quickness of the Irish and the Italian poor. Be the natural diversities of race what they may, the fact is to be explained chiefly by two causes—the quickening and elevating effect of Faith in a supernatural order in the latter, and the deadening effect of perpetual contact with material interests and calculations in the former. Such a habit of mind is adverse to Faith. S. Paul calls it, 'without God in the world.'

So far, the state of England gives little promise of any diminished hostility to the Catholic Church, if any collision should arise. On the contrary, it is to be feared that it is already far more estranged from the Catholic Faith than it was in 1688. The last recoil has taken more than a century to measure the distance it had to traverse. The insular pride, national Protestantism, Royal jealousy of any superior, the aristocratic independence and insubordination to the Church which descends from the sixteenth century,—all these are at least as strong now as in 1688. I am afraid, too, that the Anglican Church is instinct with the same animosity as broke forth sixteen years ago in such licence of tongue. There is no doubt that the Scotch Presbyterian blood which has crept into the English Establishment, has added a great intensity to the anti-Catholic spirit. About the year 1830 a curious creation arose, as by a *lusus naturæ*, out of the Scottish Presbyterian communion. Mr. Irving laid the foundation of a school which, after his death, united a servile imitation of the Catholic Church in its doctrines and ritual, with a preternatural enmity against it. Among the followers of this system, it is said, are one or two unhappy priests, who appear to have infused into it a special feeling against the Church from which they fell. Strong as is the opposition of the old Scottish Presbyterian Establishment against the Catholic Church, it is mild and gentle compared with the attitude of the 'Catholic and Apostolic Church.' The Presbyterian denounced the Catholic Church,— the Irvingite imitates it. The Presbyterian does not feel his existence in danger in the presence of the Catholic Church. The Apostolic Church stands detected when the Catholic Church appears. This raises its enmity to an instinct of self-defence.

Something of the same kind, I am afraid, must be said of the Anglican Church. The great revival of religious zeal and activity in the last thirty years, to which I have desired to do justice, has a twofold effect. All in it that is of God is in sympathy with us; all that is of man is against us. The rise and expansion of a higher mind and a more Christian aspiration after union with God and His Truth, and therefore after Faith and unity, would tend to prepare the way for a happier future and for a day of reconciliation. I am not now speaking of corporate re-union. Before corporate re-union can be verified, there must be a body to be re-united. But the upward tendency of Faith, piety, and charity among Anglicans gave and gives ground to hope for the return of multitudes to the Only Truth.

The emancipation of Catholics revived the action of the Catholic Church upon the people of England. No sooner was this felt than the old anti-Catholic spirit also revived its hostility. From 1830 to 1840, Exeter Hall took the lead. For the last twenty years it has been almost silent. The day of Apocalyptic Vials in human hands is over: but a new and remarkable opposition to the Faith has sprung up.

The Anglican Church, by the law of its being, must be opposed to Rome; and in proportion as it claimed authority to teach and govern, it denounced the Catholic Church in England as a schism and an intrus'on. This was the first of four distinct phases of opposition. In those days, from 1830 to 1840, the Catholic doctrines were denied as false, because contrary to Scripture and to the unanimous consent of the Fathers; and notably, as contrary to the Faith of the undivided Church of the first six hundred years, before the separation of the East and West. This was Jewel's challenge; and men at that day believed in it. Gradually, the examination of the Fathers, and above all of the Councils of Ephesus and Chalcedon, proved the falsehood of this position. By these General Councils,—which the Anglican Church professes to accept,—the worship of the Mother of God and the universal jurisdiction of the Roman Pontiff were incontestably proved. It was necessary therefore to shift the ground.

The second opposition was, that even these decrees of Ephesus and Chalcedon were Roman novelties, not necessary because not Apostolic; that the Roman and the Anglican Churches are both Catholic, but the Anglican purer and more primitive; that Rome had erred, and that England only waited for her Reformation to restore communion. But this theory also was rudely dispelled, chiefly by certain articles in the 'Dublin Review' on the Donatist schism, and partly by the 'Tracts for the Times,' which laid bare, with no sparing hand, the havoc of the Reformation, and the embarrassments of the Anglican system.

A third position was then taken up. About 1844 it was held that Rome had not erred, and that England had; but that the Anglican formularies, 'though not ambitious, were patient,' of a Catholic interpretation, and that they might be squared with the Council of Trent. This also, for a time, satisfied some minds; till the master-builders pulled down the house which they had built, and went away.

A fourth and last position has since been invented. It is this, that the whole Roman doctrine may be believed, and the whole Roman Ritual may be imported into the Anglican Church; that, to exclude Rome, the Anglican Church must be conformed to it by imitation: that is, by High Masses, and Low Masses, Confessions and Extreme Unction, chasubles and thuribles, and pastoral staves, berettas and Roman collars; in one word, by Unionism and Ritualism.

Now I wish to treat these two things as justly and

as fairly as possible, for many reasons; first, because in the Association for the Union of Christendom there are united many men whom I love and respect, in whose singular goodness and uprightness I have the fullest belief: again, because among the Ritualists are many who are moved by a true spirit of piety and reverence for the worship of Almighty God; and finally, because at this time ill-will, ridicule, and threats of persecution are heaped upon them. I would not by one word encourage or take part with their adversaries. My hope for their future lies in another direction. So far as this adoption of Catholic doctrine and Ritual is intended to raise and restore the ruin made by the Reformation, it has the sympathy and prayers of Catholics; so far as it is intended to supplant the Church and to deceive souls, it cannot escape our reprobation.

Now as to Unionism, the fourth Letter in this volume will say all I need at present, save only this. They desire unity. Let them learn from the Head of Catholic Unity on earth the only principles upon which it is possible, because those principles are a part of the deposit of Faith.

The Holy Father in a recent letter to the Bishops of England, dated May 31, 1866, says:—'From our letters of September 16, 1864, and November 8,

1865, it is clearly and openly manifest that no one can belong to the true Church of Christ unless he firmly adhere by free subjection of mind and heart, and open confession of the lips, to the Chair of Peter and the Roman Pontiff, who has been divinely constituted by Christ our Lord Himself as Successor of Peter, Head of His whole Church, the Centre of Unity, and Pastor with supreme power of feeding both lambs and sheep. God grant it, Venerable Brothers, that these unhappy wanderers may abjure their errors, and see the light of Catholic Truth, and hasten to the only Fold of Christ. And this we do not omit, day and night, to ask in humble and fervent prayer from the Father of mercies; and for this we, again and again, implore the powerful patronage of the Immaculate and most Holy Virgin Mary, Mother of God.' *

It is hardly possible to leave the subject of Unionism without touching on the 'Eirenicon' which was hailed by the 'Union Review' as its Magna Charta. The first half of that book is an elaborate proof of my assertion in the second Letter in this volume. I there affirm, that the Church of England appeals *from* the living voice of the Church at this hour, and

---

* Epist. S. D. N. Pii. P. IX. ad Episcopos Angliæ.

thereby denies the perpetual infallibility of the Church in all ages; and that this procedure is essentially rationalistic. The first half of Dr. Pusey's book almost repeats my words. The last half is a profuse criticism or Private Judgment, on Pontiffs, Councils, Theologians, including many Saints, and ending with an invitation to the Catholic Church to explain the Council of Trent in conformity with his view of Christianity. The friendship of past years, and a heartfelt desire to spare him all the pain I can, restrain me from all comments except these two :—

I do not recognise, in the following words, the reverence which in old days was held to be a duty in treating of sacred things; and even of errors in sacred things. 'One recently returned from Rome,' he says, 'had the impression that "some of the extreme" Ultramontanes, if they do not say so in so many words, imply a quasi-hypostatic union of the Holy Ghost with each successive Pope.' 'The accurate writer,' Dr. Pusey adds in a note, 'who reported this to me, observed in answer, " this seems to me to be Llamaism."' * I may be permitted to add, this seems to me to be profaneness. To me this savours not of the Spirit of God. The reporter

---

* Dr. Pusey's 'Eirenicon,' pp. 326, 327.

was probably a young man, and as his words show, a slender theologian. The retailer of this unseemly saying is neither young nor unprovided with the means of knowing better.

It would have been more intelligible if either Dr. Pusey or his informant had given us a sample of the language of these 'extreme Ultramontanes.' We might then have judged for ourselves. In the absence of this necessary matter, all I can do is to state in what terms those I am used to deal with express themselves on this subject. The following may serve for a sample :—

'The definitions and decrees of Pontiffs speaking *ex cathedrâ*, or as the Head of the Church, and to the whole Church, whether by Bull, or Apostolic letters, or Encyclical, or Brief, to many or to one person, undoubtedly emanate from a Divine assistance, and are infallible.

'S. Augustine argues as follows of the head and the body: "Therefore, as the soul animates and quickens our whole body, but perceives in the head by the action of life, by hearing, by smelling, by the taste, and by touch, in the other members by touch alone (for all are subject to the head in their operation, the head being placed above them for their guidance, since the head bears the personality of the soul itself, which guides the body, for there all the senses are manifested), so to the whole people of the saints, as of one body, the man Christ Jesus, the Mediator between God and man, is head." *

'Now, the Pontiffs, as Vicars of Jesus Christ, have a twofold relation, the one to the Divine Head of the Church, of Whom they are the representatives on earth, the other to the whole body. And these two relations impart a special prerogative of grace to him that bears them. The endowments of the head, as S. Augustine argues, are in behalf of the body. It is a small thing to say that the endowments of the body are the prerogatives of the head. The Vicar of Jesus Christ would bear no proportion to the body if, while it is infallible, he were not. He would bear also no representative character if he were the fallible witness of an infallible Head. Though the analogy observed by S. Augustine between the head and the members cannot strictly apply to the Vicar of Christ and the members upon earth; nevertheless, it invests him with a preeminence of guidance and direction over the whole body, which can neither be possessed by any other member of the body, nor by the whole body without him, and yet attaches to him

* *De Agone Christiano*, cap. xxii. tom. vi. p. 254.

personally and alone as representing to the body the prerogatives of its Divine Head. The infallibility of the Head of the Church extends to the whole matter of revelation; that is, to the Divine truth and the Divine law, and to all those facts or truths which are in contact with faith and morals. The definitions of the Church include truths of the natural order, and the revelation of supernatural truth is in contact with natural ethics, politics, and philosophy. The doctrines of the consubstantiality of the Son, of transubstantiation, and of the constitution of humanity, touch upon truths of philosophy and of the natural order; but, being in contact with the faith, they fall within the infallibility of the Church. So, again, the judgments of Pontiffs in matters which affect the welfare of the whole Church, such as the condemnation of propositions. In all declarations that such propositions are, as the case may be, heretical or savouring of heresy, or erroneous, or scandalous, or offensive to pious ears, and the like, the assistance of the Holy Spirit certainly preserves the Pontiffs from error, and such judgments are infallible, and demand interior assent from all.' *

If anyone can mistake 'assistance' for 'union,' it is

---

* *The Temporal Mission of the Holy Ghost*, pp. 81-84.

to be feared that he must be unconsciously Nestorian. If the doctrines above stated can be misunderstood as amounting to a hypostatic union of the Third Person of the Holy Trinity with the Vicar of Christ, it is to be feared that the hypostatic union of the Second Person with our manhood amounts, in the minds of such theologians, to little more than the union of assistance. And such, I am afraid, is the confusion implied by such highminded criticism.

The other remark is this: as in a tree full grown the sap which rises from the root replenishes the trunk, ramifies through every branch, and pervades every spray, quickening the minutest fibre of every leaf; so in this Catholicism of the study, from its first outset to its last detail, from its primary assertions to its remotest conclusions, there is one and one only principle which originates, and develops all; namely, the private judgment, or individual opinion of an isolated mind. The beginning, middle, and end is a sustained criticism. The private judgment of the ordinary Protestant is limited and chastened by the side of this boundless exercise of the private spirit. If a man were to hold the whole Catholic Theology and the decrees of the eighteen General Councils on the principle of the 'Eirenicon,' he would not be a Catholic. He would be as true a

Protestant as Luther or Calvin. It is not the believing of isolated doctrines, but the act of Divine Faith, terminating in its formal motive, the veracity of God through the living voice of the Church, that makes us Catholic Christians.

This is the affirmation of the third Letter, to Dr. Pusey; and to this the ' Eirenicon ' offers not a word of answer. In its multitudinous topics, all things are touched but this; and yet this was the one point vital to the whole question.

In like manner, it must be said that Ritualism is private judgment in gorgeous raiment, wrought about with divers colours. It is, I am afraid, a dangerous temptation to self-consciousness. I could never understand the passive endurance shown by some men when the Articles of the Baptismal creed were heretically denied, and, at the same time, their intense zeal for decorations and vestments. Ritual is seemly and proportionate as the clothing of Truth; and where the reality is present, Ritual becomes as unconscious as the light of day, or the circulation of the blood. A forest tree is hardly more unconscious of the majesty of its foliage than the Catholic Church of the splendour of its worship. Somebody well said lately of the Catholic priest —' Incense is the smell of the garden in which he is trained to work.'

But it is to be feared that the artificial perfuming of the garden is no sign of unconscious nature. Every fringe in an elaborate cope worn without authority, is only a distinct and separate act of private judgment; the more elaborate, the less Catholic: the nearer the imitation, the further from the submission of Faith. And this is openly exhibited in such words as these: 'The deceiving symbolism of Rome .. is ever lying in wait to profit by any mistakes of ours. She manifests by her undisguised hatred to all Catholic movement amongst us, how well she knows the strength we might find against Papal perversion in a satisfying amount of English Ritual.' The same speaker, in the same breath, proved that he knew well enough how little part Ritualism has in the conversion of souls, and how supremely indifferent the Catholic Church is to all such levities, by adding—'At the very gate of her spiritual dominion sit the two stern portresses, Supremacy and Infallibility; forbidding, as it seems to me, all attempt to us to enter.'* No Ritualism, however English and satisfying, would keep back one soul that believes the Catholic Church to be supreme and infallible. And Rome refuses all, Ritualists included, who deny these Divine Truths, our adver-

* Bishop Wilberforce's Charge, pp. 55, 63.

saries being witness. Little do they know of the action of the Catholic Church in England, who imagine that Unionism or Ritualism hinder the perpetual expansion which, day by day, is advancing on every side. Neither Unionism nor Ritualism would have existed but for the spread of the Catholic Church, and its action upon those who are outside its own unity. The Letters of a well-known writer, and of Lord Shaftesbury, in the 'Times,' show far more perception.

For instance :—

'It is said that I ought to have asserted the peril of the Established Church, rather than the peril of the Reformation in England.

'I plead guilty to having used the word "Reformation" intentionally, and not by oversight. The peril of the Church of England I assumed as a matter of course, but I desired to indicate a far greater peril. Deeply as I value the Established Church, I value the Reformation a vast deal more.

'Among other reasons for profound and reverential affection to the Church of England, to her Liturgy, her stated ministry, and her ordinances, I hold that she is the grand and only effective bulwark for the maintenance of the Reformation against the unceasing efforts, the indissoluble combinations, and methodical encroachments of the Papal See. I have long been, and I am still, conscientiously convinced that were the Establishment swept away a large proportion of her members would join the Church of Rome; many would remain indifferent; some, no doubt, would hold steadily to her doctrines; but even they, by their very weakness, would contribute to the progress of the great enemy.

'Highly as I appreciate the zeal, learning, talent, and principle of several of the Nonconformist bodies, I cannot see, in their organization and action, any power of presenting a systematic and continuous opposition to the Papal policy; and as for the Neological part of the community, [qu. all?] but a few of them, even of those who are not already Romanists, would probably become eventually the blind and willing disciples of the " Confession and Absolution " of a subtle and easy priesthood.'*

If, then, the *animus* of Unionism and Ritualism be to supplant the faith and worship of Rome, they must be set down as the last developments of the anti-Catholic spirit which, in the event of a future collision with the Catholic Church, would give all the intensity in their power to the rejection of the prin-

* Lord Shaftesbury in the *Times*, Dec. 29, 1866. See also Appendix IX.

ciple of Divine Faith. I hope better things for both. They have sprung from no controversial source, and their movement is towards Unity, and the only perfect worship of the Ever-blessed Trinity in the Holy Sacrifice of the Mass. We shall watch them with care and sympathy, and pray that they may not be tainted by the spirit of heresy, or schism, or turned off the path which leads to the only centre of rest—the Catholic and Roman Church.

The tendency of the Church of England to conform itself to the state of opinion among the English people, so as to reflect their subjective contradictions instead of witnessing to objective truths, has been elevated to a test of its perfection. The comprehension in one communion of all doctrines and opinions, howsoever irreconcilable, seems to have taken the place of the unity of truth. Dean Stanley has twice enunciated this in his graphic and facile style. Preaching on the eight hundredth anniversary of the dedication of Westminster Abbey, he spoke of its heterogeneous assemblage of tombs as a type of the Church of England.

'We know, how " in this temple of silence and reconciliation," are found in a strange but instructive union many renowned in their own day, and forgotten in ours; with others, once neglected, but by a late justice receiving their meed of honour; sovereigns and statesmen, divided in all but in death and in hope of a common resurrection; the ornaments of other communions, Roman, Puritan, Nonconformist, beside the uncompromising prelates of our own; the doubting sceptic hard by the enthusiastic believer; the smoking flax beside the blazing lamp; the bruised reed beside the sturdy tree.' And, afterwards describing England, he says: 'Church and State . . inextricably interwoven one with the other; opposing parties, both in Church and State, coexisting, neutralising, counteracting, completing each other, neither by the other entirely subdued, each by the other endured if not honoured.*

Again, preaching on last Christmas Day, he spoke as follows:—

'The proud Norman and the humble Saxon had been united in one nation, the great English people' . . . . 'From the first, there had been two tendencies in the English Church, but without destroying it. The Church of England was a mixed and double Church, because England was a mixed and double nation. If it were not so, it could not be a national Church. In these days there is a great conflict be-

* Dedication of Westminster Abbey, by A. P. Stanley, D.D. December 28, 1866.

tween two great parties. . . Some might regret that phrases had been left in the Prayer Book which savoured of the superstition which prevailed before the Reformation; while others might regret that phrases had been left which seemed to favour the rational spirit of modern times.'

'Both these certainly did exist together, and the only real breach of Christian faith and Christian charity was when either party thought it necessary to have the Church and nation to itself and to drive the other out. Let them take, for example, the divergence of opinion which there was on the subject of the Lord's Supper. Ever since the Reformation there had been two opposite tendencies, two separate forms of thought on this subject. Some, with the Church of Rome and the great reformer Luther had found pleasure in figuring to themselves the special nearness of Christ in the bread and wine, identifying these tokens with the body and blood of Christ himself; while with the Swiss reformer Zwinglius, and the Reformed Church, others had found pleasure in believing that the Saviour's presence was in his heart, within and not without. Traces of the conflict had been left in the very words of the Communion office. The Dean pointed out the various changes which the words of the Communion service had undergone, and showed that the policy of the Church had been not to ignore the views of either great party, but to preserve the spirit of both. . . . Since the first conflict, one party had been constantly endeavouring to drive the other out, always at a great loss to itself. . . . But the spirit of the nation and of the Church had been too strong for either of those parties, and he trusted that it would continue thus strong, in order that all might claim the blessed privilege of social intercourse and Christian communion. "If," said the Dean, "any have tried with untiring energy to drive us out, the true Christian retaliation will be with untiring forbearance to try to keep them in, even although we might be inclined most strongly to condemn their practices." . . The Dean concluded by earnestly deprecating divisions between Ritualists and Anti-Ritualists, Rationalists and Anti-Rationalists, counselling rather an appeal to Him who had been emphatically termed "the Prince of Peace." ' *

This is rather the vision of a poet than the argument of a theologian. But the same has been lately reduced to a theory and stated as the future of the Anglican Church. Lord Amberley, who may be taken as a sign of the stream of opinion among younger

---

* *Standard*, December 26, 1866.

laymen towards free thought, widening comprehension, and positivism in religion, quotes with approval Coleridge's fanciful theory of a National Church.

'The proper object and end of the National Church is civilization and freedom. . . . In relation to the National Church, Christianity, or the Church of Christ, is a blessed accident, a providential boon, a grace of God, a mighty and faithful friend. . . . Christianity is no essential part of the being of the National Church, however conducive or indispensable it may be to its well-being.' *

I have always thought that Swift was jesting when he gave as a reason against abolishing Christianity by Act of Parliament, that such abolition might remotely affect the security of the Established Church. But if Christianity be only a blessed accident, I have mistaken gravity for wit. Lord Amberley continues, 'It is, however, my profound conviction that the Church of England, if it is to continue at all, can only continue by making at least some approach to this ideal.' 'The Church of England, therefore, must either consent to some serious modification in its tenets, or it must ultimately fall beneath the weight of the profound dissent which its teaching

* *Fortnightly Review*, No. xxxvii. pp. 779, 780.

will excite.' 'It is quite true that no well-educated man can be expected to believe those (the Thirty-nine) Articles at the present day; yet compared with the Westminster confession—the approved and authorised creed of the Church of Scotland—they might be pronounced almost reasonable.' 'The Church of England is simply and entirely the creation of the State. The basis of its authority is wholly secular. No remote antiquity, no apostolic, or patristic origin, can be pretended in favour of its doctrines. They may indeed, in some cases, have an accidental coincidence with belief of an ancient date; but their authority in this country rests not upon their conformity either to Scripture or to the Fathers, or to the general opinion of Christendom, but upon the will of Parliament. The Church of England is built up from its foundation solely upon Acts of Parliament.' 'Were Parliament to abolish subscription to the Thirty-nine Articles, and to take away the penalties for teaching in opposition to them, there is no reason to doubt that they would all of them sink into oblivion as complete as that which has befallen those omitted from the series in the revision of 1562.' Did the writer remember that the subject of the first and second Articles is the Holy Trinity and the Incarnation? He adds, 'Variety rather than unity of doctrine should be its (the Established Church's) aim: for the manifold beliefs of the nation cannot be summed up in any single formula, however comprehensive.' 'The laity are defrauded of their rights when the National Church, which ought to have room for all, is, in fact, reserved for the benefit of a few.' 'Those creeds (of our ancestors) represent in part certain intellectual conditions which are past.' 'Much may be done by the mere occasional decisions of the judges, whose business it is to interpret the doctrines of the Church' 'It is eminently desirable that heresy should be taught.' 'It is not intended by this that these learned men (i.e. University Professors) must be heretics, but that they may be so, and that they shall occupy stations of authority and influence.'*

This seems to be no more than the consistent and hardy carrying out of the principles hitherto exhibited. And they are the legitimate product of the Reformation, its ultimate analysis, and a prophecy of the future. They exhibit the Rationalistic school as it will be in another generation: and the Established Church, if that school be in the ascendent. Before this comes, all that is consistent and persevering in the

---

* *Fortnightly Review*, No. xxxvii. The Church of England as a Religious body, *passim*.

Anglo-Catholic, Unionist and Ritualist movement will have found its rest and its home in the only Faith and Fold.

With such anti-Catholic elements as I have enumerated, in full activity, it is manifest that collision with the Catholic Church would be followed by a still more vehement antagonism of the National, Rationalistic, Protestant, Anglican, Anglo-Catholic spirit. These hostile arrays, often in mutual conflict, unite at once against the only true Church. They could easily stir up the depths of unbelief and secularity, which are always ready to overwhelm anything supernatural. Another rejection of the Divine authority of the Church as the witness, judge and teacher of Revealed Truth, would be followed by a still deeper rationalising of the Established Church, and a still more pronounced development of rationalistic unbelief. If 1688 generated a century of incipient Rationalism, the next rejection of the Divine authority of the Church would produce at least a century of Rationalism complete and dominant, no longer under profession of Christianity, but in the form of Deism, Secularism, Positivism, and final unbelief. The Anglican Church would, I fear, be deluged by it, and swept back towards the Dead Sea of the last century. The intellectual and doctrinal ascent which it has made would be reversed, and the labour of the last thirty years would be overthrown. It is well for all those within its pale who yearn after better and higher things, for dogma, authority, and unity, to take heed how they oppose the only immutable dogma, authority, and unity upon earth. It is a dangerous thing to indulge insular theories at such a cost. Just as the Protestant Establishment in Ireland is Calvinistic, Sacramentarian, and Puritan, because the presence of the Catholic Church elicits its perverse antagonism, so would it be in England. Jealousy distorts a fair countenance, and the presence of a superior will cloud a face which hides the consciousness of something wrong within. It is certain that Protestantism is nowhere so narrow and anti-Catholic as where it is in presence of the full Catholic Faith. The growth and expansion of the Catholicism which Anglicans so prize in their own communion, depends upon a genuine and sincere sympathy with the Catholic Church. All rivalry, or supplanting, or antagonism, will be fatal to them. Grace withers where charity is repressed or maimed. If they desire corporate union, the only way to it is to show that they love the Catholic Church. We should then have no more 'Eirenicons' discharged against the love we bear to the Mother of God, and the

Vicar of her Divine Son. Since the Papal aggression fury, we have had no popular collisions with the Catholic Church; and I will give reasons hereafter for believing that such collisions are becoming less and less imminent. Nevertheless, there is great reason to fear that a secret alienation of heart and will is widely spreading among those who, being on the threshold of the Faith, will not enter, and write 'Eirenicons' to keep others back from entering.

Such, then, are some of the reasons for fearing that the future of Faith in England may be more disastrous than the past. Now for our grounds of a better hope.

And first, the Catholic Church in England comes *sine sacculo et sine perâ*, in absolute poverty. The robberies of the Reformation have given us at least this advantage in the face of English public opinion. The Church has no worldly interest to serve. To a missionary Church, poverty is a sign of apostleship. Its priests and its bishops live on the free and willing offerings of their flocks. They have not only the independence which poverty alone can give, the freedom from suspicion of avarice and interest, but they have the generous sympathy and self-denying charity of the faithful, perpetually thoughtful and active to minister all they need. In no country under the sun is the labourer counted 'worthy of his hire' more joyfully and nobly than in England and Ireland at this day. The Catholic Church, therefore, preaches to the people of England with Apostolic freedom of speech. 'We seek not yours but you.' We are 'burdensome' to no man; and no jealousy, or envy, or ostentation of riches, tarnishes its light. Even the spoiler has no temptation to rob: 'Cantabit vacuus coram latrone viator.' The Church in England goes to and fro without fear, having nothing worth taking.

For this cause also, it is eminently in England, as the Church of God must always be in all lands, the Church of the poor. It is not the Church of the Crown, certainly. It is not the Church of the aristocracy. It is not the Church of the landlords in Ireland or in England. It is the Church of the people, springing from them, mingling with them, watching over them. In the reign of Mary it was royal and aristocratic, and multitudes were provoked and blinded to resist it. In James the Second's time, it was the Church of the Crown and of the Court, and of too many interested, venal, and worldly politicians. The people, already poisoned by a century of Protestantism, rose against it in terror, as against a French despotism and a

Spanish Inquisition. In these days it is the Church of the poor. What has the people of Ireland had to protect them or to confide in for three hundred years but its Church and its pastors? The Catholics of England are the poor of Ireland and the poor of England mingling together in poverty, labour, mutual kindness, and marriages which unite both races in the unity of Faith. In past times, since the Reformation, the Catholic Church has been an exotic in England—an air-plant suspended over the soil, without root in the earth. It is now deep in the clay, like the tap root of our old forest tree, which pierces downwards, and spreads on every side with an expanding and multiplying grasp. The million Catholics of England are interwoven with the whole population, and form a solid and sensible bulk in our cities and towns, and are more firmly rooted where these are largest, as in London, Liverpool, Manchester, and Glasgow.

Moreover, the Catholic Church re-enters England wholly free from all political action or interest. It is not bound up with any royal house, or disputed succession, or class legislation, or aristocratic privilege, or monopoly of power or wealth. It has no politics but the maintenance of legitimate authority and the widest popular beneficence. All it asks is to be let alone in the exercise of its spiritual mission. It does not petition for help or favour; but only free air and unfettered limbs. It does not invoke Royal Supremacies, Orders in Council, or Acts of Parliament to spread the Council of Trent, or to silence the Thirty-nine Articles. It has no point of contact, and therefore none of collision, with the political world. It is, moreover, visibly and evidently weak in the sphere of politics. The most timid and superstitious alarmist need have no fear of its political action. The only man who has made his celebrity by such alarms has earned for himself, both in Parliament and out of it, a reputation, but not for wisdom.

It is manifest, therefore, to the whole English people, that the Catholic Church appeals to it by no power or influence but those of conviction and persuasion; and of these it has no fear. It fancies itself to be too strong in reason and private judgment to be afraid of the Council of Trent and the claims of an infallible Church. It is, indeed, somewhat irritated and vehement when Englishmen are convinced and persuaded to submit to the Church. It is provoked with itself for being so easily perplexed, and sometimes so nearly convinced, if not that the Catholic Church is right, at least that the Church of England is wrong. Nevertheless, it has a love of fair play; and it is half willing that every man should follow his own conscience. If the Catholic Church can spread itself by fair means, by conviction of the reason and persuasion of the heart, that is, by truth and by charity, the people of England will give it a fair field, though no favour. This is all we need to ask; and within these terms the dangers of extensive collision hereafter are greatly diminished.

To this must be added, that the Rationalism of the last two centuries has so shaken the minds of men that they are both more tolerant of all forms of opinion, and more sensible of their lack of certainty as to any kind of religious belief. And though latitudinarians are proverbially the most intolerant of the Catholic Faith, because it is the most positive religion, and therefore the most opposed to them, nevertheless the vagueness of the English religion has cleared the way for the re-entrance of a coherent and intelligible rule of Faith. This constitutes a predisposition for the Catholic Church. It has become axiomatic with cultivated men of the world to say, 'If there be a visible Church it is the Church of Rome, and if there be a dogmatic religious Truth it is the Catholic Faith.'

I will not here repeat what I have so often said; namely, that Protestantism—I include Anglicanism—as a religion, is gone. It has departed from its original type, and disbanded into a multitude of irreconcileable diversities. It has always been in flux, always in transition, always endeavouring to return upon its past, never able to reproduce itself except it may be in a book, or in a handful of persons, lost in the flood which has long left its old bed, and is sweeping onwards to some new and unknown deep. In the Essay, so often quoted, occurs a remarkable recognition of this fact, though with little perception, explicit at least, of its cause. 'The names which once commanded universal homage among us—the Souths, Barrows, Tillotsons, Sherlocks—excite, perhaps, only a smile of pity. Literary taste is proverbially inconstant: but theological still more so; for here we have no rule or chart to guide us but the taste of our age. Bossuet, Bourdaloue, and Massillon have survived a dozen political revolutions. We have no classical theology, though we have not had a political revolution since 1688. For in this subject-matter, most Englishmen have no other standard of merit than the prejudices of sect.' * Where theology is floating, taste is change-

* Tendencies of Religious Thought, &c. p. 265.

ful. Where theology is always one and the same, taste is intelligent and fixed.

It is clear to all who believe the Catholic Church to be immutable in truth, or even immutable in error, that the reason of this perpetual freshness of its old writers is its immutability. It never parts from its anchors or drops down the stream of opinion.

Now, in this changed and open state of the religious intelligence of England there is another guarantee for a peaceful expansion of the Catholic Faith. And here I may also take account of the reascending of the religious mind of England as a preparation of heart for a return to the Catholic Church. Every operation of the Spirit of God in England is *in ordine ad Fidem, et in ordine ad Ecclesiam*. And it is undoubted that there was never a moment since the Reformation when the Dissenters of England were more inclined towards the Establishment, nor the Anglican body more inclined towards the Catholic Church. Such is the gravitation of men's minds. The polarity of England has been changed. The rivers which once flowed northward now run to the south. I do not overrate the importance of this. I do not conceal from myself the depths and energies of Anti-Catholic spirit, personal and corporate, which are still in strength and opposition. But over all there is a Divine Will and a Divine Power, reaching from end to end, and ordering all things sweetly, and disposing the minds of men for a happier future, if pride and malice do not mar it.

For this reason, Catholics hail with joy the professed desires of the Unionists, while they are compelled, under the highest direction upon earth, to expose the impossibility of union upon the principles of the Association, or upon any foundation but that which God has laid—the indivisible unity and perpetual infallibility of the Catholic and Roman Church. In the Appendix to this volume I have collected prayers for this intention, to which indulgences have been attached by the Holy See: and I would invite all who desire truth before peace, and peace through the truth, to unite in a daily intercession for the reunion of Christendom.

For the return of England to the Faith, the chief means will be a restored consciousness of the Personality, presence, and office of the Holy Ghost, and therein of the perpetual divine infallibility of the Catholic Church. For the reconciliation of the East, the devotion to the Blessed and Immaculate Mother of God is not only a link of union still drawing the

Oriental Churches in heart to the Holy See, but a barrier making all approximation to the Anglican system on their part impossible.*

Lastly, that we may bring all to one point, let us bear in mind that to the reunion of Christendom more is needed than the restoration of Anglicans and Greeks to faith and unity. In the East there are Nestorians and Eutychians; in the West there are Lutherans, Calvinists, and millions of other Protestants of various kinds. The Vicar of Christ is always saying, 'Other sheep I have, which are not of this fold: them also I

---

* This has been shown somewhat peremptorily by a certain Dr. Overbeck, a priest of the Russian Church, and decisively by Dr. Tait in his late Charge. 'But when we come to projects of re-uniting Christendom, we are not to be hurried on by mere feelings of romance. Of course we are not such children as to suppose that the real unity of Christendom is to be secured by the clergy in Rome, Constantinople, and London wearing similarly coloured stoles. We must ask calmly, but very seriously, how far these Churches are exerting themselves to escape from that idolatrous worship of our Lord's Mother which for centuries has made Christianity in those regions despicable in the eyes both of Jews and of Mahometans.' This is indeed a basis of reunion between Jews, Mahometans, and Anglicans, from which we Catholics are excluded, certainly more solid than ' wearing similarly coloured stoles.' Are we to understand that jealousy for the Divinity of the Incarnate Son of God be the motive common to all three? This is wild controversy, and suicidal. The Jew or the Mahometan rejecting the Incarnation, reject by consequence the honour due to the Mother of God. Let those who reject the honour due to the Mother of God search themselves and see how far the belief of the Incarnation is a part of their spiritual consciousness.

must bring, and they shall hear my voice ; and there shall be made one fold and one Shepherd.'* I confess to a deep and warm sympathy with all those who have thus been robbed of their inheritance, and above all with the Dissenters of England. In our prayers for the reunion of Christendom, we owe to them a fervent and generous intercession. There are among them noble and manly souls, full of love and of good works, over whom the heart of every Catholic pastor yearns. God grant, in His good time, that they also may be brought into the shelter and peace of the only Fold.

In this sense, and with the largest comprehension of all who are out of the unity of the Catholic and Roman Church, the following Indulgence has been asked of the Sovereign Pontiff, who in the midst of all his cares, watches over England with the love of a Father. His Holiness invites all who read these lines to pray for the reunion, under the one Visible Head on earth, of all who call themselves Christians.

The Rescript here given, in answer to the following petition, reached me as I was concluding these words :—

* St. John, x. 16.

'Most Holy Father,—In order that the faithful in England may be more and more incited to pray, day by day, with earnest hearts to the God of peace and Fountain of unity, that Christian nations, miserably rent from the One Universal Church, and all who are in schism and heresy, or deceived and wandering from the truth, may be brought back to the unity of faith and of the only fold, the Archbishop of Westminster humbly prays that your Holiness will vouchsafe to grant to all the faithful joined to Blessed Peter in the unity of faith, obedience and communion, who shall devoutly recite the *Gloria Patri* and *Ave Maria* with the intention of obtaining from the God of mercies, for the English nation, the Oriental Church, and all other nations separated from the Faith, a perfect conversion to the obedience of truth, and intimate reconciliation to the chair of Peter, an Indulgence of one year, as often as they shall recite the same; and in the Solemnity of Pentecost, and also in the Feasts of the Immaculate Conception of the Blessed Mother of God, Mary, ever-Virgin, and of the Martyr Saint Thomas of Canterbury, a Plenary Indulgence on the usual conditions.'

December 28, 1866.

We readily grant the above Indulgences on the necessary conditions. God grant that all may be 'of one lip' and one baptism; not after the mind of those who desire union by any means whatsoever, but may this union be according to the spirit of this Holy See, the Mistress of faith and truth.

PIUS P.P. IX.

Feast of Saint Thomas of Canterbury, 1866.
I attest the autograph of His Holiness,
GEORGE TALBOT,
Ab intimo cubiculo S.S.'

With these words of the Vicar of the Good Shepherd, calling His scattered flock to the one fold, I will conclude. Every baptised soul is the sheep of Jesus Christ: not those only who are within the fold, but those who are out of it. They all bear His mark. He would have them all brought back, cost what it may. It cost Him His most precious Blood to redeem them from the wilderness of sin and death. He has sent us to call them home. Shall we, then, refuse any sacrifice for the accomplishment of His will, which is the unity and sanctity of His Church? Shall any one be guiltless before Him who, for worldly interest, or fear of man, or private opinion, or love of position, or hope of high things in this world, refuses to submit to the only Church of God, and keeps open the divisions of Christendom? These are times of scattering and of gathering, *dispergendi et colligendi*. The Evil One and the mystery of impiety are at work to sow divisions on every side. The Holy Spirit of God and the mystical Body of Christ are at work to gather together in one the sheep that have been driven by the malice of men from the true Fold of Salvation. The state of England shows that the hearts of men are turning backward to a higher and happier law. Even the Association for the Reunion of Christendom is one more explicit proof that men are weary of heresy and schism.

The words of the Spirit are yet to be finally accomplished: 'As the shepherd visiteth his flock in the day when he shall be in the midst of his sheep that were scattered; so will I visit my sheep, and will deliver them out of all the places where they have been scattered in the cloudy and dark day. And I will bring them out from the peoples, and will gather them out of the countries, and will bring them to their own land: and I will feed them in the mountains of Israel, by the rivers, and in all the habitations of the land. I will feed them in the most fruitful pastures, and their pastures shall be in the high mountains of Israel; there shall they rest on the green grass, and be fed in fat pastures upon the mountains of Israel. I will feed my sheep: and I will cause them to lie down, saith the Lord God. I will seek that which was lost, and that which was driven away I will bring again: and I will bind up that which was broken: and I will strengthen that which was weak.' 'And my servant David shall be king over them, and they shall have one shepherd.'*

May He hasten the day of His promise.

Feast of the Epiphany, 1867.

* Ezek. xxxiv. 12-16; xxxvii. 24.

THE CROWN IN COUNCIL

ON

THE ESSAYS AND REVIEWS.

A LETTER TO AN ANGLICAN FRIEND

---·---

MY DEAR FRIEND,

Thirteen years ago, when the sentence of the Crown in the Gorham controversy had for a moment startled the Church of England, certain resolutions were published in the 'Times' newspaper. They were signed by thirteen members of the Anglican Establishment, of whom six afterwards submitted to the Catholic Church, four are no more, and five are still Anglicans. I well remember the long and earnest discussions which were held in preparing those resolutions, and especially the last night or early morning when, at length, they were finally agreed to, and the moment to sign them was come. They were times of great trial and pain. The men who engaged in that protest against the violation, as they believed, of the doctrine and office of the Church of

England, were I trust in earnest. They believed it to be a crisis of life or death both to the Anglican communion and to themselves. Everything, therefore, was staked upon a single issue, whether the Church of England would or would not liberate itself from a heresy imposed upon it, as they believed, by the civil power, and not by its own will. All agreed that, if bound by that heretical sentence, the Church of England would cease to be the way of truth and of salvation. Long and momentous years have now elapsed since that united Declaration, and the time is come to take account of what has passed. In order to do so more closely, we will recite the resolutions. They ran as follows:—

'1. That whatsoever at the present time be the force of the sentence delivered on appeal in the case of Gorham v. the Bishop of Exeter, the Church of England will eventually be bound by the said sentence, unless it shall openly and expressly reject the erroneous doctrine sanctioned thereby.

'2. That the remission of original sin to all infants, in and by the grace of Baptism, is an essential part of the Article: "One Baptism for the remission of sin."

'3. That, to omit all other questions raised by the said sentence, while such sentence does not deny the liberty of holding that Article in the sense heretofore received, it equally sanctions the assertion that original sin is a bar to the right reception of Baptism, and is not remitted except when God bestows regeneration beforehand by an act of prevenient grace (whereof Holy Scripture and the Church are wholly silent), thereby rendering the benefits of Holy Baptism altogether uncertain and precarious.

'4. That to admit the lawfulness of holding an exposition of an Article of the Creed, contradictory of the essential meaning of that Article, is, in truth and in fact, to abandon that Article.

'5. That, inasmuch as the faith is one, and rests upon one principle of authority, the conscious, deliberate, and wilful abandonment of the essential meaning of an Article of the Creed destroys the divine foundation upon which alone the entire faith is propounded to the Church.

'6. That any portion of the Church which does so abandon the essential meaning of an Article of the Creed, forfeits not only the Catholic doctrine of that Article, but also the office and authority to witness and teach as a member of the Universal Church.

'7. That by such conscious, wilful, and deliberate act such portion of the Church becomes formally separated from the Catholic body, and can no longer assure to its members the grace of the sacraments and the remission of sins.

'8. That all measures consistent with the present legal position of the Church ought to be taken without delay to obtain an authoritative declaration by the Church of the doctrine of Holy Baptism impugned by the recent sentence: as, for instance, by praying license for the Church in Convocation to declare that doctrine; or by obtaining an Act of Parliament to give legal effect to the decisions of the collective episcopate in this and all other matters purely spiritual.

'9. That, failing such measures, all efforts must be made to obtain from the said episcopate, acting only in its spiritual character, a re-affirmation of the doctrine of Holy Baptism impugned by the said sentence.'

Now it is here affirmed that unless the Church of England should clear itself of the heresy legalised by the Gorham judgment, it would forfeit both its authority to teach and its power to absolve. It would cease, that is, to guide its members to eternal life. I well remember that one of those who framed the above resolutions addressed the rest in these words: 'If, then, the Church of England shall not clear itself of the Gorham judgment, we are all, I suppose, prepared to leave it?' I remember likewise the answer of one who spoke, I fear, also for others. He said, come what might, he had no intention to leave the Church of England. But how any man could remain when the power to teach and to absolve no longer existed, he did not explain. Such was the first indication of what we have since witnessed. With others, however, it was a real and earnest declaration of the course they believed themselves in duty bound towards God to pursue.

At that time it was believed by all who signed these resolutions that the Church of England was a living member of the universal Church; and that it might still be able by some authoritative act of its own, either in Synod or by its Bishops, to repudiate the heresy which had been legalised by the judgment of the Crown, and thereby to release itself from the taint of heresy and the consequent forfeiture of its spiritual powers.

Such an attempt was made.

The late Bishop Blomfield introduced into Parliament a Bill to amend the Appellate Jurisdiction of the Crown in matters of doctrine. By that Bill it was provided that in all such questions the matter of doctrine should be divided from the matter of law, and that the doctrine should be adjudged by the

Bishops, the law by the Judges of the Privy Council. The debate upon the Bill was memorable. It excited the highest expectation and the greatest personal anxiety; for it was well known that on its issue the conduct of many would in no small degree depend. When the night arrived there was a great concourse at the bar and in the galleries of the House of Lords. Bishop Blomfield spoke, as he always did, with an earnest, simple, manly, and pathetic eloquence. Another of his brethren displayed his great gifts with much earnestness, warning the House that unless some redress were given, consequences which they would least desire would surely follow. 'Many,' he said, 'who were gems in the Church of England would fall from it.' Lord Carlisle answered not amiss, that these gems in its vesture must be loosely set if they could be so lightly shaken off. Words of worldly wisdom and of prophecy, for they must be indeed firmly riveted into the Establishment who could endure what has followed. Lord Brougham spoke against the Bill. He said, with plain English common sense, that the bishops would constitute no sufficient tribunal for questions of controverted doctrine. They might divide in equal numbers, and give, therefore, no decision; or by a bare majority, which would carry no moral conviction to any one.

Or the majority, however great, would not tell by force of number against a minority comprising the few of known learning and influence with whom public opinion would certainly go. The end of the Bill might have been foreseen. It was rejected with an overwhelming rejection, not only of opposition but of arguments. So utter was the defeat that it has never been heard of more. No one has ventured to introduce any like it again. The vice of the whole situation was so visible and so hopeless that it has been left without an attempt to cure it. I remember that among those who listened to the debate there was one to whom Lord Brougham's speech suggested one more question as completing the series of his objections to the scheme: 'Suppose that all the bishops of the Church of England should decide unanimously on any doctrine, would any one receive the decision as infallible?' No one; not so much as those who declared that even if the Established Church should not clear itself, they would not leave it; not even they would affirm the unanimous decision of its episcopate to be infallible. This reduced the question to the last analysis. To those who believed that God has established upon the earth a Divine and, therefore, an unerring guardian and teacher of His Faith, this event demonstrated that the Church

of England could not be that guardian and teacher,
and that no new scheme of appellate jurisdiction
could cure the fatal vice of its position, separated
from the Universal Church, and deprived thereby of
supernatural assistance and direction. Though logically evident, however, the gravity of the subject
and the fear of precipitation caused them to act deliberately and to move slowly. They felt it due to
the sacredness of Truth, to the relations of public and
private confidence and friendship, to the trusts and
duties of their past life, to the respect they owed to
many, and lastly, to themselves, to allow no passion
or precipitation to bias or to hurry them in so momentous a crisis, in which a false step might affect
not themselves only, but many others, not only for
this life, but for the life to come. What in the end
they did you know; and I shall not say more than
that they were as keenly sensible as you could desire
them to be of all the losses and sorrows which they
had to bear in following their reason and their conscience, or, I may more truly say, the Divine Voice
of the Church of God. But from that hour, what
before was a conclusion of the intellect, became a
consciousness of the soul; and an intuition of truth
based upon a divine certainty has so filled their whole
soul that not only no shadow of a momentary doubt

has ever passed over their conscience or their reason, but a sense of wonder has arisen in their minds how they could so long have failed to perceive a truth which is now self-evident. All they can say is, 'One thing I know, that whereas I was blind, now I see.'*

But my purpose is to take account of what has passed since these Resolutions were published. Has the Church of England in any way cleared itself of accepting the heresy imposed on it by the Gorham judgment? Has it made, or has it had the opportunity of doing so? Has it manifested any disposition so to do?

Let me simply narrate a few facts, and at the end we may draw some conclusions.

1. First, the Church of England has so accepted the final Appellate Jurisdiction of the Crown, that no further attempt has been made to amend it. It is self-evident that only one remedy can be found. Either all appeals must be settled within the four seas, or they must be carried beyond them; that is, the Church of England has no choice for its final appeal but the Crown or the Holy See. The attraction by which it adheres to the Crown is proportioned to the repulsion by which it flies from the Holy See. And the consciousness of this fact has made it sub-

* S. John ix. 25.

side and acquiesce under the royal supremacy as the shelter and blind to conceal the untenableness of its position: for the common sense of Englishmen would refuse to submit in appeal, on matters of faith, to the judgment of a bench of bishops, who disclaim infallibility, and are openly divided against themselves.

But I have to do with facts, not arguments.

2. Next, it was said that if the Church of England could only speak, it would clear itself, if not of the Appellate Jurisdiction of the Crown, at least of the Gorham heresy. The Church of England has spoken, and it has not cleared itself of either the one or the other. Nay, it has spoken with a publicity and a freedom and an unanimity never known before in the memory of living men. Soon after the Gorham judgment, a Declaration, signed by three names, of whom two are now no more, was sent to every clergyman and dignitary of the Church of England. The Declaration was to the effect that the Oath of Supremacy could be taken to oblige the conscience only in matters of a civil and not of a spiritual kind. Out of 17,000, some 1,800 signed it. More than 15,000 acquiesced passively in the royal supremacy, as exhibited in the Gorham judgment. But this was only a prelude. While these things were done,

the Catholic hierarchy was restored in England: and the Church of England, bishops, clergy, and laity, in ecclesiastical sections of dioceses, chapters, archdeaconries, rural chapters, diocesan meetings, with an unanimity never known till then, not only protested against the Supremacy of the Holy See, but fell for protection at the feet of the Royal Supremacy. I pass over the effusions of loyalty, devotion, adulation, the *cultus civilis* with which the Church of England embraced once more and pressed to its heart the Statute of the 24th of Henry VIII. An instinct told it that the supremacy of the Crown was the basis of its separate existence; and that it has no other shelter from the necessity and the duty of submitting to the supremacy of the universal Church.

3. But it may be said that if the Church of England could but speak in Convocation, it would clear itself of complicity in the Gorham heresy. But the Church of England has spoken in Convocation, and it has not cleared itself. It seems as if Divine providence had granted to the Church of England all the conditions it invoked as excuses, in order to expose their nullity. After a century of silence, the Convocation had liberty to speak. But of what has it spoken? I need not make a list of

its utterances. I need only say that a protest against the Gorham judgment is not one of them. *Qui tacet, assentit.* But perhaps it may be said that it was not permitted to speak on this particular subject. To this I would answer: 'If the watchman see the sword coming, and sound not the trumpet, and the people look not to themselves, and the sword come and cut off a soul from among them; he indeed is taken away in his iniquity, but his blood I will require at the hand of the watchman.'* A Church that can hold its peace in the presence of a heresy is not the Church of God. A Church that has a living consciousness of the revelation of God, and of a Divine commission to declare it to a perishing world, could not be silent. Popular tumults, the power of Governments, loss of endowments, of legal position, of life itself, could not restrain it. The creations of man may be bound and gagged. *Verbum Dei non est alligatum. Ubi Spiritus Domini, ibi libertas.* 'The Word of God is not bound.' 'Where the Spirit of the Lord is, there is liberty.' The Church of God, and the operations of His Spirit in the Church, cannot be silenced or suspended. But for thirteen years the Church of England has met, I know not how often,

* Ezekiel xxxiii. 6.

in Convocation; but on the Appellate Jurisdiction and the Gorham heresy not an act has been done, not a word has been resolved.

4. In these last years, the doctrine of the Lord's Supper has been subjected, like that of Baptism, to legal proceedings, both in England and Scotland, and with a strange result. In Scotland a higher, and if I may so say of an erroneous doctrine, a truer statement of it has been rejected by the bishops of the Episcopal Church in the case of one of their own number; whereas in England, one of the thirteen who signed the declaration that to admit contradictory doctrines on Holy Baptism was to abdicate the office of teacher of the truth, was in his own case compelled to claim the liberty of holding one of two contradictory doctrines on the Lord's Supper. Archdeacon Denison was constrained, by the necessity of his position, to be content with a liberty to hold his own opinion on the one sacrament, as Mr. Gorham had claimed on the other; and in this the Church of England has so completely acquiesced, that no effort is heard of to vindicate what it considers to be its own doctrine, or to expel its opposite.

5. Time was, the Jerusalem bishopric shocked and alarmed the members of the Church of England,

even to contemplating withdrawal from a body which had implicated itself with the congeries of heresies and schisms which make up the Evangelical Protestantism of Prussia. Since then, bishops of the Church of England have fraternised with Swiss Presbyterians and Swiss Unitarians; and four archbishops have signed a document in praise of the bishop in Jerusalem, for making proselytes from the Catholic Church, and, what is stranger for Anglicanism, from the Greek Church in the East. But who now protests against the Jerusalem bishopric? Yet who is free from complicity with this alliance and solidarity, to talk as men do nowadays, with the Protestants of Germany? Time was, that Anglicans would have protested against Luther and Calvin as much as against S. Pius V. or Pius IX. But now they are actually in union with them, and are silent.

6. Twenty years ago, Dr. Hampden was keenly censured for an obscure book against scholastic theology. Now, Rationalism is paramount at Oxford; and its teachers, though whispered against, are in honour and power.

7. The House of Commons has ceased to profess Christianity, by admitting the Jews to Parliament: but it legislates for the Church of England, and the

Prime Minister whom it chooses nominates all Anglican bishops. It has lately been discussing the expediency of altering the Prayer Book, and of abolishing subscription to the Articles.

8. The Christian law of marriage has been abolished by Act of Parliament. For the first time since the coming of S. Augustine of Canterbury, the bond of marriage is dissoluble in English law; and divorce, borrowed partly from Judaism, and partly from the schismatics of the East, has been introduced. This has been done by Act of Parliament alone; yet the Church of England has made no protest, and its clergy are bound to remarry, or to lend the church for the remarriage of, those whose husbands or wives are still living: and they do so.

9. It is no wonder, after the legal establishment of successive polygamy in England, that simultaneous polygamy should be allowed by Dr. Colenso, under the protection of Dr. Whately, to the Christians of Natal. Luther and Melanchthon granted the same to the Elector of Hesse. But time was, that members of the Anglican Church rose with indignation against the Judaising reformers. Now, divorce is publicly sanctioned, and invades their own houses, and they are silent.

10. I remember how great a storm of astonishment

and indignation was excited by the publication of Tract 90, and Dr. Ward's pamphlets on the Articles. The authors have lived to see the ' Essays and Reviews,' and to look on while a sentence in the Court of Arches absolved two of the writers from all but a residuum of censure, and a sentence of the Crown in Council absolved them from the little that remained. It was held to be non-natural and immoral in Dr. Newman and Dr. Ward to extend the Thirty-nine Articles in the direction of the Catholic Church, from which Anglicans professed they hardly differed, and never separated. But Dr. Newman and Dr. Ward were condemned. The Essayists and Reviewers have carried the interpretation of the Thirty-nine Articles into the heart of Rationalism, and they are publicly and authoritatively absolved for doing so. Such is the progress of Rationalism in the Church of England as known to the law, and such its pronounced anti-Catholic character. But to this I must return hereafter.

11. Again, in those days Anglicans or Anglo-Catholics claimed an exclusive position, as the only true and lineal descendants and representatives of the genuine Church of England. Now, they are but one among many schools, equally recognised, most of them more popular. They are now content with a

toleration, and with the permission to believe or to teach what they *hold* to be the truth in the midst of contradictions. As an example of this, and as a sign of new and strange combinations, I may mention the letter of alliance addressed to the 'Record' newspaper by one of our friends. Some years ago he would have rested his belief of eternal punishment not upon the Assembly's Catechism, but upon the faith of the Universal Church; and his instincts would have drawn him as surely in that direction to-day as they would have repelled him from what is known as the Low Church, against which he has spent his life in protesting. These changes are but too intelligible.

12. It is only justice to the Convocation to state that it has protested against the 'Essays and Reviews;' and I cannot better describe the book than in the document drawn up by the Convocation:—

'We have carefully examined the work, and we consider the following to be its leading principles:—

'1. That the present advanced knowledge possessed by the world in its manhood is the standard whereby the educated intellect of the individual man, guided and governed by conscience, is to measure and determine the truth of the Bible.

'2. That when the Bible is assumed to be at variance with the conclusions of such educated intellect, the Bible must be taken in such cases to have no Divine authority, but to be only a human utterance.

'3. That the principles of interpretation of the Bible hitherto universally received in the Christian Church are untenable, and that new principles of interpretation must now be substituted, if the credit and authority of the Holy Scriptures are to be maintained.

'We find that in many parts of the volume statements and doctrines of the Holy Scriptures are denied, called into question, or disparaged; for example :—

' 1. The verity of miracles, including the idea of creation presented to us by the Bible.

' 2. Predictive prophecy, especially predictions concerning the Incarnation, Person, and Offices of our Lord.

' 3. The descent of all men from Adam.

' 4. The fall of man and original sin.

' 5. The Divine command to sacrifice Isaac.

' 6. The Incarnation of our Lord.

' 7. Salvation through the blood of Christ.

' 8. The Personality of the Holy Spirit.

' 9. Special and supernatural inspiration.'

The Church of England has indeed so far spoken

in this case; or, more truly, those who in the Church of England are opposed to the 'Essays and Reviews' have spoken in Convocation. And yet even this has only made their case more hopeless. So little weight was given to this act that, notwithstanding the above-mentioned declaration, the Judge in the Court of Arches dismissed almost all the articles preferred against two of the writers in the book thus condemned. He declared that they did not contain matter contrary to the Articles and formularies of the Church of England, and therefore did not incur censure. We have had, then, an evidence that the Church of England in Convocation, has no power to release itself from complicity with the heresies that are in the mouths of its clergy, nor to purify itself from the infection of error. Its case in this instance is worse than before. In the Gorham contest it passively acquiesced, and was silent. Now it has protested, and in spite, I may say in defiance, of its protest, the largest congeries of heresies ever yet published by clergymen of the Church of England, at least at any one time, has been legally admitted as permissible, both within its pale and in the teaching of its clergy. More than this; the Court of Arches, after dismissing many articles, condemned Mr. Wilson and Dr. Williams for errors of the gravest kind: nevertheless, the punishment awarded was not inhibition to teach until they had retracted their errors and made reparation for the scandal, but suspension for one year. The errors thus lightly visited were no less than a denial of eternal punishment and of the inspiration of a great part of Holy Scripture.

Later still, the claim of the Church of England as a teacher of Christianity has been even more rudely and fatally destroyed. The case of the two suspended clergymen was carried, as was Mr. Gorham's case, to the Crown in Council. The whole Church of England, with all the memories of the Gorham judgment full upon it, stood looking on, and by its silence acquiesced in the process. After full hearing, the sentence given was a reversal of the judgment of the Court below; or in other words, a declaration that to deny the inspiration of any portion of the Old and New Testament, so long as no entire Book is thereby erased from the Canon, and to deny the eternity of punishment for the wicked, is not at variance with the Articles or formularies of the Church of England.

It would seem as if Divine Providence were mercifully striving to open the eyes of men by putting before them the most patent, emphatic, articulate, and self-evident proofs of the false and untenable position in which the so-called Reformation has placed them. If any Anglicans or Protestants could imagine, what no Catholic can, that the questions about Baptism and the Lord's Supper are mysterious and remote from the substance of faith, yet it is impossible to conceive for a moment that the eternity of punishment and the inspiration of Scripture are not vital to the faith of Christians. Nevertheless, both may be denied, as they have been in this case without suspension from the office of teacher, by the clergy of the Church of England.

And here I cannot omit to say that the judgment of the Court of Arches cleared the way for Dr. Colenso. What Dr. Lushington declared it was lawful to do, Dr. Colenso did. It may be that he has somewhat exceeded his permission, but *favores sunt ampliandi* is a maxim in law. While the Lushington judgment was preparing, Dr. Colenso was writing, if not printing, his illustrations of the liberty of the Church of England and of the application of the 'critical reason' to the text of Scripture. I hope I may be mistaken, and I shall with joy revoke my opinion, or rather be relieved of my fear, but my unchanging conviction is that Dr. Colenso represents the religion of the majority of English laymen. He has addressed himself pointedly to them with a style of thought and writing which reminds me of Cobbett. And I believe that the confidence, and I must add the shallowness, of his books make them singularly popular among men who have an impatience both of study and of the supernatural; and such, I fear, is the state of most educated English laymen.

We are come then to a time in which to reckon up and to review the years since we parted. In these thirteen years a crowd of events has come to pass. And surely not one of them gives reason to believe that the Church of England will or can release itself from the net of heresies in which it is involved. Somebody has likened it to the shirt of Nessus. I will not do so; for my belief is that when the Church of England lost its inherence in the universal Church, the principle of all spiritual and intellectual disease was developed in its blood, and ate into its bone. I do not believe that it is a poisoned vestment which is put upon it from without, but a morbid and manifold disease which is ever reproducing itself from within. And, certainly, the last thirteen years have multiplied the plague spots, and have shown that there is no reaction in the patient, 'no balm in Gilead, and no physician there.'

It is a mournful sight, and one to make men wise, to see the Church of England, which rose up as a reformer of the Church of God, confounded at the work of its own hands. It denounced the celibacy of the clergy as hostile to society, and it has cut through the root of society by establishing divorce. It condemned purgatory as a 'blasphemous fable,' and its own clergy deny the eternal punishment of the wicked. It rebelled against the living Church as the interpreter of Holy Scripture, and its own children are denying the Inspiration of the Sacred Books. The experiment of reforming the Church of God and purifying the salt of the earth has been tried and found wanting. And these thirteen years have added a luminous evidence of the danger and of the chastisement of those who would instruct the Church of Jesus Christ.

I will add only two other remarks to what I have said.

It seems to be a Divine Providence that the Church of England should be punished in that which was its pride. It rebelled against the living voice of the Church of God, under the pretext of honouring the Holy Scripture. 'The Bible, and nothing but the Bible, is the religion of Protestants;' from Chillingworth downwards, this has been their maxim and their boast. The Church of England rested everything on the Scriptures—its Articles, the Baptismal Creed, the whole of Christianity. False and impossible as this rule of faith is, until now no one was listened to who doubted it ; all were denounced who denied it. The Scripture was affirmed to be the foundation, *et super hanc petram* the Church of England professed to build itself. But it is precisely the Scripture which has been ruined under its feet. Its own clergy, its own bishops, protected by its own tribunals, are now denying the inspiration and intrinsic credibility of a large part of the sacred books. My object is not to write a history or a treatise, but only a brief enumeration, to you who know them already, of the phenomena of the last thirteen years, forerunners, as I believe, of a dissolution certain and inevitable. I know, indeed, and know with joy, that there are thousands of good and sincere hearts who believe and love the Holy Scriptures, and turn with pain and fear from these dishonours of the sacred books. Happily they are neither logical, nor consistent with the principles of the Anglican Reformation, or of the Anglican Church, to which, through want of light, they pay the homage of their best and highest instincts of love, dutifulness, obedience, and trust. Such souls, I trust, God in His mercy will illuminate with a more perfect faith. And you I believe to be one of them. I well remember the long hours of anxiety and fear in our lonely walks before the goodness of God led me from the city of confusion to the vision of faith and peace. You were hopeful then that great changes were near at hand, and that the Church of England would be found true and faithful as a teacher and guide of souls. Where are those fair hopes now? Every year they have receded further and further before you. And the confusions have multiplied, and a darkness has settled over the Church of England, so that 'no man can see his brother, nor move himself out of the place where he is.' *

The only other point I will touch is this. It is of no avail to say that the Court of Arches and the Crown in Council are not the Church of England. They are the tribunals of the Church of England, and by them the Church of England is bound, and for them the Church of England is responsible both to man and to God, so long (to use the words of a friend who thirteen years ago spoke in one of the last gleams of his higher aspirations) so long as the Church of England chooses for itself 'the mess of potage rather than the portion of the Bride.' It is

* Exodus x. 23.

of no use, nor is it, I must say, manly, or real, or truthful, to pretend that the Church of England or those in it are free from complicity in the decisions of its own tribunals. It is a fearful thing, seen in the light of the presence of God and of the eternal world, to acquiesce in the existence of tribunals which may legalise whatsoever doctrines appear to them to be, not true, of which they disclaim to judge, but admissible in the Church of England. The Anglican Church has, we may infer, two classes of doctrines; those which are true, and those which though false are legal; yet both equally admissible, and both equally taught to those for whom Christ died, to the simple, the poor, the little ones fresh from Baptism. Is it possible that any one who knows and loves the truth as it is in Jesus, or has any fidelity to His person, or jealousy for His honour, or love for the souls for whom He gave His precious Blood, can acquiesce even by silence or passive communion with a system which thus dishonours Him and destroys His flock? But in truth it is not the tribunals, but the Church of England, which is the source of all these evils. If the Church of England were the Church of God, the tribunals could do it no harm. It is Anglicanism which *generates* the errors. The tribunals only *legalise* them.

The Anglican system is the source of all its own confusions, which the law contemptuously tolerates.

My dear friend, S. Augustine says that the perpetual miracles of God's almighty power pass unperceived because they are daily before us. It seems to me that the tokens of His hand, and the writing upon the face of these thirteen years, in like manner, are imperceptible to those who live in the midst of them. To us, who by God's mercy look on the Anglican system from without, it seems incredible that the meaning and the purport of the warning and the call of God in these events should not speak home, and penetrate every reason and every heart with the understanding of His truth and will. You have been saying, ' If the Church of England does not do this or that, it will be bound.' But the Church of England has done neither the one thing nor the other, and it is therefore bound. ' If this or that should happen, then nothing remains.' But this supposed event has happened again and again, in ways more emphatic and more explicit than could have been conceived. It is no surprise that the descendants of Cranmer, and Hooper, and Bradford, should deny baptismal regeneration, or that the posterity of Abbot and Tillotson should deny the Real Presence. But that even the tribunals of the Church of England should permit a formal denial of the inspiration of large parts of Holy Scripture, and of the eternity of punishment, goes beyond all anticipation. It seems to have been permitted in mercy to open the eyes of men to see and know that the Church of England is not the Church of God, and that it has fallen from the unity of the faith, and holds communion with those who destroy revelation; nay, even permits them to speak in its name, and to mislead the souls of millions out of the way of eternal life. The alternative is very simple: either the Church of God is the dwelling-place of the Holy Ghost, and the organ of His perpetual, immutable teaching, or it is not. If it is, then certainly the Church of England is neither that Church nor any part of it; not only because it is separated from the whole Christian Church throughout the world, but because it contradicts it, and appeals from it to Scripture, to Fathers, to Councils past or future—it matters not to what, for an appeal is a denial of the ultimate authority of the judge whose sentence we refuse. And what is this but to deny the perpetual assistance and perpetual voice of the Spirit of God in the Church of God? And this the Church of England has done in every form: by affirming the incoherent theory of the sufficiency of Holy Scripture; by thus excluding the necessity of a living and divine teacher; by professing to purify the doctrines of the Church, which is to assume their corruption, and so to deny their immutable perpetuity. It is true, the Church of England disclaims all infallibility for itself; but it thereby still more strongly denies infallibility to the whole Church upon earth, which it professes to reform and to guide into the way of primitive Christianity. What is this but to affirm that the ultimate principle of certainty in matters of religion is the human reason exercising itself critically upon Scriptures, Fathers, Councils, history, evidences, and the like? In other words, the Church of England has based itself upon the same principle which the Essayists and Reviewers have carried out to its legitimate result. The Church of England, in the Articles, affirms that all Churches have erred, that General Councils may err; it rests the creeds upon Scripture, and Scripture, both its canon and interpretation, upon historical evidence tested by criticism. And Dr. Williams, Dr. Colenso, and Mr. Wilson have only applied the same test of critical reason to its inspiration and intrinsic credibility. The Church of England will not own its offspring, but they are its legitimate sons.

I can only pray that the Holy Spirit of Truth, who alone revealed the science of God and of His Son, and always, in every age, by His immediate presence and assistance in the one and undivided Universal Church, perpetuates, defines, and propounds the faith, may in this moment of confusion reveal Himself to many; that they may come forth from the spiritual captivity in which they are bound, and return to the liberty wherewith Christ has made them free; free not only from human errors, but from all human authority over their faith, by submission to the only Divine Truth, and the only Divine Teacher among men—the Church of Jesus Christ.

   Believe me, my dear friend,
    Always affectionately yours,
       H. E. MANNING.

March 8, 1864.

THE CONVOCATION

AND

THE CROWN IN COUNCIL.

THE CONVOCATION AND THE CROWN IN COUNCIL.

My dear Friend,

I have carefully read, so far as I could find them, all the answers which have been made to the letter I addressed to you three months ago. About six or seven have appeared in newspapers or reviews, but I have not found in them more than two points which seem to me to require any comment.

The one is the statement that I have failed to distinguish between the Church and the Establishment, and that I have charged upon the Church of England what attaches only to its legal and secular manifestation. Whether this be true or probable we shall see hereafter.

The other is a complaint that I have spoken with bitterness, and, with, I think some one wrote, 'a

savage joy,' of the confusions of the Anglican system.
Now, on this point I will say at once that I am not
conscious of it, and that if I had done so I should be
sorry for it. I had the sincerest desire to speak with
moderation and with kindness. I feel no temptation
to be bitter or unkind, I hope, towards any one; still
less towards so many old and dear friends, for whom,
though we seldom or never meet, I cherish a true
affection. Moreover, I am no believer in the efficacy
of controversial asperities; and in my last letter I
studiously erased every word which I thought could
give needless displeasure. And I asked of a friend
to read and to weigh what I had written, with the
same view. The facts I had to state were in themselves severe; and I endeavoured to follow the known
rule, τὰ σκληρὰ μαλθακῶς. Accept this as an assurance
of my intention both in the last letter and in this. I
cannot soften what in its simplest enunciation is hard:
I ought not if I could, for truth must be told truthfully; in charity, but in sincerity. If I have failed
in charity, point out the word to me; I will make
with joy the amplest reparation, though for a fault
which I had no intention to commit. In truth, my
habitual desire and daily prayer for you all is, that
you may be released from the bondage in which I
also once was held. But I know that even this will

grate upon some ears which are unused to plain speaking, and who resent even a charitable desire for their fuller illumination as an offence against their superior light and their actual perfection.

In my last letter I said that the Church of England had not repudiated either the Gorham judgment or the 'Essays and Reviews;' that Convocation had met and pronounced on many things, but on this had passed no sentence. I must now modify this statement. What I said of the Gorham judgment is still true; but the 'Essays and Reviews' have been condemned by the Convocation of the Province of Canterbury. Perhaps no event could better illustrate the argument of my last letter. You will remember I asked, 'If the Convocation should pronounce even unanimously on any doctrine, who would receive its judgment as infallible?' or, I may say, as divinely certain, or as final, or as superseding the Privy Council, or as reversing its sentence? We have now this supposition put to the test. I will not in any way diminish the importance of the condemnation by pointing out that the Upper House was equally divided, and that the condemnation passed only by the casting vote of Archbishop Longley; nor by referring to the opposition of a large minority, maintained for two or three days in the Lower House, as an evidence of the doubtfulness of the condemnation. Let me put it at the highest, as an undoubted and authoritative rejection by the Church of England in Convocation of the book and its heresies. We will assume then, for the purpose of argument, that the Church of England has spoken. Will any one modify the opinion he has hitherto entertained of the 'Essays and Reviews' because of this judgment? For instance, will the readers and followers of the 'Essays and Reviews' give up the book as unsound? Will those who have learned to disbelieve the inspiration of parts of the Scriptures, or the eternity of punishment, or the Messianic prophecies, renounce these opinions as errors because the Convocation has condemned the book? What effect will this condemnation produce upon the public opinion of the country? The 'Times' newspaper may be taken as a witness on this point: but I forbear to quote its contemptuous notice of the vote of Convocation. What legal effect will this synodical decision have? Are those clergymen who avowedly hold the condemned opinions thereby disqualified to be ministers or beneficed clergymen of the Church of England? Has this condemnation any force, or has it none? Is it a judicial decision, or a mere theological manifesto? That is, has it any real effect, or none at all?

To this a pointed answer has been given by a very exalted personage in the House of Lords. It is needless that I should do more than refer to the conversation on Lord Houghton's question as to the course the Government intended to take in respect to the proceedings in Convocation. The Lord Chancellor, in a manner which I do not commend, laid down the undoubted law of the land on the powers of Convocation. It is certain beyond controversy that by the 26th of Henry VIII. c. 1, and by the 1st of Elizabeth, c. 1, 17, 18, the Convocation cannot assemble without the Royal writ; nor, when assembled, deliberate without licence; nor, even when licence is granted, deliberate on any matter not expressed or contained in it, nor make any resolutions or constitutions of any sort, without incurring *præmunire*. The law laid down by Lord Westbury is to me evidently correct, and in perfect accordance with all that I ever read, in years past, of the post-Reformation statutes and the authoritative expositions of them by such writers as Ayliffe, Wake, Stillingfleet, and the like. And I cannot doubt that the proceedings in Convocation were illegal; or that in their result they are, to all effects and purposes, null and void. Their nullity alone will preserve those who partook in them, and every one who might endeavour to act upon them, from the penalties of *præmunire*. The dilemma is simple. Either the synodical declaration is a judicial act, or it is not. If it be not, then it is waste paper; if it be, the Convocation is in collision with the Crown in Council. Now, I dismiss all questions of *præmunire*, and all the pleasantry of the learned Lord, in which, most impartially, I have no sympathy. I wish to treat this question in its bearing upon the Church of England, and upon the religious faith and conscience of its members.

For my own part, I believe the Convocation has acted rightly. It has placed itself in direct collision with the Crown in a matter where our Divine Lord has bestowed no power upon any Crown, and all power in heaven and earth upon His Church alone. Do not mistake me. I do not recognise the Church of England as that Church in any part of it; a belief which, as Dr. Newman has said, nothing but a miracle could reproduce in me. But I place myself in your position for a moment, and view this matter in your light. I think the Convocation has done well. The Civil Power declared that clergymen of the Church of England might teach the matter contained in the 'Essays and Reviews' with impunity. The Convocation has declared these 'teachings to be contrary to the doctrine received by the United Church of England

and Ireland, in common with the whole Catholic Church of Christ.' Beyond all doubt, therefore, no clergyman of the Church of England can teach such doctrine with impunity.

We have here a full and direct variance between the Convocation and the Crown in Council.

Let it be observed that the Convocation does not limit itself to re-affirming the doctrine denied in the 'Essays and Reviews,' after the manner of the feeble and irrelevant Protest which has lately met with so just a reprobation from Dr. Thirlwall. It declares the teaching of the 'Essays and Reviews' to be contrary to the doctrine of the Universal Church; that is to say, to be false and heretical.

Not only, therefore, cannot such doctrine be taught with impunity in the Church of England, but it cannot be taught at all by its clergy without violation of their duty. What the Crown in Council permits, the Convocation prohibits. Nor let it be said that by impunity is meant only 'legal impunity;' that is, exemption from ecclesiastical proceedings and censures in the courts of law. The Convocation denies to these errors all impunity, all tolerance whatsoever. No opposition can be more point-blank: and nothing less would have saved the Convocation from the just condemnation of paltering with words, and of betraying its convictions.

The Lord Chancellor, after quoting the Acts of Henry VIII. and Elizabeth, by which all jurisdiction, spiritual and ecclesiastical, and all power of correcting 'errors, heresies, schisms, &c.,' is annexed and united to the Crown, went on to say: 'Now, if you had ten thousand times the jurisdiction attaching to Convocation, the whole of it would be taken away and annexed to the Crown. It does not remain to you, and for this plain reason: because the Statute of Henry VIII., confirmed by the Statute of Elizabeth, has declared the final charge of all this jurisdiction shall be vested in the Crown. But from you no appeal is given. Now, it is impossible that any body can exercise ecclesiastical jurisdiction without an appeal to the Crown. From you there is no appeal. You therefore can exercise no jurisdiction.' * That is to say, the Crown is the last resort, the ultimate judge: all others are inferior; Westminster Hall after its kind, the Jerusalem Chamber after its kind. But the creator and ruler of both is the Crown, the sole fountain of all jurisdiction, civil and spiritual, within these realms.

Now it is to this I wish to draw your attention.

* *Times* newspaper, July 16, 1864.

I do so the more intently, because it is the special point which in the Gorham judgment opened my eyes to the light, in which I have for these thirteen years found the peace and certainty of Divine faith.

Let me make the largest allowances. Let me say that by these Tudor Statutes all that is enacted is as follows:—

1. That the Crown should be the fountain of all *jurisdiction*—that is, of all *coercive* power by way of judicial process, *in foro externo*, before the tribunals of public law.

2. That the Crown should have power to judge in the last resort of all ecclesiastical causes, with a view to correct excesses, abuses, or errors in the Ecclesiastical Courts.

3. That the Crown should judge in appeal of all causes relating to benefices and temporal possessions.

4. That the Crown should have the power of judging in appeal of all causes of controverted doctrine, so far as to verify the fact, whether or no the doctrines in contest are *legal*, that is, recognised by law as doctrines of the Established Church.

Be it said, in passing, that I of course do not admit the power of the Crown in such points; but I state them in order to show that what was done in the Gorham case, what has been done in this, and what may be done in every case of appeal on controverted doctrine, goes far beyond all this, and amounts to a power of deciding what doctrines are or are not the doctrines of the Church of England : or, in other words, that the Crown is invested with a power to admit or to exclude doctrines upon the exercise of its own *discernment,* all the while disclaiming the power to pronounce them to be *true,* and claiming only to pronounce them to be legal.

Now I conceive that the Convocation, roused by the enormity of this claim, has pronounced to be false the doctrine which the Crown in Council declares to be legal. If the Crown disclaims the power to discern what is truth, the Convocation assumes the office as the ultimate judge of doctrine in the Church of England. The Convocation has, therefore, withdrawn itself from its Reformation settlement. It is neither under the Tudor Statutes, nor reunited to the Universal Church. It is isolated. It proclaims that the Crown has legalised doctrines contrary to its own teaching, and to the teaching of the Catholic Church of Christ. This is a heavy impeachment, and goes to the root of the whole Tudor legislation. The Royal supremacy is thereby declared to have erred in its judicial character, and the minds of men are driven to review the whole position. They have to examine whether the Royal supremacy has erred now for the first time as an ultimate ecclesiastical judge, or whether it has erred from the beginning in assuming that impossible character, of which this recent error is only the normal and legitimate result.

Whatever distinction there may be between the Establishment and the Church of England, the Church of England is clearly and visibly bound by the jurisdiction of the Crown in Council; and actually submits, though with much ill-will, to its decrees. It is unnecessary to waste time upon this, which is self-evident. I will therefore go deeper, and show that the Church of England, and not the Crown in Council, nor any legal tribunal, is the ultimate and true source of all these violations of Christian doctrine, and that the Crown in Council is only accidentally responsible for them.

To do this, I must recall you to the facts of the case.

The Church of England at the Reformation established itself upon two bases: the one, its independence of all spiritual jurisdiction upon earth; the other, its sufficiency to itself for the preservation and declaration of doctrine, and for the termination of all controversies and questions within its own limits—

that is, without appeal beyond the four seas, or to the Church throughout the world.

And yet, while claiming this power of ultimate determination, it did not claim to do so with infallibility, or a divine guidance, or divine certainty in its decisions. It even rejected formally, and in terms, the idea of such a divine and infallible guidance, not only in itself, but in any body upon earth; and built itself upon the sand, that is, upon the processes of human and historical evidence.

I cannot, therefore, blame the tribunal which has recognised the 'Essays and Reviews,' for it is the offspring of the Reformation. The claim of supremacy and of final determination in all causes, ecclesiastical as well as civil, is a primary principle of the Anglican system. It has been accepted, and even clamorously affirmed, by the Anglican Church. The appellate jurisdiction of the Crown in all causes is the same in principle, whether under the form and title of the Court of Delegates or of the Privy Council. Its machinery may vary, but the thing is identical. I notice this only to preclude an objection which is without force or weight.

Neither do I blame the writers of the book in question for using the liberty granted to them by the Church of England. As to the heresies which they have published, I have no words too keen or strong to condemn their falsehood and impiety. But for the writers I have a sincere compassion. They have done no more than Anglicanism has taught them to do. The Reformation placed them upon the inclined plane. They have but obeyed the law of their position.

The real culprit is the Anglican system, which generates the heresies which the tribunals only legalise. The Crown in Council does not create any new doctrine, nor even pronounce upon its truth. It waits passively until Anglicanism shall have cast up, from its perpetual agitations, some disputed question; and then, with the calmness of an examination *post mortem*, it dissects the Anglican system, its formularies and its history, to see if there be anything to exclude the new forms of thought which it has engendered. It does not pretend to pronounce them to be true: sometimes it even deplores them with a dignified surprise and regret. It only declares them to be not punishable. It gives them impunity, and legal establishment within the Anglican Church. The true source and fountain of all these multitudinous errors, contradictions, heresies, is Anglicanism—the Anglican Church, with its three hundred years of multiplying aberrations from Christianity, and its essential rationalism in practice and in principle. And this is the point I would dwell upon. But first let me notice two consequences of the system and position which Anglicanism has thus made or accepted for itself.

The first is, that it has two classes of doctrines: those which it believes to be true, and those which, though not true, are legal. Both true and false are equally legal, and equally taught in its name; and the teachers of the false doctrines are equally beneficed, and often more dignified, than the teachers of the true.

The second consequence is, that there is in the Anglican system a tribunal which has it always in its power to inundate the Establishment with new doctrines, avowedly not true, but only legal. This tribunal commands the established religion as a water-gate commands a plain country. At any moment the hand of a man may turn it, and the country is laid under water. Multiply appeals, and you multiply new doctrines. Every generation throws out its own forms of error, and the Crown in Council declares them to be legal.

It is in vain to say that this tribunal is not the Church of England. No; but it legalises the errors

which the Church of England generates, and the
Church of England neither condemns the error nor
the tribunal. It could not if it would. Must I add,
it would not if it could? And that, because it is
only obeying the law of its nature. To make this
evident, it is enough to take its own documents and
its own history.

My object, then, is to show that the recent Act of
the Convocation, heartily as I commend it for its intention, is absolutely without force or effect. It is
null and void, both in law and in conscience. It has
no legal effect, as the Lord Chancellor has too abundantly demonstrated. It has no spiritual effect on
the intellect or conscience of England; because the
Convocation is incapable, even by an unanimous
decision, of affording a motive of divine, or even of
human certainty. It cannot assure the members of
the Church of England that its decisions are true.
It can but give a human judgment, even on matters
of revealed faith; and therefore it can generate
in the minds of men only a fallible opinion. I
must go even further, and affirm that the principles
by which the Convocation proceeds, and those on
which the Anglican system is founded, are ultimately
rationalistic; though the good providence of God

has in England until now restrained their legitimate development. To prove this, I must enter upon some details.

I. Anglicans acknowledge readily that Protestantism is essentially rationalistic, but deny that Anglicanism is Protestant. What I wish to show is, that Anglicanism is identical in principle with all other forms of the Protestant Reformation. At one and the same time, and by one and the same movement, the Reformation sprang up in Germany, Switzerland, France, Scotland, and England. It took the form of Lutheranism, Zuinglianism, Calvinism, Presbyterianism, and Anglicanism. But these were no more than five aspects of one and the same movement. The names and the forms varied with the country in which they arose. In Germany, Switzerland, and France, it took the impression of the character of its authors. In Scotland, it was democratic and rigid; in England, aristocratic and conservative. For this reason it became episcopal and ceremonial. But the essence of all is one and the same, and their ultimate principles are identical. I will mention only three of them.

1. First, all these five forms of the Reformation alike appeal *from* the living voice of the Church. They all alike reject its divine and infallible au-

thority. It matters not *to* what they appeal; whether to Scripture, or to Fathers, or to antiquity, or to the undivided Church, as they say, before the separation of the East and West, or to General Councils in the past or in the future; for all these are but so many forms and pleas of evasion to cover the essence of their insubordination, which consists in this, namely, the refusal of the living voice of the Church as the rule of faith. For example; if a subject refuse submission to the sovereign power, and appeal to Parliaments in the past, or Princes in the future, nobody would care for the tribunal to which he appealed. To refuse obedience to the sovereign is treason. Such an act would be a capital offence. So it is with the Church. There can be no appeal from its voice without a denial of the law; ' He that heareth you heareth Me.'

2. Again, all these five forms of fragmentary Christianity alike affirm the sufficiency of Holy Scripture. The 6th of the Thirty-nine Articles declares as follows:—' Holy Scripture containeth all things necessary to salvation: so that whatsoever is not read therein, nor may be proved thereby, is not to be required of any man, that it should be believed as an article of faith.'

But this is to exclude the living voice and witness

of the Church. And if so, who is to decide what is contained in the Holy Scripture, what is to be read therein, or to be proved thereby? If the Church be not the sole ultimate judge of the contents of Holy Scripture, then that judge must be the individual; that is, each one for himself. But this is naked Protestantism, or, as we shall see hereafter, essential Rationalism.

3. Again, all these five forms of the Reformation alike proclaim a reform in doctrine. They profess to have purified the teaching of the Church: but this assumes that it was corrupted; and to have rejected additions made by man: but this denies the divine immutability of the faith. The pretension to recall the teaching of the Church to primitive purity assumes for Anglicanism what it denies to the whole Church, a higher discernment of truth.

In these three principles all forms of the Reformation are identical. They all alike appeal from the living Church, affirm the sufficiency of the Scriptures, and profess to reform the doctrines of faith. And Anglicanism is perhaps the most obtrusive in its claim to a special purity and primitiveness in its system.

Now, in this procedure, and in these pretensions, Anglicanism is either divinely, and therefore infallibly, guided, or it is not. If it be, how is it that the Anglican system is at variance not only with the Catholic Church throughout the world, but with the Greek Church, with which it endeavours in vain to make common cause; with every other form of Protestantism, which it condemns as untenable; at variance also with itself, with its past and its present, forasmuch as it is divided against itself? These are not the operations or the signs of a divine teacher. But if it be not infallible, then its basis is but human; and if so, rationalistic, for there is nothing intermediate between divine faith and human opinion.

We are not left to argue this alternative; the Anglican Church has decided for itself.

II. To prove this, we need little more than to show from its own books that it formally disclaims all infallibility.

It is remarkable that the Anglican Church, in putting forth the first reformed Prayer-book, continued to use the usual form of words, 'It appeared good to the Holy Ghost, and to us.'* But in publishing it a second time, after a few years, with extensive changes, these words appear no more. It was conscious of their unreality. Since then, the Anglican Church has not only never ventured upon any such

---

* Wheatly on the Book of Common Prayer, pp. 25, 26.

profession of a divine guidance, but has formally and dogmatically denied its existence in any Church upon earth.

In the 19th Article it declares, 'As the Church of Jerusalem, Alexandria, and Antioch, have erred; so also the Church of Rome hath erred, not only in their living and manner of ceremonies, but also in matters of faith:' that is to say, all particular Churches not only may err, but have erred; and not only the lesser Churches, but the greater—all the four great patriarchates. If so, certainly the Anglican Church does not arrogate for itself that which it denies to the four great patriarchal Churches of Christendom. If they may err and have erred, how much more the Church of two provinces isolated from all the world, and at variance with all the world, and even with itself?

But this is to deny the existence of any divine— that is, infallible—voice on earth. For the Church Universal was once made up of these patriarchal or particular Churches. By union they made one, as many stars made a constellation; but in the Anglican theory they are now disunited, and all are fallible. There is, therefore, no collective Church at this time through which the divine voice speaks to us with infallible certainty of truth. The Church

Universal is dissolved into its separate parts, and has no corporate unity of speech or action.

There is no such voice to be heard: and for want of it men are turning to the right hand and to the left, into every error that lies out of the way of faith. The Universal Church, then, no longer exists as the ultimate witness for truth. The light is put under a bushel, for it is no more seen. The city seated on a hill is hid, for it is no more visible. And what is more, the office of the Holy Ghost in the body of the Church is suspended. He does not speak through the Universal Church, for it is divided; nor through particular Churches, for they are liable to err.

The result of this is inevitable and self-evident. If there be no divine or infallible witness, then the highest and last certainty for the faith of Jesus Christ is only human. The Anglican system has shut itself up within its own circle, and has proclaimed its own sufficiency. By the 24th Henry VIII., the Act by which the schism was accomplished, the Anglican Church isolated itself from the whole Christian world, and rejected the guidance and ultimate appeal to the Universal Church. It thereby erected its own judgment in the place of the divine witness and discernment of the whole Church. The consequences of this were immediate and fatal.

The highest ordinary authority in the Anglican Church is its Episcopate. But it was never yet heard that an Episcopate of two provinces separated from the Universal Church is infallible. And the Anglican Episcopate does not so much as claim or believe in its own infallibility. Its bishops, one by one, whether in person or by their tribunals, are abundantly fallible; for, if Patriarchates may err, much more Episcopal Sees. But from them the appeal lies to the Crown in Council. I need not discuss the fallibility of a tribunal which disclaims even to judge of the truth of the matter brought before it. But it may be thought that the whole Episcopate united in Convocation has a higher assistance, and a divine direction. Yet here, also, the Anglican system is inexorable against itself. In the 21st Article it declares that 'General Councils may err, and sometimes have erred, in things pertaining to God.' But if General Councils may err, much more Convocations. Yet this is the ultimate and highest certainty for doctrine in the Anglican Church. Water cannot rise above its source. The Anglican Reformation resolves itself into the human authority from which it sprang.

III. What has been already said is enough to show that the Anglican system can afford no divine certainty in its judgments or declarations of doctrine.

But to make this more evident, it is well to examine the basis upon which it avowedly rests. The professed foundation of Anglicanism is Holy Scripture, but the real foundation is the critical reason. The ultimate certainty upon which it rests, even the Scripture, its authenticity, interpretation, inspiration, is a human, and therefore a fallible, tradition.

To prove this, it is enough to quote the 6th Article, in which it is said that 'In the name of the Holy Scripture we do understand those canonical books of the Old and New Testament of whose authority was never any doubt in the Church.'

Now, if it means 'whereof there was never any doubt' *by* the Church, it is true; because the Church never doubts as to any matter either of faith or of its divine deposit. It knows what books are canonical with a supernatural and infallible certainty. But this would go too far for Anglicanism, which has rejected several books held by the Catholic Church to be canonical. In publishing a new and amended catalogue of Canonical Books, the Church of England has destroyed its own foundation, by placing itself, not upon the divine witness of the Church, but upon the authority of mere historical evidence tried by criticism. If by 'never any doubt *in* the Church,' it means doubt by individuals, it is untrue; because the Epistle to the Hebrews, the 2nd of St. Peter, the 2nd and 3rd of St. John, and the Apocalypse, have been doubted, though by no names of weight. Anglicanism, therefore, rests the whole of Scripture, its authenticity, inspiration, and text, upon historical evidence; that is, upon a human and fallible authority. Dr. Lushington appears to me to have rightly enunciated and applied this fact. He said in his Judgment, 'The passage (of Dr. Williams) goes on to speak of the necessity of our assuming in ourselves a verifying faculty. What is the true meaning of these words? I apprehend it must mean this: that the clergy (for I speak of them only) are at liberty to reject parts of Scripture upon their own opinion that the narrative is internally incredible, to disregard precepts in Holy Writ because they think them evidently wrong. Whatever I may think as to the danger of the liberty so claimed, still if the liberty do not extend to the impugning of the Articles of Religion or the Formularies, the matter is beyond my cognizance;* that is, as official of the Archbishop of Canterbury in the highest Spiritual Court.

Again, for the interpretation of Scripture it can use no higher than human criticism. In the 20th Article it says, 'The Church hath power to decree

---

* Judgment of Court of Arches, June 25, 1862, p. 19.

rites and ceremonies, and authority in matters of faith.' But what authority? divine or human? If divine, this is a claim to infallibility, which Anglicanism has so often and so formally rejected. If human, it can bind no man to believe in its decisions; for no man can be under obligation to make an act of faith in a teacher who may err.

It says, moreover, 'And yet it is not lawful for the Church to ordain anything that is contrary to God's Word written: neither may it so expound one place of Scripture that it be repugnant to another.'* A wholesome counsel to all men; but not needed, certainly, by a divine teacher. But who is to be the judge of such repugnance? and who is to determine the true meaning of Scripture? Suppose the Anglican Church in Convocation to declare the sense of the passages which relate to the eternity of punishment: do such declarations carry a divine certainty, and require the submission of the reason and conscience of its members; or are they still at liberty to exercise their critical faculty to accept or to reject such declarations? Undoubtedly, they are still free to revise all judgments of a teacher who disclaims infallibility. The same Article declares, that the Church is the 'witness and keeper of Holy Writ.' But its testimony

* Article xx.

and guardianship are of no great avail; for according to the late Judgment, though it is not permitted to any clergyman of the Church of England to deny the inspiration of the whole of any book of Scripture, because that would erase it from the Canon, and the list thereby would be mutilated; yet it is lawful to all to deny any portion of any book, so long as any part of it remains; because the name of the book would still stand in the Canon. Nevertheless, as it is permitted to any one to deny any part of any or of all the books of the Old and New Testament, the whole of Scripture may therefore be denied with impunity, and a universal doubt cast upon the whole of the Sacred books. For example, let me suppose that two or more of the Anglican clergy should deny different parts of the same book, the whole book might be denied by both or by all together, though not by each alone. A doubt may thus be cast upon the authenticity of the whole Bible. Suppose the one to deny the beginning, another the end of any book: or some books to be doubted by some, others by others, until the whole is called into doubt. Nobody would singly deny the whole of Scripture, nor the whole of any book; but no book and no part of any book is safe from the scepticism of the critical reason; and the whole Bible, on which Anglicanism rests itself, may gradually be treated as Dr. Colenso has treated the Pentateuch and the Psalms.

The result of this is inevitable latitudinarianism and indifference. Contradiction of doctrine and negation of the Inspired books is thereby permitted by law; and not only so, but taught in the name of the Anglican Church by its ministers and bishops. Now I cannot charge the fault of this upon the Establishment, but upon the Church of England. The Crown in Council is comparatively innocent. The true and guilty cause of these multiplying errors is Anglicanism, which has denied the divine voice of the Church, and erected itself in the confidence of its human discernment and historical criticism. No system but one that is essentially rationalistic could tolerate the presence of heresies: for where a divine certainty exists, there can be no toleration of error; but when the authority is only human, it is not only a necessity, but a duty, to tolerate all forms of human opinion.

And now do not be displeased, my dear Friend, if I go on to say some things which will seem hard.

IV. The rationalistic character of the Church of England may be further abundantly proved by the fact that for three hundred years it has been in perpetual oscillation, generating new opinions which act and react upon each other. Contrast with this the last three hundred years of the Catholic Church since the Council of Trent. It has maintained throughout the world an uniform and unchanging sameness. The same faith, the same theology, unites together nations the most adverse in race, language, civilisation; races the most repugnant, often at war with each other, always divided in political interests; one, nevertheless, in all that pertains to faith. Compare this with the instability and variations of the Anglican system, which is divided in itself and against itself; so that it condemns its own past as much as the future will condemn the present. What can better illustrate the contrast of St. Paul between the unity and stability of the one Body and one Spirit, by the power of the Holy Ghost, who guides the pastors in perfecting the body of Christ, and the division and instability of those who are carried about with every wind of doctrine by the influence of human teachers? *

I am not writing a history of the variations of Anglicanism: it suffices to enumerate them. In Edward VI.'s time it was Protestant, and in sympathy with the foreign reformers. In Elizabeth's, it became Hierarchical, and began once more to teach

* Ephes. iv. 4—16.

a doctrine of sacramental grace. In the time of the Stuarts, it Romanised more or less: Popery and Prelacy were looked upon as one and the same; they who called the Roman Church Babylon, called Anglicanism its eldest daughter.

Under William III. it became Latitudinarian. It made common cause with the Dissenters. Archbishop Tillotson and Bishop Law doubted of eternal punishment; Bishop Hoadley was believed to be Socinian.

Under the Georges it became formalistic and dead. Then it swung back into Puritanism, which was a blind testimony to the interior life in an age when Christianity seemed gone from the hearts of men.

Then came the Evangelical movement; a worthy and manly effort of those who knew a few truths to obey those truths as far as they knew them.

Then followed the Oxford or Romanising movement, which for some years carried all before it; and next, by a proportionate reaction, the Rationalistic School, of which the 'Essays and Reviews' are a legitimate fruit, and Dr. Colenso the offspring.

No words will more exactly express what I feel on this subject than the following, in which I beg you not to consider the plainness of speech to imply bitterness on my part :—'During the eighteen centuries of its existence, the Catholic Church has been tried by the rise of a succession of heresies within its unity. Every century has had its characteristic heresy. From Gnosticism to Jansenism there is a line of almost unbroken succession in error, which has sprung up parasitically by the side of the Divine Truth. But the Church remained stedfast and resplendent, without change or shadow of vicissitude, ever the same, and perfect in its light as in the beginning. The errors of the human intellect have never fastened upon the supernatural intelligence of the mystical body; but every successive error has been expelled by the vital and vigorous action of the infallible mind and voice of the Church of God. All its dogmas of faith remain to this hour incorrupt, because incorruptible, and therefore primitive and immutable. The errors of men have been cast forth as humours which are developed in the human system, but cannot coexist with the principle of life and health. A living body casts off whatever assails its perfection. "They went out from us, but they were not of us; for if they had been of us, they would have continued with us, but that they might be manifest that they were not all of us." * But in the Anglican Church all is the reverse. Every error which has sprung up in it,

* St. John ii. 19.

adheres to it still. Its doctrines vanish, its heresies abide. All its morbid humours are absorbed into its blood. The Lutheranism of Edward VI., the Hierarchical Calvinism of Elizabeth, the Ceremonial Arminianism of James, the Episcopalian Antiquarianism of the two Charleses, the Latitudinarianism of William III., the Formalism and the Fanaticism of the Georges, the Anglo-Catholicism and the Rationalism of the last thirty years, all coexist at this hour, side by side, congested together, in open contradiction, and almost perpetual controversy. It would be untrue to represent any one of these schools of error as the legitimate voice or exponent of the Anglican Church. They are all equally so, and all equally not so. They each claim so to be, and deny the legitimacy of all the rest. But the Anglican Church pronounces no judgment among them. It sits mute and confounded. It puts none of them out of its pale. None of them will go out. All alike refuse to be put out, for all are equally of it, and all, therefore, by the inspired rule, alike remain with it. And this for the obvious reason already given, which to any Catholic is intuitively clear: forasmuch as the Anglican Reformation has entirely cancelled from the intelligence of the English people the whole idea of the Church divinely founded, endowed with supernatural attributes, and teaching with divine, and, therefore, infallible certainty, there is neither any principle of authority, or test of certainty by which to discern truth from error, nor any frontier or circle of unity from which error should be expelled. I believe the universal experience of all those who have exercised the Evangelical ministry in England would be this—that the last article of the Creed, which enters, and that slowly, and for a long time painfully, into the English intelligence, is the nature and office of the Church: or, to speak theologically, the formal object of faith, and the divinely-ordained conditions of its manifestation to the world.' *

These, in the fewest words, are the reasons why I must acquit the Crown in Council, and find the Church of England guilty of the heresies taught in the 'Essays and Reviews.' It has no power to condemn them, for they are its own legitimate offspring. The unlimited license of thought which has prevailed since the schism of Henry VIII. has borne its natural fruit. And its act of condemnation carries no divine certainty. It is no more than an act of human judgment, and human opinion, contrary indeed to the 'Essays and Reviews,' but within the same sphere, and upon the same level.

* Sermons on Ecclesiastical Subjects, Preface, pp. 5C–8.

During these last thirteen years, in which the Church of England has been tossed to and fro by every wind of human error, distracted by Judgments of the Crown in Council and by turbulent confusions in Convocation, the Catholic Church in England has three times met in Synod. It took up its work again after a silence of three hundred years, and reopened its proceedings with a familiarity as prompt and a readiness as calm as if it had resumed to-day the deliberation of last night. Though centuries of time had rolled away since it sat in council, the last Synod in England is but as the session of yesterday to the session of the morrow. Time is not with the Church of God; save as it works in time, and time for it. The prerogatives of the Church, like His from whom they spring, are changeless. Its Episcopate met once more as of old. It had no principles to seek, no theories to invent, no precedents to discover; from the highest obligation to the lowest usage, all is definite and sure. After centuries, the Church puts forth its divine laws and powers, and applies them to the needs of place and time, with the precision of a science and the facility of instinct. What is human stiffens and dies; the living is ever in act, as He in whose life the Church lives eternally.

I cannot forbear to quote some of the last words I

ever wrote in the Church of England, as they express, though too feebly, what I feel at this day with all the powers of my reason and of my conscience. 'It has been said that this decision [the Gorham] leaves the doctrine of the Church of England wholly untouched; that it does not alter a letter of its Formularies, and that, therefore, the doctrine of the Church is inviolate as ever.

'This has been said by so many of the highest name and note, as well as by so many who must be "esteemed very highly in love for their work's sake," that I am loath to deny it. But truth leaves no freedom. The doctrine of the Church, then, is surely not an assemblage of formularies, but the true meaning of them. Doctrine is not a written, but a living truth. "Prior sermo quam liber; prior sensus quam stylus." If books were doctrine, no sect could be in heresy so long as it retained the Bible. If creeds were doctrine, the Socinians, who recite the Apostles' Creed, must be acquitted. But books and forms without their true interpretation are nothing. Doctrine is defined " univoca docendi methodus." It is the perpetual living voice of the individual pastors uniting as one. The Church is the collective teacher, and doctrine is the oral exposition of the faith. Will any one say that this is not touched by legalising the denial of an article of the Creed ? The doctrine of the Church of England is not only its written Formularies, but the oral teaching of its twenty-eight bishops, its fifteen thousand clergy, its many more thousand school-teachers, and its two or three millions of heads of families. Doctrine is the living, ever-spreading, and perpetual sense which is taught at our altars and from house to house all the year round. If this be so, it seems to me to be a dream to say that the doctrine of the Church is untouched. For what is the effect of the latitude given by the late sentence of the Crown ? To those who believe truth to be divine, that the authority of God is in every article of faith, and that our contradictions are His dishonour, it inspires alarm to hear from such authorities that the late sentence has not touched the doctrine of the Church. Would the legalising of Arianism after the Nicene Council, leaving the Nicene Creed to stand in words, have touched the doctrine of the Church ? Would legalising Sabellianism touch doctrine so long as the words of our formularies are unchanged ? If the answer be yes, I ask why ? The formularies are still unaltered : the faithful may teach the Nicene doctrine. Lastly, I would ask, How shall we stand the test of our own standards ? By the definition of the Church of England, " the visible Church is a congregation of faithful men in which the pure Word of God is preached." '*

It is almost incredible that a writer in the 'Edinburgh Review' should have noted with satisfaction that the Gorham judgment legalised in the Church of England one school of doctrine, and that this late Judgment has legalised another. It is like rejoicing that two mortal diseases have been established in the body of a dying man. Such an opinion demonstrates the absence of all faith in the Church as a Witness, Judge, and Teacher.†

No other words of mine will better express this

---

* The Appellate Jurisdiction of the Crown in Matters Spiritual, pp. 35–37, 2nd edition, Murray, 1850.

† The following passages from the 'Edinburgh Review' read like irony:—

'. . . The Gorham judgment—the Magna Charta, as it has been truly called, of the liberties of the English Church. . . As the Gorham judgment established beyond question the legal position of the Puritan, or so-called Evangelical party, in the Church of England; as the Denison judgment would, had it turned on the merits of the case, instead of a technical flaw, have established the legal position of the High Church or Sacramental party; so the judgment in the case of Mr. Wilson and Dr. Williams established the legal position of those who have always claimed the right of free inquiry and latitude of opinion, equally for themselves and for both the other sections of the Church.' *Edinburgh Review:* The Three Pastorals. July, 1864. No. 245. pp. 270-2.

So that the only party which is not legalised is the so-called Anglo-Catholic. A strange reverse of position for those who the other day claimed, and were thought, to be the only true English Churchmen.

divine office, than the following which were spoken in the last Provincial Synod of Westminster:—

'When the Holy Ghost, on the day of Pentecost, descended upon the Apostles, the mind of God was unfolded to them. They became the witnesses of the mysteries which are hid in God : they were partakers of His thoughts, and depositories of His intentions. Then arose within them the living consciousness of the truth, which has descended lineally in the mystical body to this hour; the divine tradition of the light of Pentecost, in which all the revelation of God hangs suspended in its symmetry and perfection. For what is the Church, but the Apostolic college prolonged and expanded in its organisation and unity throughout the world, wherein the mind of the Spirit has descended to us through the perpetual indwelling of the Holy Ghost ? He preserves what He has revealed, and perpetually proposes to the world the truth which in the beginning He shed abroad upon the intelligence of man. The Church, then, is not a name of multitude, but of a supernatural unity, the head and the body, Christ mystical, of which the Holy Ghost is the life, soul, and mind.

'The Church is, as St. Augustine says, "una quædam persona," "unus perfectus vir;"or, as the

Apostle says, "the spiritual man, who judgeth all things, and himself is judged of no man." It is the fountain and the channel of light to the world; the expositor of the law and the interpreter of the truth of God. The law of God, expounded and applied in its fullness and minuteness to the souls of men within the sphere of its jurisdiction, constitutes the wonderful science of law which the legislation of the Church is perpetually elaborating. The truth of God, interpreted by the Holy Spirit, and disposed in order and harmony, constitutes the highest science of which the reason of man is capable—that is Theology, of which both the author and the object is God. But the legislator and the interpreter of these divine sciences is the Spirit of God, from whom truth and law both alike proceed. Such thoughts as these are seasonable at a time like this. All things around us draw our minds this way. The solemn invocations of the Holy Ghost are still lingering in our ears. A Synod of the Church in England, the representative of the spiritual sway of Calcyth, Finchal, Oxford, Herudford, London, and Westminster, is gathered here. It is a Council of Westminster once more. We see here the evidence of the undying life and ever-renewing power of the Church of God, calmly legislating from age to age; restoring, re-creating, what time or the sin of man has destroyed, as the exuberant life of nature perpetually re-ascends, full and ready to clothe again with fertility the bare earth which has been scathed and torn. For more than a thousand years the Church in England has witnessed for the same changeless faith. Through all vicissitudes of time and state, through sun or storm, it has spoken with one unfaltering voice. What it taught by St. Augustine it teaches now. The history of St. Bede is the transcript of the Church of God in England at this hour; and the Church of this hour is the history of St. Bede, breathing and living still. There we see the same filial reverence and dutiful submission to the Successor of St. Peter, the same divine sacrifice upon the altar, the same sacrament of penance, the same affectionate intercession for the souls purifying in the fire of God's love,—above all, the same invocation of the saints, the same loving worship of the Mother of God. A thousand years passed away, and the same Hierarchy stood in witness and in suffering for the same mind of the Spirit. In the face of princes and the powers of this world—in despite of mockery and slander, of tortures and of martyrdom—the Catholic Hierarchy of England witnessed, till by violence it was swept away from the earth.

'Three centuries again are gone, and the same truths are still living and fresh in the heart of the changeless Church. They are before us at this moment; the same dutiful and loving obedience binds this Council to the Apostle See.'*

There were no controversies about Articles of the Creed, or about the inspiration of Holy Scripture, or about eternal punishment, to be debated in that Synod. Had there been a question of doctrine or of its interpretation, the Universal Church, upon which the Catholic Church in England rests, would have solved it with a tranquil and divine certainty. 'Securus judicat orbis terrarum.' And the decree of a Provincial Council of Westminster, confirmed by the Holy See, would afford an infallible rule of faith, as the Provincial Councils of Africa did with the confirmation of S. Innocent I. in the condemnation of the Pelagian heresy.†

But it is now more than time to make an end. I will, therefore, sum up what I have written. These late proceedings have laid bare once more, as the Gorham appeal did, through God's mercy, to me

---

* Sermons on Ecclesiastical Subjects, pp. 117–120.

† Melchior Cani Opera, lib. v. c. iv. 5. Bellarm. De Conciliorum auctor. lib. ii. c. v. . . . Certè temerarium, erroneum, et proximum hæresi est, existimare, Concilia particularia a Pontifice confirmata posse errare.

some fourteen years ago, that the Statute 26th
Henry VIII. was a violation of the divine office and
unity of the Church. The local Church of England
was thereby cut from the Universal Church, and
from that hour it forfeited its participation in the
perpetual illumination and assistance of the Holy
Spirit of God, by Whom the original Revelation is
preserved and propounded in all ages whole and immutable. In that hour it lost as a body the tradition
and gift of divine faith. The Christianity of England
from that hour has rested upon a historical basis, on
human criticism, and the balance of probabilities.
Protestants appeal to the inspired books of the Old
and New Testaments; Anglicans appeal also to the
uninspired books of the Fathers; but the principle
and process are identical in both. It is historical and
critical, and generates only opinion or human faith.
The distinction between reason and faith is thus
obscured; and the generic difference between the last
act of reason and the first act of faith, so far as my
experience reaches, which is not now little or superficial, is effaced from the mind of most Anglicans.
Reason leads us to the feet of a Divine Teacher; but
thenceforward His voice, and not our balancing of
probabilities, will be the formal motive of our faith.
Historical criticism teaches us that Christianity has

penetrated the nations of the world for eighteen
hundred years, united them in one family, elevated
the intellect and purified the heart of mankind,
created the new Christian civilisation, taught immutably one dogma, and reigned inflexibly by one
divine law: that its unity and universality fulfil the
prophecies, and that the multitude of its martyrs,
saints, and penitents attest a supernatural power.
The cumulus of evidence and the ever-growing
weight of probabilities determine the reason impe-
ratively to believe that Christianity is a divine revelation, and the Church a divine kingdom upon earth.
But there is a truth, arising out of this order and
sphere of truths, which predominates over all and
draws all to itself. The same evidence which tells
me that the Church had a Divine Founder, tells me
that it is at this hour inhabited by a Divine Person;
that the witness and voice of the Church is not only
human and historical, but also supernatural and
divine. The maximum of probabilities passes upward into the divine certainty, as the taper which
leads me up out of the windings of a catacomb passes
away in the blaze of the sun at noon-day. My faith
terminates no longer in a cumulus of probabilities
gathered from the past, but upon the veracity of a
Divine Person guiding me with His presence. The
Universal Church is His dwelling-place and the organ

of His voice. It is immutable in its doctrine, because He sustains it in every age incorrupt, primitive, and changeless. So long as I submit to that Church, and through it my faith terminates in the Person and voice of the Holy Spirit of God, so long, by an act of divine faith, I infallibly know the revelation of the day of Pentecost. In the hour I fall from the Church, in that hour I lose the divine certainty of faith, and descend to the region of criticism and opinion. In like manner, in the hour the Church of England fell from the unity of the Church throughout the world, it lost the illumination of divine faith and the tradition of divine and infallible certainty. In that hour the Crown took it captive, and till this day it has been in bondage. Its chains are heavy, though they be of gold: and dearly it has paid for its fault in the spiritual atrophy of three hundred years, and the confusions which are dissolving it before our eyes.

My dear Friend, let no one who has ever looked upon me with kindness, think I write with bitterness or with the heart of an adversary. God knows it is not so. But I feel so vividly the miseries I once endured while I was in the house of bondage, and I see so intensely the dishonour which Anglicanism has done and is doing to the Name and Person of our Divine Lord, that I cannot temper my words or turn the edge of truth. I rejoice to see the Convocation openly and deliberately standing for the doctrines denied in the 'Essays and Reviews,' and condemning as false the errors legalised by a tribunal which does not derive itself either from God or from His Church. I trust none who have so far stood firm will falter. Better a thousand times to suffer the spoiling of goods, and to stand before the Lord High Chancellor, to use his courtly words, even 'in sackcloth and ashes,' than so much as to keep silence when the heresies of the 'Essays and Reviews' are declared to be admissible in any society of Christians. 'Judex damnatur cum nocens absolvitur.' I am sure that the hearts of all honest and good men, and I am sure mine most warmly and firmly, would be with Archbishop Longley, in the day when for such a cause he should stand before Lord Westbury. But this will not be. I look for no organic changes in the Church of England; but a gradual wasting away, by multiplying aberrations of its teachers and its people. The law of its dissolution is working in it irresistibly.

One effect of this last Judgment of the Crown is certain. It has revealed more and more the absence of all discernment, certainty, and authority in the Church of England, whether in its Episcopate or its

Convocations. No one looks to either as to an ultimate and final judge invested with the conditions of a supernatural office, or as to an organ of divine certainty in the matter of doctrine or of faith. The question is being pushed to its last analysis. The alternative before the present generation is no longer Anglo-Catholicism or Roman Catholicism, but between Rationalism and Christianity; that is, Rationalism or Rome. It is certain that the Anglo-Catholicism of the Oxford movement threw out, by reaction, the Rationalism of the 'Essays and Reviews.' It is certain that the Rationalistic School, now in the ascendant, will throw out a far more thorough approximation to Catholicism in all its amplitude. The alternative is self-evident: either the human certainty of history and criticism, or the divine certainty of Catholic tradition; either the human reason as a critic testing the doctrines of Revelation, or the human reason as a disciple submitting to the voice of a Divine Person, the Author and Teacher of the Faith.

Believe me, my dear Friend,
Always affectionately yours,
HENRY EDWARD MANNING.

BAYSWATER: *July* 25, 1864.

THE WORKINGS OF THE HOLY SPIRIT IN THE CHURCH OF ENGLAND.

A LETTER

TO

THE REV. E. B. PUSEY, D.D.

A LETTER, ETC.

My Dear Friend,

I do not know why twelve years of silence should forbid my calling you still by the name we used both to give and to accept of old. Aristotle says indeed

Πολλὰς δὴ φιλίας ἀπροσηγορία διέλυσεν·

but he did not know the basis and the affections of a Christian friendship such as that to which, though I acknowledge in myself no claim to it, you were so kind as to admit me. Silence and suspension of communications cannot prevail against the kindliness and confidence which springs from such years and such events as once united us. Contentions and variances might indeed more seriously try and strain such a friendship. But, though we have been both parted and opposed, there has been between us neither variance nor contention. We have both indeed been in the field where a warfare has been waging;

but, happily, we have not met in contest. Sometimes we have been very near to each other, and have even felt the opposition of each other's will and hand; but I believe on neither side has there ever been a word or an act which has left a needless wound. That I should have grieved and displeased you is inevitable. The simple fact of my submitting to the Catholic Church must have done so, much more the duties which bind me as a pastor. If, in the discharge of that office, I have given you or any one either pain or wound by personal faults in the manner of its discharge, I should be open to just censure. If the displeasure arise only from the substance of my duties, 'necessity is laid upon me,' and you would be the last to blame me.

You will perhaps be surprised at my beginning thus to write to you. I will at once tell you why I do so. Yesterday I saw, for the first time, your pamphlet on the legal force of the judgment of the Privy Council, and I found my name often in its pages. I have nothing to complain of in the way you use it. And I trust that in this reply you will feel that I have not forgotten your example. But your mention of me, and of old days, kindled in me a strong desire to pour out many things which have been for years rising in my mind. I have long wished for the occasion to do so, but I have always felt that it is more fitting to take than to make such an occasion: and as your kindness has made it, I will take it.

But before I enter upon the subject of this letter I wish to say a few words of yourself, and of some others whom I am wont to class with you.

Among the many challenges to controversy and public disputation which it has been my fortune to receive, and I may add, my happiness to refuse, in the last twelve or thirteen years, one was sent me last autumn at Bath. It was the only one to which, for a moment, I was tempted to write a reply. The challenger paid me compliments on my honesty in leaving the Church of England; denouncing those who, holding my principles, still eat its bread. I was almost induced to write a few words to say that my old friends and I are parted because we hold principles which are irreconcileable; that I once held what they hold now, and was then united with them; that they have never held what I hold now, and therefore we are separated; that they are as honest in the Church of England now as I was once, and that our separation was my own act in abandoning as untenable the Anglican Church and its rule of faith, Scripture and antiquity, which you and they hold still, and in submitting to the voice of the Catholic and

Roman Church at this hour, which I believe to be the sole authoritative interpreter of Scripture and of antiquity. This principle no friend known to me in the Church of England has ever accepted. In all these years, both in England and in foreign countries, and on occasions both private and public, and with persons of every condition, I have borne this witness for you and for others.

I felt no little indignation at what seemed to me the insincerity of my correspondent; but on reflection I felt that silence was the best answer.

I will now turn to your pamphlet, and to the subject of this Letter.

You speak at the outset of 'the jubilee of triumph among half believers' on the occasion of the late judgment of the Crown in Council ; and you add, 'A class of believers joined in the triumph. And while I know that a very earnest body of Roman Catholics rejoice in all the workings of God the Holy Ghost in the Church of England (whatever they think of her), and are saddened in what weakens her who is, in God's hands, the great bulwark against infidelity in this land, others seemed to be in an ecstasy of triumph at this victory of Satan.' * Now,

---

* Legal Force of the Judgment of the Privy Council, by the Rev. E. B. Pusey, D.D., pp. 3, 4.

IN THE CHURCH OF ENGLAND. 87

I will not ask where you intended to class me. But as an anonymous critic of a pamphlet lately published by me accused me of rejoicing in your troubles, and another more recently—with a want of candour visible in every line of the attack—accused me of being 'merry' over these miseries of the Church of England, I think the time is made for me to declare how I regard the Church of England, and events like these; and I know no one to whom I would rather address what I have to say than to yourself.

I will, then, say at once:
1. That I rejoice with all my heart in all the workings of the Holy Ghost in the Church of England.
2. That I lament whensoever what remains of truth in it gives way before unbelief.
3. That I rejoice whensoever what is imperfect in it is unfolded into a more perfect truth.
4. But that I cannot regard the Church of England as 'the great bulwark against infidelity in this land,' for reasons which I will give in their place.

1. First, then, I will say what I believe of the Church of England, and why I rejoice in every working of the Holy Spirit in it. And I do this the more gladly because I have been sometimes grieved at hearing, and once at even seeing in a handwriting which I reverence with affection, the statement that

Catholics—or at least the worst of Catholics called Converts, deny the validity of Anglican Baptism, regard our own past spiritual life as a mockery, look upon our departed parents as heathen, and deny the operations of the Holy Spirit in those who are out of the Church. I do not believe that those who say such things have ever read the Condemned Propositions, or are aware that a Catholic who so spoke would come under the weight of at least two Pontifical censures, and the decrees of at least two General Councils.

I need not, however, do more than remind you that, according to the faith and theology of the Catholic Church, the operations of the Holy Spirit of God have been from the beginning of the world coextensive with the whole human race.*

Believing, then, in the operations of the Holy Spirit, even among the nations of the world who have neither the revelation of the Faith nor the Sacraments, how much more must we believe His presence and grace in those who are regenerate by water and the Holy Ghost? To you, whose name first became celebrated for a tract on Baptism, which,

---

* Suarez, De Divina Gratia, Pars Secunda, lib. iv. c. viii. xi. xii. Ripalda, De Ente Supernaturali, lib. i. disp. xx. s. xii. and s. xxii. Viva, Cursus Theol., pars iii. disp. i. quæst. v. iii.

notwithstanding certain imperfections inseparable from a work written when and where you wrote it, is in substance deep, true, and elevating, it need not be said that Baptism, if rightly administered with the due form and matter, is always valid by whatsoever hand it may be given.*

Let me, then, say at once,

1. That in denying the Church of England to be the Catholic Church, or any part of it, or in any divine and true sense a Church at all, and in denying the validity of its absolutions and its orders, no Catholic ever denies the workings of the Spirit of God or the operations of grace in it.

2. That in affirming the workings of grace in the Church of England no Catholic ever thereby affirms that it possesses the character of a Church.

They who most inflexibly deny to it the character of a Church affirm most explicitly the presence and

---

* Concil. Florent. Decretum Eugenii iv. Mansi Concil. tom. xviii. 547. 'In causa autem necessitatis non solum sacerdos vel diaconus sed etiam laicus vel mulier, immo etiam paganus et hæreticus baptizare potest, dummodo formam servet Ecclesiæ, et facere intendat quod facit Ecclesia.' The Council of Trent repeats this under anathema, Sess. vii. can. iv. : 'Si quis dixerit Baptismum qui etiam datur ab hæreticis in Nomine Patris, et Filii, et Spiritus Sancti, cum intentione faciendi quod facit Ecclesia, non esse verum Baptismum, anathema sit.' See also Bellarm. Controversiæ, De Baptismo, lib. i. c. vii.

the operations of grace among its people; and that for the following reasons :

In the judgment of the Catholic Church, a baptized people is no longer in the state of nature, but is admitted to a state of supernatural grace. And though I believe the number of those who have never been baptized to be very great in England, and to be increasing every year, nevertheless I believe the English people, as a mass, to be a baptized people. I say the number of the unbaptized is great, because there are many causes which contribute to produce this result. First, the imperfect, and therefore invalid, administration of baptism through the carelessness of the administrators. You, perhaps, think that this is exaggerated, through an erroneous belief of Catholics as to the extent of such carelessness among the Protestant ministers, both in and out of the Church of England. It is however undeniable, as I know from the evidence of eye-witnesses, that such carelessness has, in times past, been great and frequent. This I consider the least, but a sufficient reason for believing that many have never been baptized. Add to this, negligence caused by the formal disbelief of baptismal regeneration in a large number of Protestant ministers. There are, however, two other reasons far more direct. The one is the studied rejection, as a point of religious profession, of the practice of infant baptism. Many therefore grow up without baptism who in adult life, for various causes, never seek it. The other, the sinful unbelief and neglect of parents in every class of the English people, who often leave whole families of children to grow up without baptism. Of the fact that many have never been baptized, I, or any Catholic priest actively employed in England, can bear witness. There are few among us who who have not had to baptize grown people of every condition, poor and rich; and, of children, often whole families together. There has indeed been, in the last thirty years, a revival of care in the administration of baptism on the part of the Anglican ministers, and of attention on the part of parents in bringing their children to be baptized; but this reaction is by no means proportionate to the neglect, which on the other side has been extending. My fear is that, after all, the number of persons unbaptized in England is greater at this moment than at any previous time.

Still, the English people as a body are baptized, and therefore elevated to the order of supernatural grace. Every infant, and also every adult baptized, having the necessary dispositions, is thereby placed in a state of justification; and, if they die without committing any mortal sin, would certainly be saved. They are also, in the sight of the Church, Catholics. S. Augustine says, 'Ecclesia etiam inter eos qui foris sunt per baptismum generat suos.' A mortal sin of any kind, including *prava voluntatis electio*, the perverse election of the will, by which in riper years such persons chose for themselves, notwithstanding sufficient light, heresy instead of the true faith, and schism instead of the unity of the Church, would indeed deprive them of their state of grace. But before such act of self-privation all such people are regarded by the Catholic Church as in the way of eternal life. With perfect confidence of faith, we extend the shelter of this truth over the millions of infants and young children who every year pass to their Heavenly Father. We extend it also in hope to many more who grow up in their baptismal grace. Catholic missionaries in this country have often assured me of a fact, attested also by my own experience, that they have received into the Church persons grown to adult life, in whom their baptismal grace was still preserved. How can we, then, be supposed to regard such persons as no better than heathens? To ascribe the good lives of such persons to the power of nature would be Pelagianism.

To deny their goodness would be Jansenism. And with such a consciousness, how could any one regard his past spiritual life in the Church of England as a mockery? I have no deeper conviction than that the grace of the Holy Spirit was with me from my earliest consciousness. Though at the time, perhaps, I knew it not as I know it now, yet I can clearly perceive the order and chain of grace by which God mercifully led me onward from childhood to the age of twenty years. From that time the interior workings of His light and grace, which continued through all my life, till the hour when that light and grace had its perfect work, to which all its operations had been converging, in submission to the fulness of truth, and of the Spirit in the Church of God, is a reality as profoundly certain, intimate, and sensible to me now as that I live. Never have I by the lightest word breathed a doubt of this fact in the Divine order of grace. Never have I allowed any one who has come to me for guidance or instruction to harbour a doubt of the past workings of grace in them. It would be not only a sin of ingratitude, but a sin against truth. The working of the Holy Spirit in individual souls is, as I have said, as old as the fall of man, and as wide as the human race. It is not we who ever breathe or harbour a doubt of this.

It is rather they who accuse us of it. Because, to believe such an error possible in others, shows how little consciousness there must be of the true doctrine of grace in themselves. And such, I am forced to add, is my belief, because I know by experience how inadequately I understood the doctrine of grace until I learned it of the Catholic Church. And I trace the same inadequate conception of the workings of grace in almost every Anglican writer I know, not excepting even those who are nearest to the truth.

But, further, our theologians teach, not only that the state of baptismal innocence exists, and may be preserved out of the Church, but that they who in good faith are out of it, if they shall correspond with the grace they have already received, will receive an increase or augmentation of grace.* I do not for a moment doubt that there are to be found among the English people individuals who practise in a high degree the four cardinal virtues, and in no small degree, though with the limits and blemishes inseparable from their state, the three theological virtues of

---

* Suarez, De Div. Gratia, lib. iv. c. xi. Ripalda, De Ente Supernaturali, lib. i. disp. xx. sect. xii. et seq. S. Alphonsi Theol. Moral. lib. i. tract. i. 5, 6.

Faith,* Hope, and Charity, infused into them in their baptism. I do not think, my dear friend, in all that I have said or written in the last fourteen years, that you can find a word implying so much as a doubt of these workings of the Holy Spirit among all the baptized who are separated from the Catholic Church.

I will go further still. The doctrine, '*extra ecclesiam nulla salus,*' is to be interpreted both by dogmatic and by moral theology. As a dogma, theologians teach that many belong to the Church who are out of its visible unity; † as a moral truth, that to be out of the Church is no personal sin, except to those who sin in being out of it. That is, they will be lost, not because they are *geographically* out of it, but because they are *culpably* out of it. And they who are culpably out of it are those who know—or might, and therefore ought to, know—that it is their duty to submit to it. The Church teaches that men may

---

* De Lugo, De Virtute divinæ Fidei, disp. xvii. sect. iv. v. Viva, Cursus Theol. p. iv. disp. iv. quæst. iii. 7.

† See Perrone, Prælect. Theolog. pars i. c. ii. 1, 2 :
    'Omnes et soli justi pertinent ad Ecclesiæ animam.'
    'Ad Christi Ecclesiæ corpus spectant fideles omnes tam justi quam peccatores.'
S. Augustine expresses these two propositions in six words ' Multæ oves foris, multi lupi intus.' S. Aug. tom. iii. pars ii. p. 600.

be *inculpably* out of its pale. Now they are inculpably out of it who are and have always been either physically or morally unable to see their obligation to submit to it. And they only are culpably out of it who are both physically and morally able to know that it is God's will they should submit to the Church; and either knowing it will not obey that knowledge, or, not knowing it, are culpable for that ignorance. I will say then that we hopefully apply this benign law of our Divine Master as far as possible to the English people. First, it is applicable in the letter to the whole multitude of those baptized persons who are under the age of reason. Secondly, to all who are in good faith, of whatsover age they be : such as a great many of the poor and unlettered, to whom it is often physically, and very often morally, impossible to judge which is the true revelation or Church of God. I say physically, because in these three hundred years the Catholic Church has been so swept off the face of England that nine or ten generations of men have lived and died without the faith being so much as proposed to them, or the Church ever visible to them; and I say morally, because the great majority of the poor, from lifelong prejudice, are often incapable of judging in questions so removed from the primary truths of conscience and Christianity. Of such simple persons it may be said that *infantibus æquiparantur*, they are to be classed morally with infants. Again, to these may be added the unlearned in all classes, among whom many have no contact with the Catholic Church, or with Catholic books. Under this head will come a great number of wives and daughters, whose freedom of religious enquiry and religious thought is unjustly limited or suspended by the authority of parents and husbands. Add, lastly, the large class who have been studiously brought up, with all the dominant authority of the English tradition of three hundred years, to believe sincerely, and without a doubt, that the Catholic Church is corrupt, has changed the doctrines of the faith, and that the author of the Reformation is the Spirit of holiness and truth. It may seem incredible to some that such an illusion exists. But it is credible to me, because for nearly forty years of my life I was fully possessed by this erroneous belief. To all such persons it is morally difficult in no small degree to discover the falsehood of this illusion. All the better parts of their nature are engaged in its support: dutifulness, self-mistrust, submission, respect for others older, better, more learned than themselves, all combine to form a false conscience of the duty to refuse to hear anything against 'the religion of their fathers,' 'the Church of their baptism,' or to read anything which could unsettle them. Such people are told that it is their duty to extinguish a doubt against the Church of England, as they would extinguish a temptation against their virtue. A conscience so subdued and held in subjection exercises true virtues upon a false object, and renders to a human authority the submissive trust which is due only to the Divine voice of the Church of God.

Still further, I believe that the people of England were not all guilty of the first acts of heresy and schism by which they were separated from the Catholic unity and faith. They were robbed of it. In many places they rose in arms for it. The children, the poor, the unlearned at that time, were certainly innocent: much more the next generation. They were born into a state of privation. They knew no better. No choice was before them. They made no perverse act of the will in remaining where they were born. Every successive generation was still less culpable, in proportion as they were born into a greater privation, and under the dominion of a tradition of error already grown strong. For three centuries they have been born further and further out of the truth, and their culpability is perpetually diminishing; and as they were passively borne onward in the course of the English separation, the moral responsibility for the past is proportionately less.

The Divine law is peremptory: 'To him who knoweth to do good, and doth it not, to him it is sin.'* Every Divine truth, as it shines in upon us, lays its obligation on our conscience to believe and to obey it. When the Divine authority of the Church manifests itself to our intellect, it lays its jurisdiction upon our conscience to submit to it. To refuse is an act of infidelity, and the least act of infidelity in its measure expels faith; one mortal act of it will expel the habit of faith altogether.† Every such act of infidelity grieves the Holy Ghost by a direct opposition to His Divine voice speaking through the Church; the habit of such opposition is one of the six sins against the Holy Ghost defined as 'impugning the known truth.' Nothing that I have said above modifies the absolute and vital necessity of submitting to the Catholic Church as the only way of salvation to those who know it, by the revelation of God, to be such. But I must not attempt now to treat of this point.

* S. James iv. 17.
† De Lugo, De Virtute Fidei Divinæ disp. xvii. sect. iv. 53 et seq.

Nevertheless, for the reasons above given, we make the largest allowance for all who are in invincible ignorance; always supposing that there is a preparation of heart to embrace the truth when they see it, at any cost; a desire to know it; and a faithful use of the means of knowing it, such as study, docility, prayer, and the like. But I do not now enter into the case of the educated or the learned, or of those who have liberty of mind and means of enquiry. I cannot class them under the above enumeration of those who are inculpably out of the truth. I leave them, therefore, to the only Judge of all men.

Lastly, I will not here attempt to estimate how far all I have said is being modified by the liberation and expansion of the Catholic Church in England during the last thirty years. It is certain that the restoration of the Catholic Hierarchy, with the universal tumult which published it to the whole world, still more by its steady, widespread, and penetrating action throughout England, is taking away every year the plea of invincible ignorance.

It is certain, however, that to those who, being invincibly ignorant, faithfully co-operate with the grace they have received, an augmentation of grace is given; and this at once places the English people, so far as they come within the limits of these conditions, in a state of supernatural grace, even though they be out of the visible unity of the Church. I do not now enter into the question of the state of those who fall from baptismal grace by mortal sin, or of the great difficulty and uncertainty of their restoration. This would lead me too far ; and it lies beyond the limits of this Letter.

It must not, however, be forgotten, for a moment, that this applies to the whole English people, of all forms of Christianity, or, as it is called, of all denominations. What I have said does not recognise the grace *of* the Church of England as such. The working of grace *in* the Church of England is a truth we joyfully hold and always teach. But we as joyfully recognise the working of the Holy Spirit among Dissenters of every kind. Indeed, I must say that I am far more able to assure myself of the invincible ignorance of Dissenters as a mass than of Anglicans as a mass. They are far more deprived of what survived of Catholic truth ; far more distant from the idea of a Church ; far more traditionally opposed to it by the prejudice of education ; I must add, for the most part, far more simple in their belief in the person and passion of our Divine Lord. Their piety is more like the personal service of disciples to a personal Master than the Anglican piety, which has always been more dim and distant from this central light of souls. Witness Jeremy Taylor's works, much as I have loved them, compared with Baxter's, or even those of Andrewes compared with Leighton's, who was formed by the Kirk of Scotland.

I do not here forget all you have done to provide ascetical and devotional books for the use of the Church of England, both by your own writings, and, may I not say it, from your neighbour's vineyard?

With truth, then, I can say that I rejoice in all the operations of the Holy Spirit out of the Catholic Church, whether in the Anglican or other Protestant bodies; not that those communions are thereby invested with any supernatural character, but because more souls, I trust, are saved. If I have a greater joy over these workings of grace in the Church of England, it is only because more who are dear to me are in it, for whom I never fail to pray day by day. These graces to individuals were given before the Church was founded, and are given still out of its unity. They are no more tokens of an ecclesiastical character, or a sacramental power in the Church of England, than in the Kirk of Scotland, or in the Wesleyan connexion; they prove only the manifold grace of God, which, after all the sins of men, and in the midst of all the ruins they have made, still works in the souls for whom Christ died. Such, then, is our estimate of the Church of England in regard to the grace that works not *by* it, nor *through* it, but *in* it and among those who, without faults of their own, are detained by it from the true Church of their baptism.

And here it is necessary to guard against a possible misuse of what I have said. Let no one imagine that he may still continue in the Church of England because God has hitherto mercifully bestowed His grace upon him. As I have shown, this is no evidence that salvation is to be had *by* the Church of England. It is an axiom that *to those who do all they can God never refuses His grace*. He bestows it that He may lead them on from grace to grace, and from truth to truth, until they enter the full and perfect light of faith in His only true Fold. The grace they have received, therefore, was given, not to detain them in the Church of England, but to call them out of it. The grace of their past life lays on them the obligation of seeking and submitting to the perfect Truth. God would ' have all men to be saved, and to come to the knowledge of the truth.' * But His Church is an eminent doctrine and mystery of that truth; and all grace given out of the Church is

* 1 Tim. ii. 4.

in order to bring men into the Church, wheresoever the Church is present to them. If they refuse to submit to the Church they resist the Divine intention of the graces they have hitherto received, and are thereby in grave danger of losing them; as we see too often in men who once were on the threshold of the Church, and now are in Rationalism, or in states of which I desire to say no more.

2. Let me next speak of the truths which the Church of England still retains. I have no pleasure in its present trials; and the anonymous writer who describes me as being 'positively merry' over its disasters little knows me. If I am to speak plainly, he seems to me to be guilty of one of the greatest offences—a rash accusation against one whom he evidently does not know. I will further say, that I lament with all my heart whensoever what remains of truth in the Anglican system gives way before unbelief.

I do not, indeed, regard the Church of England as a teacher of *truth*, for that would imply that it teaches the truth in all its circumference, and in all its divine certainty. Now this is precisely what the Church of England does not, and, as I will show presently, has destroyed in itself the power of doing. I am willing to call it a teacher of *truths*; because many fragmentary truths, shattered, disjointed from the perfect unity of the Christian revelation, still survive the Reformation, and, with much variation and in the midst of much contradiction, are still taught in it. I have been always wont to say, and to say with joy, that the Reformation, which has done its work with such a terrible completeness in Germany, was arrested half-way in England; that here much of the Christian belief and Christian order has survived. Until lately I have been in the habit of saying that there are three things which missionaries may take for granted in England: first, the existence of a supernatural world; secondly, the revelation of Christianity; and thirdly, the inspiration of Scripture. The Church of England has also preserved other doctrines with more or less of exactness, such as the doctrine of the Holy Trinity, the incarnation, baptism, and the like. I will not now enter into the question as to what other doctrines are retained by it, because a few more or a few less would make little difference in the final estimate a Catholic must make of it. A teacher of Christian truths I gladly admit it to be. ·A teacher of Christian truth—no; because it rejects much of that truth, and also the Divine principle of its perpetuity in the world. Nevertheless, I rejoice in every fragment of doctrine which remains in it; and I should lament the diminution of any particle of that truth. I have ever regarded with regret the so-called Low-Church and Latitudinarian schools in the Anglican Church, because I believe their action and effect is to diminish what remains of truth in it. I have always regarded with joy, and I have never ceased to regard with sympathy, notwithstanding much which I cannot either like or respect, the labour of the High-Church, or Anglo-Catholic party, because I believe that their action and effect are 'to strengthen the things that remain, which were ready to die.' For myself, I am conscious how little I have ever done in my life; but as it is now drawing towards its end, I have at least this consolation, that I cannot remember at any time, by word, or act, to have undermined a revealed truth; but that, according to my power, little enough as I know, I have endeavoured to build up what truth I knew, truth upon truth, if only as one grain of sand upon another, and to bind it together by the only bond and principle of cohesion which holds in unity the perfect revelation of God. A very dear friend, whose friendship has been to me most instructive, the loss of which was to me one of the hardest sacrifices I had to make, has often objected to me, with the subtlety which marks his mind, that my act in leaving the Church of England has helped forward the unbelief which is now invading it. No doubt he meant to say, that the tendency of such an act helped to shake the confidence of others in the Church of England as a teacher of truth. This objection was like his mind, ingenious and refined. But a moment's thought unravelled it, and I answered it much in these words:

I do not believe that by submitting to the Catholic Church any one can weaken the witness of the Church of England for the truth which it retains. So far as it holds the truth, it is in conformity to the Catholic Church. In submitting to the Catholic Church, I all the more strongly give testimony to the same truths which the Church of England still retains. If I give testimony against the Church of England, it is in those points in which, being at variance with the truth, the Church of England is itself undermining the faith of Christianity.

It was for this reason I always lamented the legalising of the sacramentarian errors of the Low-Church party by the Gorham Judgment; and that I lament now the legalising of the heresies of the 'Essays and Reviews,' and the spreading unbelief of Dr. Colenso. I believe that anything which undermines the Christianity of England is drawing it further and further from us. In proportion as men believe more of Christianity, they are nearer to the perfect truth. The mission of the Church in the world is to fill up the truth. Our Divine Lord said, 'I am not come to destroy, but to fulfil;' and S. Paul did not overthrow the altar of the Unknown God, but gave to it an object of Divine worship and a true adoration. For this cause I regard the present downward course of the Church of England and the Christianity of England with great sorrow and fear. And I am all the more alarmed because, of those who are involved in it, so many not only refuse to acknowledge the fact, but treat us who give warning of the danger as enemies and accusers.

One of my critics has imagined, that I propose to myself and others the alternative of Catholicism or Atheism. I have never attempted to bring any one to the perfect truth by destroying or by threatening the imperfect faith they might still possess. I do not believe that the alternative before us is Catholicism or Atheism. They are lights of the natural order, divine witnesses of Himself inscribed by the Creator on His works, characters engraven upon the conscience, and testimonies of mankind in all the ages of the world, which prove the existence and perfections of God, the moral nature and responsibility of man, anterior to Catholicism, and independently of revelation. If a man, through any intellectual or moral aberration, should reject Christianity, that is, Catholicism, yet the belief of God and of His perfections stands immutably upon the foundations of nature. Catholicism, or Deism, is indeed the only ultimately logical and consistent alternative; though, happily, few men in rejecting Catholicism are logically consistent enough to reject Christianity. Atheism is an aberration which implies not only an intellectual blindness, but a moral insensibility. The Theism of the world has its foundation on the face of the natural world, and on the intellect and the heart of the human race. The old Paganism and modern Pantheism are reverent, filial, and elevating compared with the Atheism of Comte and of our modern Secularists. It would be both intellectually and morally impossible to propose to any one the alternative of Catholicism or Atheism. Not only, then, do I lament to see any truth in the Church of England give way before unbelief, but I should regard with sorrow and impatience any attempt to promote belief in the whole revelation of Christianity by a mode of logic which undermines even the truths of the natural order. The Holy See has authoritatively declared that the existence of God may be proved by reason and the light of nature,* and Alexander VIII. declared that men who do not know of the existence of God are without excuse.† Atheism is not the condition of man without revelation. As Viva truly says in his comment on this declaration, Atheists are anomalies and exceptions in the intellectual tradition of mankind.

Nay, I will go further. I can conceive a person to reject Catholicism without logically rejecting Christianity. He would indeed reject the Divine certainty which guarantees and proposes to us the whole revelation of the Day of Pentecost. But as Catholic theologians teach, the infallible authority of the Church does not of necessity enter into the essence of an act of faith.‡ It is, indeed, the Divine provision for the perfection and perpetuity of the faith, and, *in hac providentia*, the ordinary means whereby men are illuminated in the revelation of God; but the known and historical evidence of Christianity is enough to

---

* 'Ratiocinatio Dei existentiam, animæ spiritualitatem, hominis libertatem, cum certitudine probari potest.' Theses a SS. D. N. Pio IX. approbatæ, 11 Junii 1855. Denzinger's Enchiridion, p. 448. Ed. 1856.

† Viva, Propos. damnatæ, p. 372. Ripalda de Ente Supernaturali, disp. xx. s. 12, 59.

‡ De Lugo, De Virtute divinæ Fidei, disp. i. sect. xii. 250–53. Viva, Cursus. Theol. p. iv. disp. i. quæst. iv. art. iii. Ripalda, De Ente Supern. disp. xx. sect. xxii. 117.

convince any prudent man that Christianity is a Divine revelation. It is quite true that by this process he cannot attain an explicit faith in all the doctrines of revelation, and that in rejecting Catholicism, he reduces himself to human and historical evidence as the maximum of extrinsic certainty for his religion, and that this almost inevitably resolves itself in the long run into Rationalism. It is an inclined plane on which, if individuals may stand, generations cannot. Nevertheless, though the alternative in the last analysis of speculation be Catholicism or Deism, the practical alternative may be Catholicism and fragmentary Christianity.

I have said this to show how far I am from sympathising with those, if any there be, and I can truly say I know none such, who regard the giving way of any lingering truth in the Church of England under the action of unbelief with any feeling but that of sorrow. The Psalmist lamented over the dying out of truths: 'Diminutæ sunt veritates a filiis hominum;' and I believe that every one who loves God, and souls, and truth, must lament when a single truth, speculative or moral, even of the natural order is obscured; much more when any revealed truth of the elder or of the Christian revelation is rejected or even doubted. Allow me also to answer, not only for myself, which is of no great moment, but for an eminent personage to whom you have referred in your pamphlet. I can say, with a personal and perfect knowledge, that no other feeling has ever arisen in His Eminence's mind, in contemplating the troubles of the Anglican Church, than a sincere desire that God may use these things to open the eyes of men to see the untenableness of their position ; coupled with a very sincere sorrow at the havoc which the advance of unbelief is making among the truths which yet linger in the Church of England.

3. It is, however, but reason that I should rejoice when whatsoever remains in it of imperfect truth is unfolded into a more perfect faith: and that therefore I desire to see not only the conversion of England, but the conversion of every soul to whom the more perfect truth can be made known. You would not respect me if I did not. Your own zeal for truth and for souls here speaks in my behalf. There are two kinds of proselytisers. There are the Jews whom our Lord condemned. There are also the Apostles whom He sent into all the world. If by proselytising be meant the employing of unlawful and unworthy means, motives, or influences to change a person's religion, I should consider the man who used such means to commit *lèse-majesté* against Truth, and against our

Lord who is the Truth. But if by proselytising be meant the using all the means of conviction and persuasion which our Divine Master has committed to us to bring any soul who will listen to us into the only faith and fold, then to this I plead guilty with all my heart. I do heartily desire to see the Church of England dissolve and pass away, as the glow of lingering embers in the rise and steady light of a reviving flame. If the Church of England were to perish to-morrow under the action of a higher and more perfect truth, there would be no void left in England. All the truths hitherto taught in fragments and piecemeal would be still more vivedly and firmly impressed upon the minds of the English people. All of Christianity which survives in Anglicanism would be perfected by the restoration of the truths which have been lost, and the whole would be fixed and perpetuated by the evidence of Divine certainty and the voice of a Divine Teacher. No Catholic desires to see the Church of England swept away by an infidel revolution, such as that of 1789 in France. But every Catholic must wish to see it give way year by year, and day by day, under the intellectual and spiritual action of the Catholic Church; and must watch with satisfaction every change, social and political, which weakens its hold on the country: and would faithfully use all his power and influence for its complete and speedy removal.

4. But lastly, I am afraid we have reached a point of divergence. Hitherto I hope we may have been able to agree together; but now I fear every step of advance will carry us more wide of each other. I am unable to consider the Church of England to be ' in God's hands the great bulwark against infidelity in this land.' And my reasons are these :—

1.) First, I must regard the Anglican Reformation, and therefore the Anglican Church, as the true and original source of the present spiritual anarchy of England. Three centuries ago the English people were in faith *unius labii*: they were in perfect unity. Now they are divided and subdivided by a numberless multiplication of errors. What has generated these? From what source do they descend? Is it not self-evident that the Reformation is responsible for the production of every sect and every error which has sprung up in England in these three hundred years, and of all which cover the face of the land at this day? It is usual to hear Anglicans lament the multiplication of religious error. But what is the productive cause of all? Is it not Anglicanism itself which, by appealing from the voice of the Church throughout the world, has set the example to its own people of appealing from the voice of a local and provincial authority?

I am afraid, then, that the Church of England, so far from being a barrier against infidelity, must be recognised as the mother of all the intellectual and spiritual aberrations which now cover the face of England.

2.) It is true, indeed, that the Church of England retains many truths in it. But it has in two ways weakened the evidence of these very truths which it retains. It has detached them from other truths the contact of which gave solidity to all by rendering them coherent and intelligible. It has detached them from the Divine voice of the Church, which guarantees to us the truth incorruptible and changeless. The Anglican Reformation destroyed the principle of cohesion, by which all truths are bound together into one. The whole idea of Theology, as the science of God and of His revelation, has been broken up. Thirty-nine Articles, heterogeneous, disjointed, and mixed with error, are all that remain instead of the unity and harmony of Catholic truth. Surely this has been among the most prolific causes of error doubt, and unbelief. So far from being the bulwark against it, Anglicanism appears to me to be the cause and spring of its existence. As I have already said, the Reformation placed the English people upon an inclined plane, and they have steadily obeyed the law of their position, by descending gradually from age to age, sometimes with a more rapid, sometimes with a slower motion, but always tending downwards. Surely it would be unreasonable to say of a body always descending, that it is the great barrier against reaching the bottom.

I do not, indeed, forget that the Church of England has produced writers who have vindicated many Christian truths. I am not undmindful of the service rendered by Anglican writers to Christianity in general, nor, in particular, of the works of Bull and Waterland in defence of the Holy Trinity; of Hammond and Pearson in defence of Episcopacy; of Butler and Warburton in defence of Revelation, and the like. But whence came the errors and unbeliefs against which they wrote? Were they not generated by the Reformation abroad and in England? This is like the spear which healed the wounds it had made. But it is not the Divine office of the Church to make wounds in the faith that it may use its skill in healing. These writers were only quelling the mutiny which Protestantism had raised, and arresting the progress of the Reformation which, like Saturn, devours its own children.

Moreover, to be just, I must say that if the Church

of England be a barrier against infidelity, the Dissenters must also be admitted to a share in this office, and in the praise due to it. And in truth, I do not know among the Dissenters any works like the 'Essays and Reviews,' or any Biblical criticism like that of Dr. Colenso. They may not be very dogmatic in their teaching; but they bear their witness for Christianity as a Divine revelation, for the Scriptures as an inspired book, and, I must add further, for the personal Christianity of conversion and repentance, with an explicitness and consistency which is not less effectual against infidelity than the testimony of the Church of England. I do not think the Wesleyan Conference or the authorities of the Three Denominations would accept readily this assumed superiority of the Anglican Church as a witness against unbelief. They would point, and not unjustly, to the doctrinal confusions of the Church of England as causes of scepticism, from which they are comparatively free. And I am bound to say that I think they would have an advantage. I well remember that while I was in the Church of England I used to regard Dissenters from it with a certain, I will not say aversion, but distance and recoil. I never remember to have borne animosity against them, or to have attacked or pursued them with unkindness. I alawys believed many of them to be very earnest and devoted men. I did not like their theology, and I believed them to be in disobedience to the Church of England; but I respected them, and lived at peace with them. Indeed, I may say that some of the best people I have ever known out of the Church were Dissenters or children of Dissenters. Nevertheless, I had a dislike of their system, and of their meeting-houses. They seemed to me to be rivals of the Church of England, and my loyalty to it made me look somewhat impatiently upon them. But I remember, from the hour I submitted to the Catholic Church, all this underwent a sensible change. I saw that the whole revelation was perpetuated in the Church alone, and that all forms of Christianity lying round about it were but fragments more or less mutilated. But with this a sensible increase of kindly feeling grew upon me. The Church of England and the dissenting communions all alike appeared to me to be upon the same level. I rejoiced in all the truth that remains in them, in all the good I could see or hope for in them, and all the workings of the Holy Spirit in them. I had no temptation to animosity towards them; for neither they nor the Church of England could be rivals of the imperishable and immutable Church of God. The only sense, then, in which I could regard the Church of England as a barrier against infidelity I must extend also to the dissenting bodies; and I cannot put this high, for reasons I will give.

3.) If the Church of England be a barrier to infidelity by the truths which yet remain in it, I must submit that it is a source of unbelief by all the denials of other truths which it has rejected. If it sustains a belief in two Sacraments, it formally propagates unbelief in five; if it recognises an undefined presence of Christ in the Sacrament, it formally imposes on its people a disbelief in Transubstantiation and the Sacrifice of the altar; if it teaches that there is a Church upon earth, it formally denies its indissoluble unity, its visible Head, and its perpetual Divine voice.

It is not easy to see how a system can be a barrier against unbelief when by its Thirty-nine Articles it rejects, and binds its teachers to propagate the rejection, of so many revealed truths.

4.) But this is not all. It is not only by the rejection of particular doctrines that the Church of England propagates unbelief. It does so by principle, and in the essence of its whole system. What is the ultimate guarantee of the Divine revelation but the Divine authority of the Church? Deny this, and we descend at once to human teachers. But it is this that the Church of England formally and expressly denies. The perpetual and ever-present assistance of the Holy Spirit, whereby the Church in every age is not only preserved from error, but enabled at all times to declare the truth, that is, the infallibility of the living Church at this hour—this truth the Anglican Church in terms denies. But this is the formal antagonist of infidelity, because it is the evidence on which God wills that we should believe all His veracity reveals. Do not be displeased with me. It appears to me that the Anglican system, by this one fact alone, perpetually undoes what it strives to do in behalf of particular doctrines. What are they, one by one, when the Divine certainty of all is destroyed? Now, for three hundred years the Anglican clergy have been trained, ordained, and bound by subscriptions to deny not only many Christian truths, but the Divine authority of the ἡ ἀεὶ ἐκκλησία, the living Church of every age. The barrier against infidelity is the Divine voice which generates faith. But this the Anglican clergy are bound to deny. And this denial opens a flood-gate in the bulwark, through which the whole stream of unbelief at once finds way. Seventeen or eighteen thousand men, educated with all the advantages of the English schools and Universities, endowed with large corporate revenues, and distributed all over England, maintain a perpetual protest, not only against the Catholic Church, but against the belief that there is any Divine voice immutably and infallibly guiding the Church at this hour in its declaration of the Christian revelation to mankind. How can this be regarded as 'the great bulwark in God's hand against infidelity?'

It seems to me that the Church of England, so far from being a bulwark against the flood, has floated before it. Every age has exhibited an advance to a more indefinite and heterogeneous state of religious opinion within its pale. Even in our memory, the downward progress of the Church of England is manifest. That I may not seem to draw an unfavourable picture from my own view, I will quote a very unsuspected witness. Dr. Irons, in a recent pamphlet, says: 'The religion of the Church has sunk far deeper into conscience now than the surviving men of 1833-1843 are aware of. *And all that Churchmen want* of their separated brethren is that they accept nothing, and profess nothing, and submit to nothing which has " no root" in their conscience.' * If this mean anything, it means that objective truth has given place to subjective sincerity as the Anglican

* Apologia pro vita Ecclesiæ Anglicanæ, p. 22.

Rule of Faith. You will know better than I whether this be the state of men's minds among you. To me it is as strange as it is incoherent, and a sign how far men have drifted. This certainly was not the faith or religion that we held together in the years when I had the happiness of being united in friendship with you. Latitudinarian sincerity was not our basis; and if the men of 1833 and 1843 have arrived at this, it is very unlike the definite, earnest, consistent belief which animated us at that time. You say in your note (page 21), kindly, but a little upbraidingly, that my comment on your letter to the 'Record' was not like me in those days: forasmuch as I used then to join with those with whom even then you could not. It was this that made me note your doing so now. It was this which seemed to me to be a drifting backward from old moorings. For myself, it is true, indeed, that I have moved likewise. I have been carried onwards to what you then were, and beyond it. What I might have done then, I could not do now. What you do now seems to me what you would not have done then. I did not note this unkindly, but with regret; because, as I rejoice in every truth, and in every true principle retained in the Church of England, it would have given me great joy to see you maintaining with all firmness, not only all the particular truths you held, but also the impossibility of uniting with those who deny both those truths and the principles on which you have rested through your laborious life of the last thirty years.

I will add only a few more words of a personal sort, and then make an end. It was not my fate in the Church of England to be regarded as a contentious or controversial spirit, nor as a man of extreme opinions, or of a bitter temper. I remember indeed that I was regarded, and even censured, as slow to advance, somewhat tame, cautious to excess, morbidly moderate, as some one said. I remember that the Catholics κατ' ἐξοχὴν used to hold me somewhat cheap, and to think me behindhand, uncatholic, over-English, and the like. But now, is there anything in the extreme opposite of all this which I am not? Ultramontane, violent, unreasoning, bitter, rejoicing in the miseries of my neighbours, destructive, a very Apollyon, and the like. Some who so describe me now are the same who were wont then to describe me as the reverse of all this. They are yet catholicising the Church of England, without doubt more catholic still than I am. Well, what shall I say? If I should say that I am not conscious of these changes, you would only think me self-deceived. I will therefore only tell you where I believe I am unchanged, and then where I am conscious of a change, which, perhaps, will account for all you or others have to say of me.

I am unconscious, then, of any change in my love to England in all that relates to the natural order. I am no politician, and I do not set up for a patriot; but I believe, as S. Thomas teaches, that love of country is a part of charity, and assuredly I have ever loved England with a very filial love. My love for England begins with the England of S. Bede. Saxon England, with all its tumults, seems to me saintly and beautiful. Norman England I have always loved less, because, though more majestic, it became continually less Catholic, until the evil spirit of the world broke off the light yoke of faith at the so-called Reformation. Still, I loved the Christian England which survived, and all the lingering outlines of dioceses and parishes, cathedrals and churches, with the names of Saints upon them. It is this vision of the past which still hovers over England and makes it beautiful, and full of memories of the kingdom of God. Nay, I loved the parish church of my childhood, and the college chapel of my youth, and the little church under a green hill-side, where the morning and evening prayers, and the music of the

English Bible, for seventeen years, became a part of my soul. Nothing is more beautiful in the natural order, and if there were no eternal world I could have made it my home. But these things are not England, they are only its features, and I may say that my love was and is to the England which lives and breathes about me, to my countrymen whether in or out of the Church of England. With all our faults as a race, I recognise in Englishmen noble Christian virtues, exalted characters, beautiful examples of domestic life, and of every personal excellence which can be found, where the fulness of grace and truth is not, and much, too, which puts to shame those who are where the fulness of grace and truth abounds. So long as I believed the Church of England to be a part of the Church of God I loved it: how well, you know; and I honoured it with a filial reverence, and laboured to serve it, with what fidelity I can affirm, with what, or if with any utility, it is not for me to say. And I love still those who are in it, and I would rather suffer anything than wrong them in word or deed, or pain them without a cause. To all this I must add, lastly, and in a way above all, the love I bear to many personal friends, so dear to me, whose letters I kept by me till two years ago, though more than fifty of them are gone into the world unseen. All these things are sweet to me still beyond all words that I can find to express it.

You will ask me then, perhaps, why I have never manifested this before? It is because when I left you, in the full, calm, deliberate and undoubting belief that the light of the only Truth led me from a fragmentary Christianity into the perfect Revelation of the day of Pentecost, I believed it to be my duty to walk alone in the path in which it led me, leaving you all unmolested by any advance on my part. If any old friend has ever written to me, or signified to me his wish to renew our friendship, I believe he will bear witness to the happiness with which I have accepted the kindness offered to me. But I felt that it was my act which had changed our relations, and that I had no warrant to assume that a friendship, founded upon agreement in our old convictions, would be continued when that foundation had been destroyed by myself; or would be restored upon a foundation altogether new. I felt, too, a jealousy for truth. It was no human pride which made me feel that I ought not to expose the Catholic Church to be rejected in my person. Therefore I held on my own course, seeking no one, but welcoming every old friend—and they have been many—who came to me. This has caused a suspension of nearly fourteen years in which I have never so much as met or exchanged a line with many who till then were among my nearest friends. This, too, has given room for many misapprehensions. It would hardly surprise me if I heard that my old friends believed me to have become a cannibal.

Perhaps you will say, This does not account for your hard words against us and the Church of England. When I read your late pamphlet I said to myself, Have I ever written such hard words as these? I will not quote them, but truly I do not think that, in anything I have ever written, I have handled at least any person as you, my dear friend, in your zeal, which I respect and honour, have treated certain very exalted personages who are opposed to you. But let this pass. It would not excuse me even if I were to find you in the same condemnation.

One of my anonymous censors writes that 'as in times past I had written violently against the Church of Rome, so now I must do the same against the Church of England.' I wish he would find, in the books I published when out of the Church, the hard sayings he speaks of. It has been my happiness to know that such do not exist. I feel sure that my accuser had nothing before his mind when he risked this controversial trick. I argued, indeed, against the Catholic and Roman Church, but I do not know of any railing accusations. How I was preserved from it I cannot tell, except by the same Divine goodness which afterwards led me into the perfect light of faith.

But I have written, some say, hard things of the Church of England. Are they hard truths or hard epithets? If they are hard epithets, show them to me, and I will erase them with a prompt and public expression of regret; but if they be hard facts, I cannot change them. It is true, indeed, that I have for the last fourteen years incessantly and unchangingly, by word and by writing, borne my witness to the truths by which God has delivered me from the bondage of a human authority in matters of faith, I have borne my witness to the presence and voice of a Divine, and therefore infallible, Teacher, guiding the Church with His perpetual assistance, and speaking through it as His organ. I have also borne witness that the Church through which He teaches is that which S. Augustine describes by the two incommunicable notes—that it is 'spread throughout the world' and 'united to the Chair of Peter.'* I know that the corollaries of these truths are severe, peremptory, and inevitable.

* S. Aug. Opp. tom. ii. pp. 119, 120; tom. x. p. 93.

If the Catholic faith be the perfect revelation of Christianity, the Anglican Reformation is a cloud of heresies; if the Catholic Church be the organ of the Holy Ghost, the Anglican Church is not only no part of the Church, but no church of divine foundation. It is a human institution, sustained, as it was founded, by a human authority; without priesthood, without sacraments, without absolution, without the Real Presence of Jesus upon its altars. I know these truths are hard. It seems heartless, cruel, unfilial, unbrotherly, ungrateful so to speak of all the beautiful fragments of Christianity which mark the face of England, from its thousand towns to its green villages, so dear even to us who believe it to be both in heresy and in schism. You must feel it so. You must turn from me and turn against me for saying it; but if I believe it, must I not say it? And if I say it, can I find words more weighed, measured, and deliberate than those I have used? If you can, show them to me, and so that they are adequate, I will use them always hereafter. God knows I have never written a syllable with the intent to leave a wound. I have erased many, I have refrained from writing and speaking many, lest I should give more pain than duty commanded me to give. I cannot hope that you will allow of all I say.

K

But it is the truth. I have refrained from it, not only because it is a duty, but because I wish to disarm those who divert men from the real point at issue by accusations of bitterness and the like. It has been my lot, more than of most, to be in these late years on the frontier which divides us. And— why I know not—people have come to me with their anxieties and their doubts. What would you have done in my place? That which you have done in your own; which, *mutato nomine,* has been my duty and my burden.

And now I have done. I have a hope that the day is coming when all in England who believe in the supernatural order, in the revelation of Christianity, in the inspiration of Holy Scripture, in the Divine certainty of dogmatic tradition, in the Divine obligation of holding no communion with heresy and with schism, will be driven in upon the lines of the only stronghold which God has constituted as 'the pillar and ground of the truth.' This may not be, perhaps, as yet; but already it is time for those who love the faith of Christianity, and look with sorrow and fear on the havoc which is laying it waste among us, to draw together in mutual kindness and mutual equity of judgment. That I have so ever treated you I can truly say; that I may claim it at your hands I am calmly conscious; but whether you and others accord it to me or not, I must leave it to the Disposer of hearts alone to determine. Though we are parted now, it may not be for ever; and morning by morning, in the Holy Sacrifice, I pray that the same light of faith which so profusely fell upon myself, notwithstanding all I am, may in like manner abundantly descend upon you who are in all things so far above me, save only in that one gift which is not mine, but His alone who is the Sovereign Giver of all Grace.

Believe me, my dear friend,
Always affectionately yours,
HENRY EDWARD MANNING.

ST. MARY'S, BAYSWATER:
Sept. 27, 1864.

P.S. My attention has just been called to the concluding pages of the last number of the *Quarterly Review*, in which I am again described by a writer who evidently has abilities to know better, to be in 'ecstasies.' The writer represents, as the sum or chief argument of my 'Second Letter to an Anglican Friend,' the passing reference I there made to the Lord Chancellor's speech. I quoted this to prove that the late judgment is a part of the law, both of the land and of the Church of England. But the whole of the Letter, excepting this single point, is an argument to show that the vote of the Convocation carries with it no Divine certainty, and resolves itself into the private judgment of the majority who passed it. For all this argument the writer has not a word. I cannot be surprised that he fills out his periods with my 'ecstasies,' 'shouts of joy,' 'wild pæans,' a quotation from 'Shylock,' and other things less fitting. This is not to reason, but to rail. Is it worthy? Is it love of truth? Is it good faith? Is it not simply the fallacy of evasion? Controversy of this kind is work that will not stand. We are in days when personalities and flimsy rhetoric will not last long. Neither will it bear to be tried by 'the fire,' nor will it satisfy, I was about to say, nor will it mislead, men who are in earnest for truth or for salvation. I had hoped that this style of controversy had been cured or suppressed by a greater sincerity, and reality of religious thought in these days of anxiety and unbelief. There either is, or is not, a Divine Person teaching perpetually through the Church in every age, and therefore now, as always, generating faith with Divine certainty in the minds of men. This question must be answered; and, as men answer it, we know where to class them, and how to deal with them. All the evasions and half-arguments of such writers are becoming daily more and more intolerable to those of the English people —and they are a multitude—who would give all that they count dear, and life itself, to know and to die in the full and certain light of the revelation of God in Jesus Christ.

H. E. M.

THE

REUNION OF CHRISTENDOM

A PASTORAL LETTER TO THE CLERGY, &c.

BY

HENRY EDWARD

ARCHBISHOP OF WESTMINSTER.

REUNION OF CHRISTENDOM.

REVEREND AND DEAR BRETHREN:

In the Synod of the Diocese held on the 14th of December in last year, I published a Letter of the Supreme Congregation of the Holy Office, in reply to a communication of the Bishops of England relating to a society called an 'Association for Promoting the Unity of Christendom,' to which certain Catholics had become unwarily united. I made known to you also at the same time that the Holy Office had transmitted another document on the same subject, which it was my intention at a future time to communicate to the Clergy of the Diocese, together with certain instructions on the subject. This promise I will now fulfil.

It is not our practice in any official way to take cognisance of the affairs of those who are without; nor is there in the above-named Association any intrinsic importance to lead me to depart from our usual path. But special reasons induce me to do so; and they are the two documents which have been elicited from the supreme judicial authority of the Church, and the principles enunciated in them.

Inasmuch, Reverend and dear Brethren, as some of you may not be aware of the precise nature of the Association in question, I will begin with describing it; and that the description may be unimpeachable, it shall be given in the words of its own declaration. The founders and promoters of it announce it as follows:

‘ *Association for the Promotion of the Unity of Christendom.*

‘ An Association has been formed under the above title, to unite in a bond of intercessory prayer members both of the clergy and laity of the Roman Catholic, Greek, and Anglican communions. It is hoped and believed that many, however widely separated at present in their religious convictions, who deplore the grievous scandal to unbelievers, and the hindrance to the promotion of truth and holiness among Christians, caused by the unhappy divisions existing amongst those who profess to have " One Lord, one Faith, one Baptism," will recognise the consequent duty of joining their intercession to the Redeemer's dying prayer, " that they all may be one, as Thou, Father, art in Me, and I in Thee, that they also may be one in Us, that the world may believe that Thou hast sent Me." To all, then, who, while they lament the divisions among Christians, look forward for their healing mainly to a corporate reunion of those three great bodies which claim for themselves the inheritance of the priesthood and the name of Catholic, an appeal is made. They are not asked to compromise any principles which they rightly or wrongly hold dear. They are simply asked to unite for the promotion of a high and holy end, in reliance on the promise of our Divine Lord, " that whatsoever we shall ask in prayer, believing, we shall receive ; " and that " if two or three agree on earth as touching anything that they shall ask, it shall be done for them of my Father who is in heaven." The daily use of a short form of prayer, together with one " Our Father," for the intention of the Association, is the only obligation incurred by those who join it; to which is added, in the case of priests, the offering, at least once in three months, of the Holy Sacrifice, for the same intention.'

Certain Catholic names appeared in the list of its members, and its chief promoters were understood to assert that not a few Catholics were inscribed in its books. This is perhaps not far from accurate, inasmuch as it is known that the promoters of the scheme had manifested much activity in seeking the names of Catholics, especially on the Continent; and that Catholics abroad are hardly on their guard against enterprises, not unfrequent among us, of which their own countries afford no example. Moreover, both abroad and in England the very name of unity is dear to every Catholic heart, and every one who utters it speaks the password to our goodwill. A Catholic, in proportion to his love of the Church of God, and of Jesus, Who in dying for us laid upon us the law of unity, will always mourn over the schisms which men have made, and be ready to give not his name only, but his life, if he could heal them. It is not wonderful, therefore, if some fervent minds should have consented to unite in this Association. Others again were involved in it with more simplicity on their own part, and I fear, from their statements, less on that of those who invited them.

A *Review* setting forth the principles of the Association, and the opinions of individuals composing it, is published every two months. Certain Catholics were induced to write in it; and statements purporting to come from Catholic hands have appeared in it, which compelled the Bishops of England to take cognizance of the *Review* and of the Association.

The matter was therefore referred by the united act of the Episcopate in England to the Holy Office, in the month of April 1864. The answer was dated on Sept. 16, 1864, and contains an enunciation of the following principles:

1. That the theory that Christendom or the Christian Church consists of three parts, the Roman, the Greek, and the Anglican, is a heresy overthrowing

the nature of unity and the Divine constitution of the Church. 'Fundamentum cui ipsa innititur hujusmodi est quod divinam Ecclesiæ constitutionem susque deque vertit. Tota enim in eo est ut supponat veram Jesu Christi Ecclesiam constare partim ex Romana Ecclesia per universum orbem diffusa et propagata, partim vero ex schismate Photiano et ex Anglicana hæresi, quibus æque ac Ecclesiæ Romanæ unus sit Dominus, una fides, et unum baptisma.'*

2. That to unite in an association of prayer with those who hold this theory is unlawful, inasmuch as it is an implicit adhesion to heresy, and to an intention stained with heresy. 'At quod Christi fideles et ecclesiastici viri hæreticorum ductu, et, quod pejus est, juxta intentionem hæresi quam maxime pollutam et infectam pro christiana unitate orent, tolerari nullo modo potest.' †

3. That such association favours indifferentism, and is therefore scandalous. 'Conspirantes in eam indifferentismo favent, et scandalum ingerunt.' ‡

The Holy Office therefore concludes by strictly prohibiting the faithful to inscribe themselves in it, or in any way whatsoever to show it favour. 'Maxima igitur sollicitudine curandum est ne Ca-

---

* S. R. I. Epist. ad omnes Angliæ Episcopos. † Ibid. § Ibid.

tholici, vel specie pietatis vel mala sententia decepti, societati de qua hic habitus est sermo aliisque similibus adscribantur, vel quoquomodo faveant.'

On the publication of this answer, the promoters of the Association addressed a letter to His Eminence Cardinal Patrizi, by whom, as Secretary of the Holy Office, the letter had been signed; saying that they had read it with great sorrow; that they had never affirmed that there are three Churches which with equal right (*æquo jure*) claim the name of Catholic; that they spoke only of *fact*, not of *right* (*facti, non juris*); that they never contemplated the reunion of three bodies holding discordant doctrines, but a reunion in truth; that the *Union Review* had no more than a fortuitous connection with the Association, and conveyed only the opinions of individuals.

This address was signed by 198 Clergy of the Church of England.

The answer, dated Nov. 8, 1865, contains a luminous and precise enunciation of Catholic principles, of which I give a brief analysis, exhorting you to study with exactness the whole document, which is given in the Appendix.

It affirms that all labour for unity is in vain, unless it be reduced to the principles upon which the Church was constituted by Christ in the beginning. Those principles it declares to be as follows:

1. That the unity of the Church is absolute and indivisible, and that the Church has never lost its unity, nor for so much as a moment of time ever can. ' Christi Ecclesia suam unitatem numquam ne brevissimo quidem temporis intervallo amittet.' There is, therefore, both *de jure* and *de facto*, only one Church; one by a numerical and exclusive unity.

2. That the Church of Christ is indefectible, not only in duration, but in doctrine; or in other words, that it is infallible, which is a Divine endowment bestowed upon it by its Head; and that the infallibility of the Church is a dogma of the faith. ' Quod si Ecclesia Christi indefectibilis prorsus est, sponte sequitur eam infallibilem quoque dici et credi debere in Evangelica doctrina tradenda; quam infallibilitatis prærogativam Christum Dominum Ecclesiæ suæ, cujus Ipse est caput, sponsus, et lapis angularis, mirabili munere contulisse inconcussum est Catholicæ fidei dogma.' *

3. 'That the Primacy of the Visible Head is of Divine institution, and was ordained to generate and to preserve the unity both of faith and of commu-

---

* Second Letter of the Holy Office addressed to Members of the Association, &c. &c.

nion, that is, both internal and external, of which the See of Peter is the centre and the bond. 'Jam non minus certum atque exploratum est Christum Jesum, ut fidei communionisque unitas in Ecclesia gigneretur ac perpetuo servaretur, utque capite constituto schismatis tolleretur occasio, Beatissimum Petrum præ cæteris Apostolis, tamquam illorum principem et ejusdem unitatis centrum et vinculum conspicuum, singulari providentia elegisse.'

4. That therefore the Catholic and Roman Church alone has received the name of Catholic. 'Ecclesia sancta, Ecclesia una, Ecclesia vera, Ecclesia Catholica, quæ Catholica nominatur non solum a suis, verum etiam ab omnibus inimicis, sicque ipsum Catholicæ nomen sola obtinuit.'

5. That no one can give to any other body the name of Catholic without incurring manifest heresy, 'citra manifestam hæresim.'

6. That whosoever is separated from the one and only Catholic Church, howsoever well he may believe himself to live, by this one sin of separation from the unity of Christ, is in the state of wrath. 'A qua quisque fuerit separatus, quantumlibet laudabiliter se vivere existimet, hoc solo scelere quod a Christi unitate disjunctus est, non habebit vitam, sed ira Dei manet super eum.'

7. That every several soul, under pain of losing eternal life, is bound to enter the only Church of Christ, out of which is neither absolution nor entrance into the kingdom of heaven. 'Quicumque ab unitate fidei vel societate illius [Beati Petri] quolibet modo semetipsos segregant, tales nec vinculis peccatorum absolvi nec januam possint regni cœlestis ingredi.'

Such are the principles on which the Supreme Authority of the Holy Office exhorts the members of this Association to hasten from their disinherited separation into the inheritance of Christ. 'Ab exhæredata præcisione fugientes in hæreditatem Christi.'

Inasmuch, then, as these two letters of the Holy Office have been communicated to me both for my guidance and for yours, it is my duty to draw out the reasons which have called them forth, and the course which it is our duty to pursue towards those to whom these letters refer.

On the first principle of the former letter of the Holy Office, namely, ' that the theory that Christendom or the Christian Church consists of three parts, the Roman, the Greek, and the Anglican, is a heresy, overthrowing the nature of unity, and the Divine constitution of the Church,' we will for the present refrain from speaking, as it will fall more properly under the comments required hereafter by the second letter.

The second principle follows by necessity; 'that to unite in such an Association with those who hold this theory, is unlawful, inasmuch as it is an implicit adhesion to heresy, and to an intention stained with heresy.'

I will therefore dwell upon the third, inasmuch as it makes practical application of the two former; namely, 'that such an Association favours indifferentism, and is therefore scandalous.'

The sum of these three principles is briefly this, that the indivisible and exclusive unity of the Church is a dogma of faith, and that all association in prayer with those who deny it is unlawful. It is on this that I purpose more fully to speak.

And in so doing I shall be compelled to treat not only of the matter of the declaration given above, but also of the principles and opinions put forward in the *Union Review*, and in other works which are but repetitions of the same. They represent a school: and though in the letter to the Cardinal Secretary of the Holy Office certain members of the Association affirm that it has only an accidental relation to the *Union Review*, it is my duty to treat of both, as the errors are identical: and therefore, whether they be related or no, we are in conscience bound to deal with both. What I say therefore, will apply to all works containing the same errors, by whomsoever written, whether he be of the Association or not. As my object is first truth, and then unity, and as I know that both unity and truth are obscured by any breach of charity, I shall treat of errors, not of names, impersonally, and as they exist, not in any particular writer, but in themselves; and I shall endeavour to treat them with as little severity as duty to truth admits.

That an Association to promote the reunion of England with the Catholic and Roman Church should exist, and that nearly two hundred clergymen of the Church of England, describing themselves as 'Deans, Canons, Parish Priests, and other Priests' of the Church of England, should address the Cardinal Secretary of the Holy Office, expressing this desire, are facts new in our history since the separation of England from Catholic unity. We do not regard this as a merely intellectual or natural event. We gladly recognise in it an influence and an impulse of supernatural grace. It is a wonderful reaction from the days within living memory when fidelity to the Church of England was measured by repulsion from the Church of Rome. It is as wonderful an evidence of the flow in the stream which has carried the minds of men onward for these thirty years nearer and nearer to the frontiers of the Catholic faith. It is a movement against the wind and tide of English tradition and of English prejudice; a supernatural movement like the attraction which drew those who were once farthest from the kingdom of heaven to the side of our Lord. A change has visibly passed over England. Thirty years ago its attitude towards the Catholic Church was either intense hostility or stagnant ignorance. It is not so now. There is still much hostility and much ignorance. But the hostility is more civilised, and the ignorance is breached on all sides. We do not, however, overestimate the importance of the movement of which this Association is the advanced column. It must never be forgotten that the Church of England represents only one-half of the English people, and that the Anglican school represents only a portion of the Church of England, and that the Anglo-Catholic movement represents only a section of the Anglican school, and that the Unionist movement represents only a fraction of that section. Two hundred clergymen are a small proportion upon some seventeen thousand; and supposing many to agree with them who did not sign the letter to Rome, and many more to wish well to them, the whole is hardly an appreciable quantity upon the Church of England, and an inappreciable quantity upon the English people. We say this to moderate the anticipations of inconsiderate hope, not to chill the warmth of our sympathy with those who are feeling their way to the truth. One soul, as S. Charles was wont to say, is diocese enough for a bishop; and a mere remnant stretching out their hands towards unity have a right to all our care. At the same time we must not forget that our mission is not only to a section or to a fraction who may be approaching nearer to us, but to the whole mass of the English people. If the handful who have come so near have a claim upon our sympathy, much more have the millions who are as sheep without a shepherd, wandering to and fro in 'the cloudy and dark day.' Moreover, we owe an especial duty to the class of the English people in which descends the mid-stream of traditional hostility to the Catholic Church—that is, the middle class of educated and industrious men, the heart of English national life, vigorous, calm, intelligent, and benevolent, though darkened by inherited prejudices, and narrowed by anti-Catholic faults. To this class above all we have a mission of charity, that is, to preach the truth in patience, and to wait till they will listen. From circumstances of birth and education, from historical contacts, and approximations of opinion, from social and political neighbourhood, and from manifold bonds of kindred, the Anglican system is more nearly related to the Catholic Church than the Baptist, Independent, Wesleyan, and other Nonconformist bodies. And yet to the Catholic Church the millions who are in separation from the Established Church are an object of the profoundest sympathy and charity. They are souls for whom Christ died, robbed of their inheritance by the Anglican separation, from which they by legitimate process have separated in turn. Their state of privation is all the less culpable, as they have been born into a diminished inheritance of truth, with a greater difficulty of rising to it again. They are, moreover, marked by a multitude of high qualities of zeal, devotion to duty, conscientious fidelity to what they believe. If they are rougher in their language against the Catholic Church, they are more generous and candid adversaries; more vehement but less bitter, and altogether free from the littleness of personality and petty faults which sometimes stain the controversy of those who are intellectually nearer to the truth. For such men it is our duty to cherish a warm charity and a true respect, and not disproportionately to waste upon those who stand nearer to us the time and the sympathy which is their due. The time is come that the Catholic Church should speak, face to face, calmly and uncontroversially to the millions of the English people who lie on the other side of the Establishment.

It may seem a strange and invidious thing for us, who witness for the unity of the Church throughout the world, to be tardy in going forth to meet those who approach us with invitations to union. This slowness is not, God knows, from indifference to division, or from disregard to the miseries and dangers of schism, or from insensibility to the dishonour done to our Divine Master. For my own part, if I may speak of myself, it is more than a quarter of a century since the thought and name of unity so filled my whole mind that it has been often turned to my reproach. In all these years it has been my heart's desire and prayer, not only to see the members of the Anglican body gathered into Catholic unity, but the millions of Dissenters, that is, the whole English people, especially the multitude of its noble-hearted poor, united once more in the bond of peace and truth. We believe union to be a very precious gift, and only less precious than truth. There is nothing we would not do or suffer, by the grace of God, to effect or to promote the reunion of all or of any who are out of the fold, to the unity of the Church. We heartily pray, therefore, that He who has inspired and nurtured this desire of union may mature and perfect it; that He will remove all that hinders its accomplishment, purifying the hearts of men from all attachment to their errors and their separations, and cleansing their intelligence to see the immutable faith and sole unity of the Catholic and Roman Church. On our part, all that can cherish and foster these yearnings shall be done. The vision of England Catholic once more; its true and energetic people once more elevated by faith to the higher instincts of the Catholic Church; our domestic schisms healed, our bitter controversies ended, and all our powers turned from mutual conflict, upon the subjugation of the sin and unbelief which, day and night, devours souls on every side: all this is as beautiful and fascinating as the image of the Heavenly Jerusalem which the Apostle saw coming down from heaven. There is only one thing more beautiful and more commanding, and that is the Heavenly Jerusalem itself, not in image, but in reality; the Holy Church throughout the world in all the perfect symmetry of unity and truth, indefectible and infallible, incorruptible and changeless, the mother of us all, the kingdom of God on earth.

We are ready to purchase the reunion of our separated brethren at any cost less than the sacrifice of a jot or a tittle of the supernatural order of unity and faith. When, some fifty years ago, a writer more zealous than circumspect spoke of a reunion of the Anglican and Catholic Churches, Bishop Milner, with his vigorous common sense and his high Catholic instinct, answered, 'If we should unite ourselves with it, the Universal Church would disunite itself from us.' This is the only price we cannot give for even so great a happiness as the reconciliation of England. Nor must we be misjudged for this. It is not that we will not, but that we cannot. We cannot barter or give that which is not our own. The Divine and infallible authority of the Church sets the limits to our powers and our desires. We can offer unity only on the condition on which we hold it—unconditional submission to the living and perpetual voice of the Church of God. If this be refused, it is not we who hinder unity. For it is not we who impose this condition, but the Spirit of Truth who abides in the Church for ever.

Thus much we have said, lest we should seem to

forget our mission to the great people of England, in our contact with the little band who are advancing with swords wreathed in myrtle. Nevertheless, with them we are willing to deal in all charity, though from the right and centre of their array we still hear the cry of 'No peace with Rome.' We thank God that there are to be found ten men who desire to be restored to the centre of unity. We should have to answer to the Good Shepherd, if so much as one of His sheep were frayed away from the fold by harsh voices or rough handling on our part. Charity, in all its forms and instincts, of patience, tenderness, forbearance, hopefulness, and gentleness, is our duty as Pastors. But we owe them more than this. They have a right to the whole truth, and we are bound in duty to declare it to them. In this the beloved Disciple is our pattern, the apostle of charity and of dogma, the most ardent in love to all men, the most inflexible for the doctrines of faith. It is startling to hear the Disciple who lay upon the breast of Jesus say, 'If any man come to you, and bring not this doctrine, receive him not into the house, nor say to him God save you: for he that saith unto him God save you, communicateth with his wicked works.' *

* 2 S. John, 10, 11.

It would be contrary to charity to put a straw across the path of those who profess to desire union. But there is something more divine than union; that is, the Faith. It was to declare this law of His kingdom that our Divine Lord said, 'Do not think that I came to send peace upon earth : I came not to send peace, but the sword': * a Divine saying, most necessary in these days, when precision of doctrine is denounced as uncharitable, and dogma as the bar to union. It is this which the Holy Office has detected, with the true instinct of Rome, in the Association before us.

It is not lawful, then, for a Catholic to hold himself in a passive attitude towards any error contrary to faith. Therefore, it is not lawful for him to unite in prayer with those who hold such error. The fidelity he owes to the dogma of faith forbids it. 'Lex orandi,' as S. Augustine teaches, ' est lex credendi.' And this we shall see more clearly by drawing out briefly what dogma is, and what are its obligations upon the conscience. It is the more necessary to do so, because it is precisely on this point that the Catholic Church is diametrically in conflict with the mind of the nineteenth century,

* S. Matth. x. 34.

and, so far as it utters itself in clamour, with the popular opinion of England. The Church is definite, precise, and peremptory in its declarations of doctrine. It refuses all compromise, transaction, or confusion of the terms and limits of its definitions. It is intolerant not only of contradiction, but of deviation. It excludes every formula but its own. The world is moving in the reverse direction. It is throwing everything open, levelling boundaries, taking in all forms of opinion, comprehending all sects of Christians, by eliminating their differences, and finding a higher generality, a *summum genus* which embraces all. The Humanitarians merge all religion in Naturalism, the Unitarians in Christian morality, the Latitudinarians in the residuum of Christianity which survives the elimination of differences among Protestants, the Anglicans in an imaginary faith of the undivided Church, the Unionists in an agreement of the universal Church which shall neither be the Thirty-nine Articles as they are understood by Englishmen, nor the Council of Trent as understood by Catholics, but the text of both, understood in a sense known neither to the Church of England nor to the Church of Rome; a doctrine wider than either, compared with which the faith and theology of the Church is denounced as narrow and sectarian. Such are the pretensions of a series and gradation of irreconcilable schools, in conflict with one another, agreed in nothing but common hostility to the only Church which is inflexible in dogma, immutable in refusing all comprehension by way of compromise, and all contact with those who are without its unity. No wonder we are thought to be narrow, sectarian, and uncharitable. Nothing but a divine law could justify such a course. But such a law there is, which more than justifies. It binds the conscience of every member of the Church, from the Sovereign Pontiff to the little child in a Catholic school, to the Divine unity of truth. For what is dogma but the true intellectual apprehension, and the true verbal expression of the truths and facts of the Divine Revelation? It is an eternal truth that there is one God in three Persons; the doctrine of Trinity in Unity is a dogma. It is a Divine fact that the Son of God was made Man; the Incarnation is a dogma. It is a Divine fact that the Holy Ghost came on the day of Pentecost, perfected and animated the Church with His presence, endowed it with an indivisible unity and a continuous infallibility, in virtue of His own perpetual presence and assistance; the conception and expression of all these Divine operations is dogma. So I might enumerate all the doctrines of the Faith. They are outlines traced upon the intelligence of the mystical body by the Spirit of God; the reflection of the mind of God in the mind of the Church, and the enunciation of the Divine truths and facts so apprehended, in words which truly and adequately express them. The perpetual knowledge and perpetual enunciation of these truths and facts, by the perpetual presence and assistance of the Holy Ghost, is the infallibility of the Church, or, in other words, the perpetuity of the Divine Revelation, in virtue of a Divine guidance to the Church in all ages, in the nineteenth as in the first. How, then, can the Church cease to be dogmatic, without betraying its Divine trust, and ceasing to witness for God?

It is also in behalf of the human reason itself, of its freedom and its perfection, that the Church is jealous in its custody of dogma. What axioms are to science, dogma is to theology. As there can be no science without fixed principles and primary certainties, so there can be no knowledge of God, nor of His revelation, without fixed and primary truths. Such are the doctrines of the faith delivered to us by the perpetual and Divine office of the Church. The intellect of man is feeble and vacillating until it has certain scientific principles to start from. These once given, it acquires firmness and power of advance.

One truth scientifically proved, becomes the basis of many. The physical sciences, each in their kind, are proof of this. The same is true in the science of God. The truths of the natural order are confirmed and perfected by revelation. On the basis of natural truths rests, by the Divine disposition, the order of revealed truths; such as the Holy Trinity, the Incarnation, the Church and its supernatural endowments. The horizon of the human reason is therefore expanded by revelation, and the reason is elevated above its natural powers. And in this both its freedom and its perfection is secured. It is no bondage to know the truth, and no freedom to be in doubt. And yet they who know the truth are not free to contradict it; and they that are in doubt have the liberty of wandering out of the way. The law of gravitation once demonstrated, took away the liberty of contradicting it: and yet no man considers himself to be in bondage. All science limits the reason by the boundaries of its own certainty; but we do not therefore think men of science to be intellectual slaves. So is it with the science of God. We are limited by Divine Revelation, and by the infallibility of the Church, to believe in the Holy Trinity, the Incarnation, and the whole dogma of faith; yet we are not therefore slaves, but freemen. We are redeemed from doubt and error, and from that which is both at once, from the guidance of the blind, the theology of human teachers, by the presence and office of a Divine. 'You shall know the truth, and the truth shall make you free.' And not free only, but perfect; for the human reason advances to its perfection in proportion as it is conformed to the Divine. The dogma of faith is the mind of God, and theology is the science of God; and they that are most fully illuminated by it, are the most conformed to the Divine intelligence, which conformity is the perfection of the reason of man.

And once more, as the Holy Office affirms, there is no unity possible except by the way of truth. Truth first, unity afterwards; truth the cause, unity the effect. To invert this order is to overthrow the Divine procedure. The unity of Babel ended in confusion; the unity of Pentecost fused all nations in one body by the one dogma of faith. To unite the Anglican, the Greek, and the Catholic Church in any conceivable way could only end in a Babel of tongues, intellects, and wills. The intrinsic repulsions of the three are irresistible. Union is not unity. Heterogeneous and repugnant things may be arbitrarily tied together, but this is not unity. Union has in itself no assimilating power. Closer contact elicits the repugnances which rend all external bonds asunder. Truth alone generates unity. It was the dogma of faith which united the intellects of men as one intelligence. The unity of truth generated its universality. The faith is Catholic, not only because it is spread throughout the world, but because throughout the world it is one and the same. The unity of the faith signifies that it is the same in every place. If it were not the same it would not be universal. Identity is the condition both of unity and of universality. From this springs the supernatural harmony of the human intelligence, spreading throughout the Church and reaching throughout all its ages. The dogma of faith has made it one by the assimilating power of the one science of God. From this unity of intellects has sprung the unity of wills. The unity of the Church is created by the submission of all wills to one Divine Teacher through the pastors of the Church, especially the one who is supreme on earth. Submission to one authority by an inevitable consequence draws after it unity of communion. One authority and one communion; 'One body, one spirit;' indivisible because intrinsically one; united both in intellect and will by the indivisible truth and charity of the Holy Ghost, by whom the Church is compacted, animated, and sustained. To countenance the assumption of the name of Catholic by any bodies in separation from, and in contradiction to, the one only Church, by so much as a silent or passive association, cannot be free from an implicit adhesion to heresy.

For this cause the Holy Office forbids the faithful to be united, or in any way whatsoever to show favour to an Association which puts union before truth, contradicting thereby the Divine order of grace, and inverting the process by which the Church has been founded and perfected. They who seek truth before union are in the path in which the Son of God has always led His disciples to suffer for His sake. They who seek union before truth fall into heresy, or into indifference, and 'the rent is made worse.'

Once more: dogma is the way of salvation, and the Church is bound to its inflexible maintenance, not only by the obligation of truth, but also by the obligation of charity for the salvation of mankind. It is a dogma of faith that 'there is no other name under heaven given among men whereby we must be saved.' Salvation through the Name of Jesus is an absolute and exclusive condition.

Again: that there is 'one baptism for the remission of sins,' and that there is no salvation for those who reject it, is a dogma necessary to salvation, on which the Church could not falter without violating both truth and charity, and incurring the guilt of losing souls for whom Christ died.

In like manner, that there is 'one fold under one Shepherd,' and that the one fold is undivided and indivisible, is a dogma as divine and as inflexible as the unity of the Saving Name and the necessity of baptism. We are as much bound, under pain of eternal death, to bear witness that without the Church is no salvation, as that without baptism is no regeneration, and without the Name of Jesus no entrance into eternal life. In the Old Law it was written, 'Cursed be he that removeth his neighbour's landmarks.' * And what is the visible unity of the Church but the landmark which God has set up to bound the Fold of Salvation? They who deny its numerical and indivisible unity remove the landmark of God. They who teach that the Anglican separation and the Greek schism are parts of the Catholic Church violate a dogma of faith, destroy the boundaries of truth and falsehood, and 'make the blind to wander out of his way.' † The inflexible and exclusive dogmatic teaching of the Church, intolerant of all compromise

---

* Deut. xxvii. 17. † Ibid. xxvii. 18.

and of all contact with error, is the voice of charity. As lighthouses are set up along dangerous coasts to guard seamen in the storms of night, so are the exclusive dogmas of the one Name, one Baptism, one Fold. To obscure these lights, much more to quench them, is cruelty to man. They who destroy sea-lights are enemies of the human race; much more they who cloud and confuse the distinctions which mark off the truths of God from the errors of men.

Not only charity to men but fidelity to God binds us to the most explicit and exclusive declaration of the truth, and the most vigilant refusal to unite even passively in any association with error. For truth is the Word of God; our Divine Lord identifies it with Himself and Himself with it. He says, 'I am the Truth.'* The truth is, therefore, not a theory, but a Person, and we owe to it a personal fidelity. Every particle of His word, and every precept of His will, is a personal obligation on our conscience. The exclusive unity of His Church is both a Divine truth and a Divine precept, from which we cannot swerve without personal infidelity to Him.

Moreover, dogma is the mind of the Spirit of Truth, Who inhabits the only Church of God, and makes it the organ of His voice. To unite in prayer

* S. John, xiv. 6.

with those who deny the unity of His temple and the organ of His voice, who affirm that He is silent, and that because of schism He cannot speak, or, worse than all, that He speaks through three *de facto* Churches in perpetual contradiction and in perpetual conflict, is an infidelity to the Person of the Spirit of Truth, and a dishonour to His presence and His office.

Lastly, it is an infidelity to the Father of Lights, who has so revealed His mind and His will as to make His Church the light of the world, that is, the self-evident witness, more manifest than all reasonings, more luminous than all proofs, as 'a city seated on a mountain,' visible to all whose eyes are open.

The first theological virtue infused into us in our baptism—the grace of faith, and the union of our hearts to the Divine truth delivered by the Church—forbids even a passive union with those who violate an article of the Baptismal Creed, and obscure the way of salvation.

The Holy Office has declared with a dignified calmness of language, that for 'the disciples of Christ and the ministers of His Church to pray for the unity of Christendom, at the invitation of those who are in heresy, and in union with an intention eminently depraved and infected by heresy, can in no way be tolerated.' We may pray for them, but not with them ; and all the more pray for them as we are bound to bear active and explicit witness against all heresy, material or formal, and the peril in which its teachers stand, by refusing all communion with them even in prayer. The only association of prayer founded by God is the Church of God.

Such, then, is the substance of the first letter.

We may now proceed to the second.

The adherents of the Association complained, as I have said, in their letter to his Eminence Cardinal Patrizi, that they had been misunderstood ; that they did not affirm the existence of three Churches, or of three parts of the Church, 'æquo jure,' but only 'de facto ;' that they did not desire reunion with a permanence of conflicting doctrines, from which, they admitted, discord under the same roof, rather than ecclesiastical unity, would arise.

To this the Holy Office answered, that there is but one principle of unity which is before all and generates all union ; namely, Truth, working through the one and only Church united to its centre and bond of unity, the See of Peter. It affirmed also that to pray for the reunion of the Church is to assume that it can be divided ; that such an assumption is contrary to faith; that the unity of the Church never has been lost, nor ever can be; and that as its unity is perpetual, so is its infallibility, in the nineteenth century as in the first.

Now it is not my intention to enter into these propositions in detail. For you, Reverend and dear Brethren, it is needless. They are the principles of your whole life, the instinctive laws of your minds. For others I cannot now attempt an adequate treatment; and can only refer to what I have endeavoured to say as to the doctrine of the Church on the Temporal Mission of the Holy Ghost. But it is possible within our present limits to apply the principles of the Holy Office to the particular form of error which this Union movement has cast up. The error may be stated as follows:—The Church of Christ is one in origin, succession, and organisation; but not necessarily in communion. For six centuries or more it was united, till the East separated from the West: since then, it has indeed lost its perfection, but both parts continue to be the Church. While united it was infallible, and the faith received universally was certainly Divine. After its division it continued to be infallible in all that was infallible before; but in all questions emerging after the division, it had no infallible voice or judgment to decide: neither could any decision be tested by the reception of the whole Church: the later divisions of the Reformation only reproduce the same anomalies in the West; the Anglican Church stands upon the same basis as the Greek; both contain the infallible truth of the undivided Church of the beginning; neither claims to be infallible in questions emerging now: the Church of England has not erred in its Thirty-nine Articles; and the Roman Church has not erred in its decrees at Trent; both are capable of a true interpretation, and both need a more perfect interpretation than either has yet received. Such interpretation in the future is the basis of reunion, and the hope of Christendom; such was the position of Bossuet, and such they claim as their own; but the great hindrance to reunion is the perpetual expansion of Roman opinions, and their transformation into new articles of faith, as for instance, the Immaculate Conception, and the Ultramontane theories which make the Pope personally infallible, and the temporal power a dogma of faith.

Let us draw out what these propositions contain.

1. First, they deny the indivisible unity and perpetual infallibility of the Church, which are affirmed by the Holy Office in precise terms. This was not the position of Bossuet, who lays down as follows:—

'In the year 1542, when the Lutheran pestilence began to make havoc in this most Christian kingdom, the Doctors of Paris, assembled in Faculty, published these Articles:—

'Every Christian is bound firmly to believe that the Universal Church is One, visible on earth, which in faith and morals cannot err, and which all the faithful, in whatsoever pertains to faith and morals, are bound to obey.'

'It is certain that a General Council legitimately gathered together, representing the Universal Church, cannot err in its decisions in faith and morals.'

'Nor is it less certain that in the Church Militant there is, by Divine right, one Roman Pontiff, whom all Christians are bound to obey. This rule of faith, delivered by all the Gallican Bishops and Churches, received also by Royal authority and the consent of all Orders, has been published and preserved by the same.' *

2. Next, they deny the infallibility of the Council of Trent, of which Bossuet thus writes to Leibnitz:—

'To give a clear and final resolution of the doubts which are raised about the Council of Trent, certain principles must be presupposed:—

'1. That the infallibility which Jesus Christ has promised to His Church resides in the whole body.

'2. That this infallibility, inasmuch as it consists, not in receiving, but in teaching the truth, resides in the order of Pastors, who succeed the Apostles, to whom the promise of Jesus Christ was made.

'3. That Bishops or Pastors, who are not ordained by and in this succession, have no part in the promise.

* Defens. Declarat. Cleri Gallicani, ed. Luxemb. 1730, tom. i. p. 3.

'4. That the Bishops or principal Pastors, who have been ordained in that succession, if they renounce the faith of their consecrators, that is to say, the faith which is in vigour in the whole body of the Episcopate and of the Church, would renounce at the same time their part in the promise, because they renounce the succession, the continuity, and perpetuity of the doctrine.

'5. That the Bishops and principal Pastors instituted in virtue of the promise, and abiding in the faith and the communion of the body where they have been consecrated, are able to bear witness to their faith, either by their unanimous preaching throughout the Catholic Church dispersed, or by an express judgment made in a legitimate Council. In either way their authority is equally infallible, and their doctrine equally certain. In the former way, because it is to that body thus outwardly dispersed, but united by the Holy Ghost, that the infallibility of the Church is attached; in the latter, because that body, being infallible, the Assembly which truly represents it, that is to say, the Council, has the same privilege, and can say, after the manner of the Apostles, "It seemed good to the Holy Ghost and to us."

'6. He adds that such a Council truly represents the Catholic Church, if its decrees be received by it.'

Bossuet sums up with this judicial sentence:—

'Those who will not accept these principles must never hope for any union with us, because they would never accept, but in words, the infallibility of the Church, which is the only solid principle of the reunion of Christians.

'On these principles it is easy to resolve all the doubts concerning the Council of Trent in that which regards the faith, it being certain that it is received and approved in that respect by the whole body of the Churches united in communion with that of Rome, which alone we recognise as Catholic; which Churches would no more reject its authority than they would that of the Council of Nice.' *

3. Lastly, they deny the Council of Trent to be œcumenical, which Bossuet recognised as of equal authority with the Council of Nice. His words seem to be written for the present day, and for this peculiar phase of anti-Catholic thought.

In his project for the reunion between the Catholics and Protestants of Germany, he says:—

'As to the objection of the Protestants that the Council of Trent was not œcumenical, because they did not sit in it as judges together with the Catholic Bishops, but sentence was passed by the adverse party; if their complaints were admitted there could never have been any Council, nor ever can be, inasmuch as neither did the Council of Nice admit as judges the Novatians and Donatists, or others already in any way separate from the Church; nor can heretics be ever judged, except by Catholics; nor they who secede from the Church, except by those who maintain its unity. Neither did the Lutherans, when in their synods they condemned the Zwinglians, have them as assessors; nor did justice permit that the Catholic Church should be judged by the English, Danish, Swedish Bishops, who professed open enmity against it, and had seceded from the Roman Church as impious, idolatrous and antichristian.

* Projet de Réunion entre les Catholiques et les Protestants d'Allemagne. Lettre XXII. See Appendix VIII.

The sum of Bossuet's judgment is given in these words:—'Nothing, therefore, will ever be done either by the Roman Pontiff, or by any Catholic whatsoever, by which the Tridentine decrees of faith can be shaken.'*

To what end, then, do men appeal to Bossuet, if they do not believe with Bossuet? Is it for the purpose of opposing the infallibility of the Pope? But that will not evade the infallibility of the Church. If Bossuet thought that the infallibility of the Pope *ex cathedrâ* could in his day be denied *salva fidei compage*, most assuredly he taught that no man could deny the infallibility of the Church without explicit heresy. If he taught that the reception of definitions by the Church was the test of their infallible certainty, he believed that Church to be the sole Catholic and Roman Church, in union with the See of Peter and exclusive of the Greek and Anglican schisms. What do they gain who appeal to Bossuet, but a greater condemnation? Out of their own mouth comes the sentence. Not only those who hold the infallibility of the Roman Pontiff condemn them, but all those who hold the infallibility of the

---

* Bossuet, Projet de Réunion entre les Catholiques et les Protestants d'Allemagne, par. iii. art. 2. Œuvres de Bossuet, tom. viii. p. 637. Paris, 1846.

Church. Gallicanism, the minimum of Catholic truth, condemns them as peremptorily as the highest Ultramontane theology. It is dangerous to use arguments *ad invidiam*, and for those who are without to appeal to any tribunal within the Catholic unity. We may say to them as S. Augustine said to the Donatists, who quoted the example of S. Cyprian against him: 'You object to us the letters of Cyprian, the judgment of Cyprian, the council of Cyprian; why put forward the authority of Cyprian for your schism, and reject his example which witnesses for the unity of the Church?'* We see Bossuet in Catholic unity; we see you in separation. Place yourselves where Bossuet lived and died, and then quote Bossuet. Being where you are, his name is a sentence against you.

The denial of the perpetual Divine assistance by which the Church is preserved from error, has led some to say that they accept the decrees of the Council of Trent, but not the interpretation of them. The Church of England is supposed to be found, not in the multitudinous contradictions of its living teachers, but only in the passive letter of its formularies. The Church of Rome is supposed not to be found in its dogmatic decrees, but in any obscure writer whose books may

* S. Aug. de Baptismo contra Donatistas, lib. ii. sec. 4.

not be censured. Still, even here truth is justified. The Church is to be found in its living voice; and its living voice is the true, and only true, and only authoritative interpretation of its formularies. By a law of natural production the formularies of the Church of England have generated contradictions over its whole surface; by a law of supernatural progression the decrees of Trent have expanded into a wide-spread and exuberant theology, dogmatic and mystical, pervading both the head and the heart, reaching far beyond the letter, as the spread of a cedar reaches on all sides beyond its centre, but is firmly and intrinsically united to its root, from which it derives life, symmetry, and substance.

When we call this living mind of the Church the true interpretation of the dogma of the faith, we need not remind you, Reverend Brethren, that in the Bull of Pius IV., confirmed and published by the Holy Council of Trent, the Sovereign Pontiff explicitly reserved to himself the interpretation of its decrees, as follows:—

'And further, to avoid perversion and confusion, which might arise if it were permitted to every one according to his will to put forth his commentaries and interpretations of the decrees of the Council, we inhibit by apostolical authority to all persons of whatsoever order, condition, or degree, whether ecclesiastical or lay, with whatsoever power they may be invested, if they be prelates, under the pain of interdict of entering the Church, and others, whosoever they be, under pain of excommunication *latæ sententiæ*, that no one, without our authority, venture to put forth any commentaries, glosses, annotations, *scholia*, or any kind of interpretation on the decrees of the same Synod, or to determine anything under whatsoever title, even under pretext of a greater confirmation or furtherance of the decrees, or any pretended reason. But if any one shall find in the same decrees any obscurity of language or of law, and for that cause any interpretation or decision shall seem to be needed, let him ascend into the place which the Lord hath chosen, that is, to the Apostolic See, the Guide of all the Faithful, whose authority the Holy Synod itself so reverently acknowledged. We therefore reserve to ourselves, according as the Holy Synod itself enjoined, the declaration and decision of all questions which may arise from its decrees.' *

* Bulla *Benedictus Deus* Pii IV. sup confirm. Conc. Trid. : 'Ad vitandum præterea perversionem et confusionem, quæ oriri posset, si unicuique liceret, prout ei liberet, in decreta concilii commentarios et interpretationes suas edere, apostolica auctoritate inhibemus omnibus, tam ecclesiasticis personis, cujuscumque sint ordinis, conditionis, et gradus, quam laicis, quocunque honore ac potestate præditis, prælatis quidem sub interdicti ingressus ecclesiæ, aliis vero quicumque fuerint, sub excommunicationis latæ sententiæ pœnis, ne quis sine auctoritate nostra audeat ullos commentarios, glossas, annotationes, scholia, ullumve omnino interpretationis genus super ipsius concilii decretis quocunque modo edere, aut quicquam quocunque nomine, etiam sub prætextu majoris decretorum corroborationis aut executionis, aliove quæsito colore statuere. Si cui vero in eis aliquid obscurius dictum et statutum fuisse, eamque ob causam interpretatione aut decisione aliqua egere visum fuerit, ascendat ad locum quem Deus elegit, ad sedem videlicet apostolicam, omnium

We have, therefore, a body of principles which govern the interpretation of dogmatic definitions, and regulate the living teaching of the Church.

1. All interpretations emanating from Pontifical authority are certainly infallible.

2. All decisions and doctrines taught by inferior tribunals or by theological schools, so long as they are not condemned by the Church, being publicly known and held in the presence of the supreme authority, may be presumed to be free from all error against faith or morals.

Of the first class are the copious and luminous decisions of the Pontiffs, S. Pius V., Innocent X., and Alexander VII., on the doctrines of grace contained in the condemned propositions of Baius and Jansenius, and the like.

Of the second class are all theological and devotional works which the Church has not censured. If they be publicly known and tolerated they may be presumed to be comformable to the dogma of faith, and to be innocent. They might not, perhaps, deserve it. They might enjoy rather impunity than toleration. Yet, till noted with censure they are in

fidelium magistram, cujus auctoritatem etiam ipsa sancta synodus tam reverenter agnovit. Nos enim difficultates et controversias, si quæ ex eis decretis ortæ fuerint, nobis declarandas et decidendas, quemadmodum ipsa quoque sancta synodus decrevit, reservamus.'

possession; as, by our common law, a man is innocent till he is found guilty. It is, indeed, a part of fidelity to truth, and of charity to souls, not to give impunity to errors in theology or devotion; and the Catholic instincts of pastors and people are quick and vigilant to detect any unsoundness, and to bring it under judicial examination. No great error passes undiscovered. And this is a presumption that whatsoever is publicly known and tolerated, whatever may be thought of it, cannot be contrary to faith or morals. But this does not make such teaching authoritative.

Nevertheless, we have no hesitation in saying, that whosoever shall rise up to condemn as pernicious what the public authority of the Church tolerates as innocent, is thereby guilty of temerity, and of immodesty. In so doing he would be ascribing to himself the supreme discernment which belongs to the Church alone. 'The spiritual man judgeth all things, and he himself is judged by no one.'* It would be the illuminism of the individual revising the discernment of the Church; the climax and efflorescence of the private judgment which criticises all things— first Scripture, then Fathers, then Churches, then Councils, then Pontiffs; finally, the accumulated

* 1 Cor. ii. 15.

living Christianity of the Catholic Church, in which the heart and mind of Fathers, Councils, and Pontiffs breathe, and teach, and worship.

It would be, then, a want both of prudence and of charity to encourage those who indulge this habit of mind in looking for concessions and explanations, to make tolerable to them the decrees of the Catholic Church. Such a course simply indulges and confirms the habit of private judgment, brings those who practise and those who indulge it under the censure of several Pontiffs, and obscures the only true principle of Divine faith.

To profess a readiness to accept the Council of Trent, if it be interpreted according to our own opinion, is not to subject ourselves to the authority of the Council, but to subject it to our own judgment. To say we will accept it as the basis of reunion if it mean so and so, is to say we will not accept it if it mean otherwise. Or, again, if the Pope would declare that the Council of Trent never meant what we object to, we would receive it. But what if it should mean otherwise? To ask for an authoritative interpretation, without engaging to submit to it, is to play fast and loose. If the authoritative interpretation agree with our own, well and good. But what if it differs? In this way we should not receive it because of its authority, but because of its agreement with our private judgment. If it differ, it would not be authoritative to us. Is it possible that men of any clearness or coherence of mind can fail to see through the obscurity and inconsequence of this procedure? In what does it differ from the private judgment of the common and consistent Protestant, who judges for himself of the meaning of Scripture, except only in this, that he confines himself to one book, and they claim to judge of all the Fathers, Theologians, Councils, Pontiffs, and the whole Church in every age? The common Protestant passes dryshod over all these, without asking whether he agrees with them or not: the Anglo-Catholic summons and convenes them all before him; professes to recognise them for what they are, Fathers, Theologians, Councils, Pontiffs; acknowledges their special illumination, commission, and authority; but after all, analyses, criticises, accepts, rejects their writings and their teaching with a final sentence that is an absolute superiority of judgment. In his opinion the Council of Trent is tolerable if it mean only what he means; intolerable if it mean anything else: tolerable if it agree with 'Tract XC.;' intolerable if it be in harmony with the faith, piety, devotion, and public worship of the Catholic and Roman Church throughout the world. Can private judgment exalt and enlarge itself beyond this girth and stature? Is there anything left on earth to be judged of; anything yet to pass under its analysis and its sentence; any tribunal standing, before which it is silent, or to which it inclines? It seems strange that good men do not perceive the moral fault of such pretensions, and men of intellect their incoherence. To read the pages of Holy Writ, luminous and simple as in great part they are, and, knowing no other teacher, neither Church nor Council, to walk humbly by the light of a few Divine truths, reverently adoring many incomprehensible mysteries—this is intelligible, coherent, and comparatively modest. But to profess to believe in Saints, Doctors, and Councils, which, if they may err, still have a special guidance, and in the Church of God, inhabited by the Spirit of God, infallible for six hundred years, assisted still in its decrees, superior to all individual minds, the chief authority on earth, divinely ordained to guide men; and yet after this to criticise all its acts and utterances from the Canons of Nice to the Decrees of Trent, from the Canon of Scripture declared by Pope Gelasius, to the Immaculate Conception declared by Pope Pius IX., and to propose this as the basis of reunion in the midst of the confusions of Anglicanism, is a process which I must refrain from characterising as it would demand. We should offend against both truth and charity if we were not to show with all fidelity and at all costs the impossibility of reunion on such terms. To receive the whole Council of Trent upon the principle of private judgment would make no man a Catholic. To receive the Council of Trent only because we critically believe its decrees to be true, and not because its decrees are infallible, is private judgment. We should not be submitting to them, but approving them. The formal motive of our approval would be not the Divine authority of the Council, but the judgment of our private spirit. God forbid, Reverend and dear Brethren, that minds be so brought within the unity of the Church. It would multiply our number, but not multiply the faithful. It would be to introduce among us a new and un-Catholic element, a show of material agreement disguising a formal and vital contrariety. Much as we desire to gather souls into the only Ark of Salvation, we dare not do so at the sacrifice of truth. The admission of those who deny the infallibility of the living Church Catholic and Roman of this hour, would not be salvation to them. They would be as S. Augustine said, 'intus corpore, corde foris.' All encouragement to such habits of mind can only end in disappointment, and miseries worse than disappointment. It could only end in apostacies, and complaints not unjust that they had been deceived. They would 'go out from us but they would not be of us.' It is far more truthful and charitable to say, firmly and plainly: The Church of God admits of no transactions. Recognition of its Divine office, acknowledgement of previous error, submission to its Divine voice—these and no others are the conditions of reunion.

Trusting to the unpopularity of what is called Ultramontanism, and to the popularity of all that encourages Nationalism, efforts have been studiously made for some years, and by writers of all kinds, sometimes, I grieve to say, by those who bore the name of Catholic, to represent as extreme, exclusive, and Ultramontane, all who believe the Holy See to be the Supreme Fountain of Faith and jurisdiction. This has been lately renewed under the form of seeking reunion on a Gallican basis, rejecting Ultramontane excesses, and appealing to the higher authority of the universal Church, to be ascertained hereafter by some process neither stated nor conceivable. You will not need, Reverend and dear Brethren, that I should point out to you that to refuse the Divine authority of the Church, speaking by its visible Head, and to appeal from that authority even to a Council in the future, falls under the sentence of excommunication reserved to the Pope.

On a point of such gravity I think it well to give the summary of the Pontifical law. The appeal from the Pope to a future General Council is described by Canonists as the crime of sacrilege against the primacy of the Sovereign Pontiff. Pius II. excommunicates all who so offend, and reserves their absolution to the Pope; declaring further that all who knowingly give counsel, help, or favour to those who so offend, incur the same pains and censures as the abettors of high treason and of heretical pravity.

And Julius II. declared that the same are to be held as true and undoubted schismatics, and of unsound opinions concerning the Catholic faith. Moreover, he extended all the above-named pains and censures to those who, by resolution, counsel, or deliberation, have either approved the words of others, or have given their opinion that an appeal from the Pope to a future General Council may, can, or ought to be made.*

* Thesaurus: De Pœnis Ecclesiasticis, ed. Giraldi, Romæ, 1831, p. 95:—

CAPUT I.

Appellantes a summo Pontifice ad futurum Concilium Generale.

Hoc est crimen sacrilegii contra primatum Pontificis Romani, *Cujet.* &c. Est autem jure declaratum non licere appellare a sen-

And further, it must be always borne in mind, and explicitly declared to our flocks, that the infallibility of the Pope, speaking *ex cathedrâ*, is an opinion protected by the highest authority. Alexander VIII., by a decree of December 7, 1690, that is, eight years after the Gallican declaration of 1682, condemned the following proposition: 'The assertion of the authority of the Roman Pontiff over General Councils,

tentia Romani Pontificis, *cap.* Nemo, *cap.* Aliorum facta, *cap.* Ipsi sunt, *cap.* Cuncta per mundum, &c. . . Præterea in dicta Bulla Pii II. incipit *Execrabilis*, statutum est, ut appellantes a Papa ad futurum Concilium, vel scienter consilium, auxilium, aut favorem ad id praestantes, eas pœnas et censuras incurrant, quas rei læsæ majestatis et hæreticæ pravitatis fautores incurrere dignoscuntur.

Et Julius II. dicta Bulla, incipit *Suscepti*, § 5, confirmavit dictam Constitutionem Pii II. supplendo omnem defectum solemnitatis, etiam publicationis forte omissæ; et, § 6, declaravit dictos contravenientes non solum ipso facto incurrere in pœnas in dicta Bulla *Execrabilis* impositas, sed ipsos pro veris et indubitatis schismaticis, et de catholica fide male sentientibus habendos, pœnisque canonicis et legalibus contra tales impositis subjacere. Item omnes supradictas pœnas et censuras extendit ad eos qui decreverint, consuluerint, deliberaverint, aut aliorum dicta approbaverint, aut vocem dederint, ut ad futurum Concilium universale a Papa appellare liceat, possit vel debeat.

Et merito quidem haec statuta sunt: nam appellans a Papa ad Concilium in crimen rebellionis incurrit, quatenus sic appellando se subtrahit ab obedientia supremi sui Principis in damnum ejusdem Principis, ejusque supremi dominii, illud ad alium procurando convertere . . . Similiter quod tales sint schismatici, et de fide male sentientes, ait *Sylvest.*, &c. et alii communiter. . . . Et quod asserens licitum esse appellare a Papa ad futurum Concilium sint hæretici formaliter, tenet *S. Antonin.*, &c. . . . Unde sequitur tales incurrere in censuras et pœnas latas contra hæreticos.

and his infallibility in determining questions of faith, is futile and has been often refuted.' The lightest censure inflicted by the decree on this proposition is that of temerity, and whosoever shall in public or in private maintain it incurs excommunication reserved to the Pope. I say the lightest, because inasmuch as theologians, such as Suarez and Bellarmine, hold the contrary of this proposition to be proximate to faith, it may be maintained with much reason that it is scandalous, savouring of heresy and proximate to heresy, and it is certain that to maintain it or to believe it, is a sin.*

But once more: we have said that this procedure obscures the principle of Divine faith, which is the veracity of God proposing His revelation to us through the medium of His Church. It is no question at this day how God proposed His truth to man before His Church was instituted through the incarnation of His Son, nor how He may propose it now among those to whom His Church is not present. The question is for England at this day. The Catholic Church is present among us, visible and audible, proposing the whole revelation of God by the Divine voice of His Holy Spirit. To criticise the decrees of Trent, before they believe or disbelieve their Divine veracity, is eva-

---

* Viva, Damnatæ Theses. Patavii, 1737, p. 495.

sion. To put forward lamentations over the onward course of the Church by accusing it of turning private opinions into dogmas of faith, is to beg the question. To accuse the Church of making new truths, is like accusing it of worshipping a wafer. A Catholic major premiss and a Protestant minor makes a poor syllogism. To complain of Ultramontanism as the great obstacle to reunion, is to hide the true issue of the controversy. If the Pope be not infallible, at least the Church is. Let men submit to the infallibility of the Church, and we may then hear what they have to say of the infallibility of the Pope. It is not Ultramontanism that demands their submission, but even Gallicanism. And it is Gallicanism that bars their way, until they have submitted with heart and head in faith both to the exclusive and indivisible unity, and to the exclusive and perpetual infallibility of the Catholic and Roman Church.

Divine faith consists in an infusion of supernatural grace illuminating the intelligence to know and the heart to believe all that God has revealed and proposed to be believed. The proposition of the Church is the test of the revelation of God. The Church proposes all that God has revealed, and nothing that He has not revealed. We have no contact with the revelation of God, except through the proposition of the Church. We are in contact with the Scriptures, because the Church proposes them to us as the written word of God; we are in contact with tradition, because the Church proposes tradition to us as the unwritten word of God. We are in contact with antiquity, because the Church proposes antiquity as its own past experience. Antiquity is no more than a period in the mind of the Church : for the mind of the Church is continuous. It proposes to us now what it proposed in antiquity. Every age has its truths, terms, definitions; and all are guarded and laid up in the Divine custody of the Church, and are proposed in every age as the master of the house 'bringeth forth new things and old;' the old new, because ever fresh; the new old, because they were from the beginning; though new errors demand new terms to meet them, and old truths need new fences to exclude new perversions. As Vincent of Lerins said, 'Non nova sed novè.'

The principle, or rule of Divine faith, then, is that the enunciation of the Church of this hour is the test and evidence of the original Revelation. By this God speaks to our reason and our faith. To refuse this, is to reject the voice of God in the world. We have, in that case, no choice but to turn to human teachers and to human criticism.

It is strange that men of consecutive minds, who seem to have mastered the principle that the Church alone possesses the key of Scripture, and that the true mind of Scripture is to be known only as it is interpreted by the living mind of the Church, should not see that, *a fortiori*, by the same law, the sense of antiquity is to be known from the Church alone. It is in vain to answer to the Catholic: But we have antiquity before us, Fathers and Councils, facts and doctrines. The Protestant says the same to them in turn: We have Scripture before us, the Evangelists and the Apostles, the very words and deeds of our Divine Lord. The Protestant is comparatively consistent in rejecting the Church, and interpreting both Scripture and antiquity for himself. How is it coherent to interpret Scripture by the Church, and antiquity by private judgment; to affirm the Church to be the interpreter of Scripture, but not of antiquity —that is, of the written word of God, but not of its own words and acts, its own experience, and its own intentions? This is surely a confusion into which nothing but the stress of controversy could have driven cultivated and thoughtful men. Was it that the one theory was necessary against Dissenters, the other against Catholics?

The ultimate cause, indeed, probably is, that such

reasoners have no adequate perception of the unity and continuity of the mind of the Church; and this, because they have no adequate perception of the perpetual presence and office of the Spirit of Truth in the Church. This one truth once fully seen, solves all, not only by way of authority, but by way of intelligent explanation. The Fathers were but the disciples of the Church; 'Doctores fidelium ecclesiæ discipuli.' What they taught they first learned; and the Church who taught them, both recognises her own teaching in their writings, even when the language may be less exact, and can correct it where it is equivocal, obscure, or erroneous.

The same is true of Councils, which are its own assemblies, and express its collective mind, with the sanction of its public authority. The Church of to-day sees its own mind, faith and morals, doctrine and discipline, not only in the first four Councils appealed to by Anglicans, but in the seven held to be General by the Greeks, and in the eleven which have continuously legislated and decreed, from the Second Council of Nice down to the Council of Trent. As the British Empire knows the mind of its own legislature from its earliest parliaments to this day, and permits no man, be he subject or prince, to contravene its authoritative interpretations; so, even in the natural order, the Catholic Church knows its own ancient statutes, and the acts of its own senate.

But more than this: the lineal and living consciousness of the Church has a higher fountain than the natural order. The perpetual knowledge and certainty of the revelation committed to its custody comes by a Divine assistance, as the revelation itself came by a Divine gift. The perpetuity of its infallibility is the permanence of the original revelation, by the perpetual presence of the same Divine Person from whom it flowed. Its onward progression in the explicit definition of truth is a property and an evidence of its perpetual Divine office. When we enunciate these axioms of Catholic faith, we are accused of putting assertions for proofs. But it is the office of a Divine teacher to assert and not to argue. The assertions of men are indeed no argument, but the assertion of the Church is proof in itself.

The denial of the perpetual Divine assistance of the Church has its newest form in the assertion that though the assistance be perpetual, yet we do not know when its exercise is to be expected. This comes strangely from those who say that the Church is divided, and that its divisions make the exercise of its infallible office at present impossible. They seem to admit that the assistance of the Holy Spirit is perpetual, but yet they affirm that it is not always. They appear to hold an intermittent operation of the Spirit of Truth, which gives no tests whereby it is to be discerned from the operation of human authority and of human teachers. The definition of the Immaculate Conception is accused as novel, unseasonable, and a hindrance to the reunion of Christendom. If true, why was it not defined before? If not necessary, why defined now?

To this we answer: When the disciples asked of our Divine Lord, 'Wilt Thou at this time restore again the kingdom to Israel?' He said, 'It is not for you to know the times or moments which the Father hath put in His own power. But you shall receive the power of the Holy Ghost coming upon you.'* In these words He declared the sovereignty and secrecy of His government over the Church. He reserved to Himself the time and the season of His operations; but when they came, all men recognised in them His presence and His action. During the ten days between the Ascension and the day of Pentecost, they were in uncertainty as to the future, and what His words might mean. When the Holy Ghost descended, all was manifest. No man could doubt

* Acts, i. 7, 8.

that it was the operation of His will. So it may be said of the course and action of the Church. In the succession of its history, from the declaration of the Consubstantiality of the Son to that of the Immaculate Conception of His Blessed Mother, there has been a line of definitions reaching through fifteen centuries of time. They who ask why the Immaculate Conception has been defined in the nineteenth century, would have asked why the 'Homoousion' was defined in the fourth, or the two Natures in One Person in the fifth. To those who deny the perpetual Divine office of the Church, all this may indeed cause perplexity; but the perplexity arises not from the exercise of its Divine office by the Church, but from their denial of it. They are the makers of their own difficulties. To those who believe that the words of Jesus are verified to the letter, and that the Spirit of Truth perpetually abides with us in all the fulness of His operations, it is as obvious and as certain that the Church should infallibly declare the doctrines of the Faith in the nineteenth as in the sixth or the fourth century. Nay, more; we believe that the discernment not only of the truth, but of the opportunity of declaring it, are both contained in the Divine assistance which guides the Church. We are sure that the 'Homoousion' is true, and that the fourth century was the opportunity divinely chosen for its declaration. We know with the certainty of faith that the Immaculate Conception is true, and we are certain that this time was the opportunity divinely chosen for its definition. The event is proof. The times and the moments were uncertain before the event; after it, they form a part of the Divine operation, and are declared by the fact. It is remarkable that the two questions proposed by the Sovereign Pontiff to the Bishops throughout the world were, not whether the doctrine of the Immaculate Conception were true; but first, whether it were definable, and second, if so, whether the time for defining it were come. Is it from want of knowledge, or accuracy of mind, that some have represented the Bishops of the Catholic world as divided about the truth of the Immaculate Conception? They all alike and with one voice proclaimed, and, as we are told even by an adversary, ostentatiously proclaimed, their belief in it. Some of them indeed doubted before the event, whether the time and the moment for the definition were come. And this has been used to create a rhetorical impression, on the minds of those who do not know the facts of the case, that they were opposed to the doctrine to be defined. The unreserved freedom with which a small number of the Bishops expressed their opinion, either that the doctrine was not capable of definition, or that the time for defining it was not opportune, made all the more striking their unanimity in believing it to be true, and the unhesitating firmness with which the Sovereign Pontiff proceeded to define it. A hostile critic has acutely remarked that the Pope knew the mind of his communion better than the few who counselled otherwise. And the event has justified his act. The whole Catholic Church has not only received the definition as certain, but acknowledged the time to be opportune. No shade of any of the anticipated dangers has been verified; but many momentous consequences to the Faith and to the Church have followed on this Pontifical act. Inasmuch as those who are out of the unity of the Church lament over the Immaculate Conception as a stumbling-block in their own way, and a source of unknown evils to come hereafter to us, it may be well, at a more fitting time, to trace out the evident marks of the Divine hand in this event. We do not assume to know that which the Father has put in His own power; but, as we may know that the key which answers to the wards belongs to the lock, so when the *clavis scientiæ* corresponds minutely with the intellectual demands both of error without the Church and of truth within it, we may with certainty predicate that it is 'the Key of David,' which alone 'openeth and no man shutteth, and shutteth and no man openeth.'*

We are told that the doctrine of the Immaculate Conception has no foundation in Scripture or tradition, and is contradicted by antiquity. How then is it that the whole Church, East and West, from the beginning, has always affirmed the Blessed Mother of God to have been sanctified with a pre-eminent and exceptional sanctification; that even those who affirm her to be of sinful flesh, *ex massa peccatrice*, affirm the same also of her Divine Son, and therefore not as affirming personal sin; that in affirming her to be free from actual sin, they affirmed by implication the absence of sin altogether; that the very term and phrase 'original sin' are technical and of Western origin; that as the nature of sin was more explicitly analysed in the Pelagian controversies, she was always more explicitly excepted from all affirmation of original sin; that the fact of her sanctification does include, and not contradict, as has been most preposterously said, her Immaculate Conception, which is no more than sanctification in its sovereign fulness; that the whole Episcopate, whensoever it has

* Apoc. iii. 7.

approached the question, has always affirmed it ; that the Councils of Ephesus and of Francfort recognised her as sinless ; that the Councils of Basil and of Avignon framed decrees to declare the Immaculate Conception ; that the Universities of Christendom always taught it, and bound their Doctors to teach it ; that every great Religious Order, but one, defended it ; that of the one only which hesitated, a majority of its theologians, as 130 to 90, maintained it ; that those who objected to the terms Immaculate Conception, held that Mary was Immaculate in her Nativity ; that is, that she was not only free from all actual sin, but from all original sin, and that by a sanctification which preceded birth into this world ; that this is the doctrine of S. Bernard, who is always made to contradict himself to serve the ends of controversy, in the very same letter to the Canons of Lyons in which he opposes their introducing, without authority of the Holy See, the Feast of the Immaculate Conception, instead of the Immaculate Nativity ; that, finally, thirty-three Pontiffs, in seventy Constitutions, have protected and promoted the belief of the Immaculate Conception, on which Pius IX. did no more than impress the image and superscription of the Divine and universal tradition of the Church of God ? It would have inspired more confidence in the candour and pacific aims of those who write against us, if these things had at least been recognised by so much as a statement and rejection.

The case then stands thus. The pre-eminent sanctification of the Mother of God is a tradition which has descended from the earliest traceable antiquity in the universal belief or passive infallibility of the Church of God. The active infallibility of the Church, as diffused throughout the world in the Episcopate, taught it. Six times, Bishops gathered in Council have implied or affirmed it. Twice they actually proposed to define it, in the very form of the Immaculate Conception; and now, lastly, the Sovereign Pontiff, after consulting the whole Episcopate throughout the world, receiving and weighing maturely the answers of some six hundred Bishops, defined the dogma *ex cathedrâ*, and the definition has been received not only with assent, but with joy, by the whole Catholic world. We have here more than a General Council, by way of protracted and universal consultation, and universal reception following. The requirements of Gallicanism are here more than satisfied. Bossuet would now judicially pronounce any man to be a heretic who should refuse to accept the Immaculate Conception as a dogma of faith. For Bossuet, in unwisely extolling General

Councils above the Pope, was not unwise enough to extol them above the Church; neither was he so superficial as to believe that the Church derives its infallibility from Councils, a theory seven-fold incoherent in those who maintain that General Councils may err. He did not hold the Church to be infallible because of the infallibility of Councils; but Councils to be infallible because of the infallibility of the Church. The Church is the fountain, the Council the pool into which the supernatural gift of infallibility flows. The universal reception of the Church was to him the test of that which the universal faith or passive infallibility of the Church already believed. Council or no Council, this was to Bossuet divinely and infallibly certain. The Church diffused throughout the world is always both passively and actively infallible. Councils are accidental, not necessary, to it. The Church is a perpetual Council in itself, containing not only all that the eighteen Councils have defined, but the whole revelation of truth which may ever be defined, and the Divine discernment to define it. Bossuet held, as of faith, every Pontifical definition received by the whole Church, though no General Council had intervened. The doctrine of original sin declared by S. Innocent I., and received by the whole Church; the doctrines of grace declared in the condemnation of Baius by S. Pius V., and likewise universally received, were to him infallible utterances of the Church. The remonstrances of Pelagians in early times, and of Greeks and Protestants in his own day, were to him the voice of strangers, separate from Catholic unity, and therefore excluded from the reception of the Church. How then can those who are separated from the only Church which Bossuet recognised, say, 'We and Bossuet rest on the same foundation'?

And what is the intelligible sense of saying, that though all Churches have erred, the universal Church is infallible? What is this universal Church, and where? If the Church be divided into three parts, and each part has erred, where is the Church which cannot err? Where is it to be seen? where heard? Where does it teach? How does it witness? Whom does it govern? Who submits to it? Is it the Church before the division, or the Church after the reunion? Where, then, is it now, but in the imagination? It would seem to me that this position is of all the least tenable. It admits that the Church of God must be infallible; it rejects the exercise of its infallibility. It is, therefore, as Giraldus says, both a heresy and a treason; a treason in appealing from the ultimate sovereignty of the Church of this hour, and a heresy in denying that ultimate sovereignty to be infallible. The Church has shown its unerring instinct in rejecting all who hold this error with pertinacity.

And here we have the precise point of contact between the error of the Unionist school and the faith of the Catholic Church. The Church teaches that its infallibility, whether in or out of the Council, is perpetual. The Unionist school teaches that its infallibility is intermittent, from Council to Council, and that by reason of its present divisions a General Council is impossible. The Church holds that a General Council is possible to-morrow, and that if convened and confirmed by the Sovereign Pontiff it would be infallible. But, whether a Council be held or no, the Church diffused and the Church in its Head is permanently and perpetually infallible; the ultimate and highest witness, both in the natural and supernatural order, of the original revelation, of the sense of Scripture, of the testimony of antiquity, of the mind of Councils; the supreme judge of truth and falsehood in all matters of faith and morals, and of all facts and truths in necessary contact with them. There is no obscurity as to the faith of Catholics, in relation to the Church, its nature, notes, properties, or gifts. We may be denounced as peremptory, exclusive, unreasonable;

but men know what we say, because we know what we mean.

It would seem to me an unwise course for those who approach us with professions of peace and desires of reunion, to cast stones at even the least in the household of faith. It is still less wise to assail the highest and most sacred person upon earth. It is dangerous and a sign of heresy to represent the Immaculate Conception defined by the Sovereign Pontiff as a hindrance to reunion. It is dangerous also to ascribe to any man opinions visibly absurd. It is indeed true that the portion of the Catholic Church most devoted to the 'cultus' of the Blessed Virgin is most persuaded of the personal infallibility of the Pope. But in no part of the Church, even among the most Ultramontane Catholics, is there to be found even one who believes that there is a continual flow of inspiration to change at any time popular opinion into infallible truth. If by this be meant into a dogma of faith, it is a simple confusion arising from want of common catechetical knowledge. No dogma is definable as of faith unless it have the first essential condition, namely, that it was revealed by God. Therefore Pius IX. in the definition of the Immaculate Conception did not declare the doctrine to be true, but to be revealed. It is hard to acquit such controversialists of a culpable want of knowledge, or of a culpable rashness in accusing.

But if this statement be intended to affirm only that popular opinion may become by the authority of the Church infallibly certain, it is most sound and Catholic doctrine. We would give as an example of an 'infallible truth,' which was once only a popular opinion, and has become infallibly certain, though it can never become a dogma of faith, the necessity of the temporal power of the Holy See to the freedom of the Church and of its Head. It shows no exactness to impute to any one that he has made the temporal power a part of his creed.

For ourselves, Reverend and dear Brethren, it is hardly needful that I should say that as yet I have never known of any Catholic so ignorant of the Act of Faith which he learnt in childhood as to incorporate the proposition of the temporal power with the doctrines of the Faith. My own mind on this subject was declared clearly enough four years ago to all who may wish to know it, or may desire not to misrepresent it. I then said:

'Inasmuch as it is better to err by excess of caution than by defect of explicitness, I will here say what I must ask all Catholics to pardon as needless to them, but necessary perhaps for those that are without.

'In the parallel I have drawn between the gradual definition of the doctrines of the Holy Trinity and of the Immaculate Conception, and the subject of the temporal power of the Sovereign Pontiffs, I have in no way and in no sense expressed or implied that the temporal power constitutes the material object of a dogma of faith.

'The first of the two conditions of a dogma of faith is, that it was revealed by God to the Apostles.

'The local sovereignty of the Vicar of our Lord over Rome and the Marches was a fact in Providence many centuries afterwards, and as such can form no proper or direct matter of a dogma of faith. The instinct of a Catholic child would perceive this; and Catholics will forgive my pointing it out only for the sake of those who either have not the light of faith, or who are given to the spirit of contention.

'Nevertheless, the temporal sovereignty affords abundant and proper matter for a definition, or judgment, or authoritative declaration of the Church, like the disciplinary decrees of General Councils; or, finally, the authoritative sentences in the Bulls of Pontiffs—as, for instance, in the Bull *Auctorem fidei*—of which many relate to discipline, to ecclesiastical and mixed questions bearing on temporal things.

'And to such an authoritative utterance, under anathema, and by the voice of the whole Church through the Supreme Pontiff, the subject of the temporal power of the Vicar of Jesus Christ may legitimately, and not improbably, attain; and such a *judicium Ecclesiæ*, or authoritative sentence, would be binding on the consciences of all the faithful, and the contrary would be noted as "propositio falsa, juribus Conciliorum Generalium et Summorum Pontificum laesiva, scandalosa et schismati favens." And yet the subject-matter may not be among the original articles of revealed doctrine, but of the nature of a dogmatic fact attaching to a Divine doctrine and institution, viz. the Vicariate of St. Peter and his successors; and therefore, after declaration, it would be of incontrovertible certainty and universal obligation, so that the denial of it would involve grave sin.' *

The necessity of the temporal power in this sense might, perhaps, be called a popular opinion until the Encyclical allocutions of the Sovereign Pontiff in 1859 and 1860. The declaration of nearly three hundred Bishops in Rome in the year 1862, and the reception of their words by the whole Episcopate of the Church, would even in Bossuet's judgment raise this opinion to the rank of a truth, which, though not a dogma of faith, is yet incontestably certain. The words of the Bishops are as follows:—'We recognise the civil princedom of the Holy See as a thing necessary, and manifestly instituted by the providence of God; nor do we hesitate to declare that in the present state of human affairs that civil princedom is required for the good and free government of the Church and of souls. For it is fitting that the Roman Pontiff, the Head of the whole Church, should be subject to no prince, nor be guest

---

* 'The Temporal Power of the Vicar of Jesus Christ,' by Henry Edward Manning. D.D. Second edition, with a preface, p. xxiv.

of any, but that he should dwell in his own dominions and kingdom in full personal sovereignty; and that he should protect and defend the Catholic faith, and rule and govern the whole Christian commonwealth in a dignified, tranquil, and beneficent liberty.' . . . 'But on this grave matter it hardly becomes us to say more, forasmuch as we have heard yourself not so much discoursing as teaching concerning it. For your voice has proclaimed . . . to the whole world that by "a singular counsel of the providence of God it has been ordered that the Roman Pontiff, whom Christ constituted as Head and Centre of His whole Church, should have a civil princedom." It is, therefore, to be held by us as a most certain truth, that this temporal government accrued to the Holy See not by chance, but was by a special Divine disposition conferred upon it, and by a long series of years, by an unanimous consent of kingdoms and empires, and by almost a miracle, has been confirmed and preserved.' *

They who deplore Ultramontanism as a modern opinion and the extravagance of a party, must have superficially read the history of the Church, and can hardly know the one-and-twenty folio

---

* Declaration of the Bishops, &c. Acta Canonizationisa a Pio IX. P.P. peractæ. Rom. 1864. Pp. 544, 545.

volumes of Rocaberti's 'Bibliotheca Pontificia.' And as the name of Turrecremata has been carelessly used in this sense, it may be well to hear his own words.

In his treatise *de Potestate Papali*, Turrecremata affirms that the Roman Pontiff is Vicar of Christ, in a special and exclusive sense (ch. xxxvi.), because he alone receives the plenitude of power neither from the Apostles, nor from Councils, but *immediately* from Christ (ch. xxxviii. xl. xli.); that the power of the Pope can be enlarged or restricted by no other than God alone (ch. xliv.); that all jurisdiction is derived to the whole Church from the Pope (ch. liv.); that the Pope is the immediate Prelate, and judge of all the faithful, and can do everywhere, in all the world, whatsoever inferior Prelates can do in their several jurisdictions (ch. lxv.); that the Pope is superior to the whole Church in power, authority, and jurisdiction (ch. lxxx.); that it belongs to the Pope to determine matters of faith, and the interpretation of Scripture, and to approve or to condemn the words and writings of the teachers of the Church (ch. cvii.); and that the judgment of the Holy See in matters of faith, and things necessary to salvation, is infallible (ch. cix.)

In his treatise *de Conciliis* Turrecremata affirms

that the authority of General Councils is derived from the Roman Pontiff (ch. xxviii,); that the authority of Councils is not immediately from Christ, but the authority of the Pope is (ch. xxxi.); that whatever is defined or determined by Councils has its authority principally from the Roman Pontiff (ch. xxxii.); that the Roman Pontiff is superior to Councils in the authority of jurisdiction (ch. xliv.); that it is unlawful to appeal from the Pope to a General Council, but lawful to appeal from a General Council to the Pope (ch. xlvii.); that a Council has no power against a decree of the Pope; finally, that the Pope is the interpreter of laws, and can dispense from them, and can abolish them (ch. lii. liii. liv.)

I will add a few sentences from the oration of Turrecremata in the Council of Florence, on the power of the Supreme Pontiff and of General Councils. He affirms that if the Apostolic See or Roman Church contradict a Council, we must adhere to the Apostolic See (ch. lxv.); that the Roman Church cannot err (ch. lxvi.); that God alone is the superior of the Roman Pontiff (ch. lxxx.); that God has reserved the judgment of the Pope to Himself alone (ch. lxxxi.); that the Roman Pontiff has the primacy of the whole world, as Successor of Peter, Head of the whole Church, Father of the Faithful,

Doctor, Pastor and Ruler, as instituted by Christ in the person of Peter (ch. lxxxix.)

I will only add a few words from his explanation of this last assertion, which is in fact the substance of the Decree of the Council of Florence:—

'Clearly these things cannot stand together, that the Roman Pontiff be Primate of the whole world, and yet subject to a General Council which represents the world.

'That he be Prince of the Apostles or Christian people, and yet subject to them in Council.

'That he be the Vicar of Christ's presence, immediately constituted by Him, and yet subject to any other than Christ alone.

'That he be Head of the whole body of the Church, and yet be judged and ruled by a Council representing the body of the Church.

'That he be Father of all Christians, and yet be bound to obey the commands of his sons under pain of condemnation.

'That he be the Doctor of all the Faithful, and yet be inferior to a General Council, the College of his Disciples.

'That he have received from Christ the full power of feeding, ruling, and governing the universal Church, and yet that a General Council, representing the Church, be superior to him in the power of rule and government.'*

This, at least, Turrecremata does not hold to be the language of flattery which 'equals the Popes, as it were, to God.'

It is an ill-advised overture of peace, then, to assail the popular, prevalent, and dominant opinions, devotions, and doctrines of the Catholic Church with hostile criticism, and to appeal from them to some authoritative censure to be hereafter pronounced against them. What is this but to say, you must all come to my mind before I can unite with you? And who shall say this with modesty except he be an inspired person or an infallible judge? To claim this universal censorship in the same breath which denies the infallibility of the living Church is hardly reasonable. If *sentire cum Ecclesia* be a test of conformity to the mind of the Spirit, *Ecclesiæ dissentire* is no sign of illumination; for the presence and assistance of the Holy Ghost, which secures the Church within the sphere of faith and of morals, invests it also with instincts and a discernment

---

* Rocaberti, *Bibl. Pontif.* tom. xiii. p. 281, &c.: De Potestate Papali, De Conciliis, De Summi Pontif. et Gen. Concil. Potestate. In the first edition of this Pastoral a passage from a treatise by Turrecremensis was inserted, by an error, for the above from Turrecremata.

which preside over its worship and doctrine, its practices and customs. We may be sure that whatsoever is prevalent in the Church, under the eye of its public authority, practised by the people and not censured by its pastors, is at least conformable to faith, and innocent as to morals. Whosoever rises up to condemn such practices and opinions, thereby convicts himself of the private spirit, which is the root of heresy.

But if it be ill-advised to assail the mind of the Church, it is still more so to oppose its visible Head. There can be no doubt that the Sovereign Pontiff has declared the same opinion as to the temporal power as that which is censured in others, and that he defined the Immaculate Conception, and that he believes in his own infallibility. If these things be our reproach, we share it with the Vicar of Jesus Christ. They are not our private opinions, nor the tenets of a school, but the mind of the Pontiff, as they were of his predecessors, as they will be of those who will come after him. To appeal from the Pope to an 'Eighth' General Council of Greeks, Anglicans, and Romans, who shall put down Ultramontism, relegate the Immaculate Conception to the region of pious opinions without foundation in Scripture and antiquity, declare the Pope to be fallible, and subject to General

Councils which may err, reunite Christendom on the basis of the Russian Catechism, the Thirty-nine Articles, and the decrees of Trent, interpreted, not as they were intended, but by the rule of a Catholicism which the Catholic world has never known, elaborated by the criticism or illuminism of uncatholic minds nurtured in an anti-Catholic religion,—all this is to us no harbinger of unity, no voice of peace, because no sign of humility, no evidence of faith. The Holy Office, with unerring discernment, has declared that the tendency of the Association for Promoting the Reunion of Christendon is indifferentism; that it is an attempt to widen the unity of truth by the comprehension of those who differ. The universal Church is in these days denounced as sectarian. We are reproached for narrowness by those who would explain away the decrees of Trent, and bring them down to the Greek 'orthodoxy' and the Anglican formularies. And this, too, is narrow to those who are incorporating the Anglican religion with the semi-rationalism of Germany. Unionism is outwardly a reaction against Latitudinarianism; inwardly it promotes it. There can be but two principles and two tendencies. The one, divine faith, which perpetually expands into greater bulk, opens into more explicit fulness, ascends into a loftier stature, as, for instance, in the popular 'cultus' of the Mother of God, and the dominant faith of the infallibility of the Church, which rest upon the decrees of Trent, as I have said, like the cedar upon its root. The other, of human criticism, disguise it as you may in texts of Scripture, or in patristic learning, or in sceptical history, or rationalistic interpretation; the tendency of which is always to wider formulas and diminished truth, to comprehension of communion, and loss of faith. There can be no doubt that the peril of the next ten years will be latitudinarian Christianity in all its forms. So long as men are approaching to the Catholic Church they hold the necessity of precise and inflexible dogma. The moment they waver in their approach, fidelity to dogma declines; they then feel about for a new basis. As it cannot be precision, it must be vagueness. Dogma is against them; they must be against dogma. Theology excludes them; they must hold theology cheap. From that moment (we write what we have seen) men move off from the path of truth, insensibly for awhile, unconsciously to themselves. The Catholic faith is 'Latin Christianity;' the Catholic Church is Rome; Trent is occidental; theology a transient phase of mediæval thought; Christianity the education of the world, the joint contribution of nations, wide as the human race, old as creation, intolerant of visible forms, impatient of mixture with the earthly elements of government and temporal power, purer than the Church of God, awaiting its redemption from the bigotries of sects and churches, its investiture in the theology of the nineteenth century, and the Church of the future. Such is the tendency of the day, of which the theory of union before truth is the one extreme, and the rationalism of freemasonry is the other. All other forms of thought are but intermediates, one in principle, all alike irreconcilable with the principles of Divine faith, the presence of a Divine Teacher, and unconditional submission to His voice.

In your dealings, then, with persons of those opinions, Reverend Brethren, you will keep steadily to one point, namely, the perpetual infallibility of the Church, whether diffused or in Council, whether speaking by the Council of Trent or by its Head. It is necessary to be on your guard against two modes of argument by which this affirmation is evaded. The one is to lead away into details, such as the devotion to the Blessed Virgin, or the Temporal Power of the Pope. This has the effect of diversion, while the main issue is left without an answer. The other is to admit the perpetual Divine office of the Church, denying the infallibility of its Head, and of the Councils held since the schism of the Greek Church. The sure test of this is to ask, Do you believe in the infallibility of the Council of Trent? Do you believe the Pontifical declarations of doctrine since the Council of Trent, received as they are also by the Catholic Church, to be infallible? If the answer be Yes, you will know how to proceed. If it be No, you will have the proof that this supposed perpetual office or infallibility of the Church is a private imagination, like the doctrine of consubstantiation, or of particular redemption, or of divided unity.

Another test by which the absence of real faith or of real knowledge respecting the Divine office of the Church may be detected, is the objection which is made to the alleged definitions of new doctrine, and the making them to be new terms of communion. If the Church be fallible, then such new definitions may, and in all probability would be, human opinions; and to make them articles of faith and communion would be tyrannous and schismatical. A supreme power claiming to regulate the faith and conscience of men, if liable to error, is an usurpation and a despotism. None would deprecate and abjure such new definitions so inflexibly as Catholics. They died rather than accept them under Henry VIII. and Queen Elizabeth.

But if the authority which defines these doctrines have a Divine assistance to preserve it from error, every new definition is a fuller declaration of truth, a broader light, and a more perfect knowledge of the Revelation of God. To object to such accessions of knowledge proves that the Divine source and certainty of them is denied; for no man of sound or pious mind would deprecate a clearer and more perfect knowledge of the mind of God. It would be like saying, 'Let the Holy One of Israel cease from before us.'* When these men desire to stay the onward course and growth of the living Church, and to keep down the explicit mind of the Church to a minimum as a means of reunion with their maximum—a strange dialect in matters of faith—as it is impossible, without great severity of judgment upon them, to imagine that they wish to bind the operations of the Holy Spirit, or to refuse His perpetual voice, it is evident that they deny His presence and His operations in the perpetual offices of the Church. But this is what we affirmed and they denied from the beginning.

* Isaias. xxx. 11.

An impartial critic, further from the Catholic Church than from Anglicanism, well observed, that it is strange for men who proclaim so constraining a desire for unity to keep open a separation, for the difference between a maximum and a minimum which is supposed to be almost coincident. The critic further adds, with great perspicuity, that the question of a little more or a little less of dogma can be nothing to those who accept the principle of infallibility, and that to those who do not accept it there is no question of more or less.

I cannot refrain from noticing a letter lately published with the signature of Prince Orloff,* the Russian Minister at the Court of Brussels, detailing the discussions held at a meeting on the 15th of November last, at which certain Anglican Bishops and 'about eighty persons, chiefly clergymen of High Church principles,'. were assembled for the purpose of promoting union with the Russo-Greek Church. I notice it only to draw out certain points in confirmation of what has been hitherto said.

First, it is evident that if the Anglican clergy there present are willing to unite with the Russian Greeks, the mass of the Anglican Church and of the English people have no such will. Out of this

* 'Times' newspaper, Dec. 28, 1865.

project of union a domestic disunion of the gravest kind at once arises.

Next, it is equally certain, by the steady refusal of the Greeks to communicate with the Protestant or Reformed bodies, expressed again and again, as in the case of Cyril Leuchar in the seventeenth century, and in the overtures of Dr. Basire, and lately of Mr. William Palmer, and of the Anglican clergyman who went the other day to Servia, and most transparently shown in the conduct of Prince Orloff, detailed in his letter, that the Greek Church absolutely refuses all contact with those who are out of its communion, and at variance with its traditional 'Orthodoxy,' in which the Seven Sacraments, and the honour due to the Mother of God are primary and essential points.

Again, there is but little reliance to be placed in the professions of desire of reunion with Rome, while they who make them are courting union with those who for a thousand years have made animosity to Rome a test of fidelity to Constantinople.

But, lastly, the strangest revelation in this affair was the proposal of instant communion, despite of all differences of doctrine or of faith. Prince Orloff wisely proposed that truth should prepare the way for unity. But this slow process was too tardy for some who were present. They proposed immediate communion in the Lord's Supper, postponing the adjustment of doctrinal differences; urging that 'we should not content ourselves with preparing the ground, leaving the harvest to be reaped by future generations, but, deferring all dogmatical debates, proceed to celebrate the Lord's Supper by intercommunion.' The Holy Office was not wrong, therefore, in pronouncing that Unionism implies indifferentism. The comments which these proceedings have elicited both in England and Scotland, show how little this country is disposed for any such enterprises, and how impracticable and unreal it holds them to be.

These things we have written, Reverend and dear Brethren, under a constraining sense of duty towards our Divine Master, and the souls of our brethren in separation. God knows that the desire of our hearts and prayer to God is that they may be saved. If our life would reconcile this land, which we love so well, to the unity of the faith and of the Church, we trust that life would not be dear. But truth is better than life; and truth alone can restore us to unity. 'I am the way, and the truth, and the life; no man cometh to the Father, but by Me.'* Compromise,

---

* S. John, xiv. 6.

concession, conditions, transactions, explanations which soften Divine decrees, and evade the precision of infallible declarations of the Church, are not inspirations of the Holy Ghost. To hold out hopes of impossible events is deception and cruelty. A true love of souls dictates another course. Clear, open, patient, loving exhortations, definite and precise declarations of truth, without sharpness, and without controversy; holding up the light of faith, which by a sacramental power of its own enters into men and illuminates them when they are least aware; confidence in the supernatural grace and the divine mission of the Church, in its authority to teach and its power to save—these are our nets to let down into the sea, our sickles to reap in the Master's field. We are put in charge with the whole Revelation of God, and of all the souls around us. We must labour for them, though they smite us. We must 'gladly spend, and be spent for them; although, loving them more, we be loved less.'* Jesus did not lift a hand to shade His face from the shame and spitting; not even to ward the blow from His cheek, much less to return the buffet which smote Him on the mouth. We have greater things at stake; nobler things in

---

* 2 Cor. xii. 15.

charge. We are guardians of the unity of the Truth, of the purity of the fold, of the infallible rule of faith, of the sovereign jurisdiction of Jesus Christ. We speak in the name of the universal Church of God, which is the same in every place, which even by us here, in our fewness and weakness, speaks with the voice of the Church throughout the world, and binds and looses with the keys of the kingdom of heaven. We received them from the Vicar of Christ; he from the Son of God. We cannot open or shut but as He wills. If we close the door to those who approach it as critics, teachers, and reformers, it is for their sakes, that one day we may open it wide, with joy and thanksgiving, when they shall have learned to know its voice to be the voice of the Son of God. 'Therefore let Christ speak, because in Christ the Church speaks, and in the Church Christ speaks; both the body in the Head, and the Head in the body.'* And in the day when this is known, they will see that we have not been uncharitable, narrow or exclusive; but that they have thought to stay up the Ark by laying their hands upon it. The Church of God accepts of no support, or service, except from its own divine power and commission:

---

* S. Aug. in Psalm. xl. tom. iv. p. 344.

and truth can be spread in no way but that which our Lord has consecrated. 'If any man will come after Me, let him . . . take up his cross and follow Me.' He called men one by one. He so calls them still.

It is not for us to ask, 'Lord, what shall this man do?' The voice of Truth is articulate and clear, 'Follow thou Me.' To question about others is to forget ourselves. To check our own convictions is to resist a Divine grace. To wait for others is to assume a control over the dispensations of the Spirit. God calls whom, and as, and when He wills. We shall die alone, and be judged one by one. It is, therefore, by the obedience of the whole soul, all alone with God, detached from kindred and home, from all human traditions, from even spiritual bonds, by the witness of our whole being, at all costs and sorrows, by sufferings for the Truth, and that to the apparent overthrow of the work of a life, and the forfeiture of all usefulness to come ; it is only by this that we can testify to the faith and make men believe it to be true, and believe that we believe it ourselves. So our Divine Master testified 'a good confession,' and so His disciples in every time and land have obeyed the Spirit of Truth, and won souls from error. It is not by 'corporate' movements, nor by convictions merged in parties, that truth is served and souls saved. Much less is it so that schism can be healed, or errors cast out. The act of conforming our own intelligence to the truth, and our own will to obedience, is the highest, the most divine, the only way in which we can promote the unity of the Church and the supremacy of faith. And this we shall do all the more powerfully and deeply in proportion as we suffer for it, and suffer, if so it be, one by one. I cannot doubt that of those who have addressed the Holy Office, and of those who are united in this movement, there are many who sincerely desire to be reunited to the Apostolic See, the mother of all churches, and believe that they are advancing to this end. They have a zeal of God, but not according to knowledge. 'Magni passus,' as S. Augustine says, 'sed extra viam.' So far as this movement shall lead to the submission of individuals to the truth, it is of God ; so far as it leads to the suppression of individual convictions and individual responsibility, it is not of God.

And now to make an end.

Thus far I have been constrained by the imperative law of truth to lay bare the impossibility and the unlawfulness of all union except that which is based upon the only and infallible Church of God. 'Other

foundation can no man lay than that which is laid.'*
Nothing else will endure the day of His judgment.
All other work will be burnt up. But I cannot so
dismiss the thought of union; the vision, distant as
it may be, of seeing my brethren, countrymen, friends,
and kinsmen once more in the bond of peace, of
kneeling with them once, before I die, in the
presence of Jesus upon the altar. God knows that
for this I have prayed and laboured; for this I have
incurred their displeasure and borne many a wound.
For this I am ready to bear many more, and to bear
them to the end. Every affection of nature and
of grace binds me to desire, next after the glory of
God, their salvation and the conversion of England.
To this I gladly give the few years that remain to
me in life. I know what it will cost me by what it
has cost me already. 'Am I then become your
enemy in telling you the truth?' But truth unites
or divides. It is never neutral; it never returns void.
It kindles charity or enmity, and is 'unto God the
good odour of Christ in them who are saved, and in
them who perish. To some, indeed, the odour of death
unto death; but to the others, the odour of life unto
life. And for these things who is so sufficient?'†

* 1 Cor. iii. 11. † 2 Cor. ii. 15, 16.

The Holy Office concludes its letter with words full of charity; calling on those who addressed it to return into the bosom of the One only Church which from its intrinsic nature can never be divided. It assures them that the Sovereign Pontiff with all his heart implores this grace for them continually from the Father of Light and of all Mercy. To this prevailing prayer let us add our own daily supplications, that the Spirit of Unity and Truth will out of the darkness of our country show to all men His marvellous light, and out of the confusions of this moment, and in the midst of the faults of men, call forth once more a new creation of unity in truth. And for this the prayers of saints and martyrs are ascending, and, above all, the prayers of those whose tears and whose blood have sunk into the soil of England. They so loved unity that they died for it: they so loved truth that they laid down their lives for its sake. Their tears and their blood have not been shed in vain. They are ascending up before God with the intercession of His Immaculate Mother for the land which has so long forgotten to call her blessed. I might say more, but I refrain. Grant this, O Lord, in Thine own good time and way: the souls so dear to us are dearer still to Thee, for

Thou hast redeemed them in Thy most precious blood.

I remain, Reverend and dear Brethren,

Your affectionate Servant in Christ,

✠ HENRY EDWARD,

ARCHBISHOP OF WESTMINSTER.

Epiphany 1866.

APPENDIX.

I.

A Letter of the Supreme Holy Roman and Universal Inquisition to all the English Bishops.

It has been notified to the Apostolic See that some Catholics, and even ecclesiastics, have given their names to a Society established in London in the year 1857, 'for promoting' (as it is called) 'the unity of Christendom;' and that several articles have been published in the daily papers, signed with the names of Catholics, in approval of this Society, or supposed to have been written by ecclesiastics in its favour. Now, the real character and aim of the Society are plain, not only from the articles in the journal called the 'Union Review,' but from the very prospectus in which persons are invited to join it, and are enrolled as members. Organised and conducted by Protestants, it has resulted from a view, put forth by it in express terms, that the three Christian communions, the Roman Catholic, the schismatic Greek, and the Anglican, though separated and divided one from another, have yet an equal claim to the title of Catholic. Hence, its doors are open to all men whencesoeover—Catholics, schismatic Greeks, or Anglicans—on condition of none mooting the question of the several points of doctrine in which they differ, and each following undisturbed the opinions of his own religious profession. It appoints, moreover, prayers to be said by all its members, and Masses to be celebrated by priests, according to its particular intention; namely, that these three Christian communions, constituting, as by hypothesis they do, the Catholic Church collectively, may at some future time coalesce to the formation of one body.

The Supreme Congregation of the Holy Office, to whose scrutiny the matter has been referred as usual, has judged, after mature consideration, that the faithful should be warned with all care against being led by heretics to join with them and with schismatics in entering this Association. The Most Eminent Fathers the Cardinals, placed with myself over the Sacred Inquisition, entertain, indeed, no doubt that the Bishops of those parts address themselves already with diligence, according to the charity and learning which distinguish them, to point out the evils which that Association diffuses, and to repel the dangers it is bringing on. Yet they would seem wanting to their office, did they not, in a matter of such moment, further enkindle the said Bishops' pastoral zeal; this novelty being all the more perilous as it bears a semblance of religion, and of great concern for the unity of the Christian society.

The principle on which it rests is one that overthrows the divine constitution of the Church. For it is pervaded by the idea that the true Church of Jesus Christ consists partly of the Roman Church spread abroad and propagated throughout the world, partly of the Photian schism and the Anglican heresy, as having equally with the Roman Church, one Lord, *one faith*, and one baptism. To take away the dissensions which distract these three Christian communions, not without grievous scandal and at the expense of truth and charity, it appoints prayers and sacrifices, to obtain from God the grace of unity. Nothing indeed should be dearer to a Catholic than the eradicating of schisms and dissensions among Christians, and to see all Christians '*solicitous to keep the unity of the Spirit in the bond of peace*' (Eph. iv.). To that end, the Catholic Church offers prayers to Almighty God, and urges the faithful in Christ to pray, that all who have left the Holy Roman Church, out of which is no salvation, may abjure their errors and be brought to the true faith, and the peace of that Church; nay, that all men may, by God's merciful aid, attain to a knowledge of the truth. But that the faithful in Christ, and that ecclesiastics, should pray for Christian unity under the direction of heretics, and, worse still, according to an intention stained and infected by heresy in a high degree, can no way be tolerated. The true Church of Jesus Christ is constituted and recognised as such by those four 'notes,' belief in which is asserted in the Creed, each note being so linked with the rest as to be incapable of separation. Hence, the Church Catholic, truly so called, must be luminous with all the high attributes of unity, sanctity, and apostolical succession. The Catholic Church therefore is One, in the manifest and perfect unity of all nations of the world; that is, the unity of which the supreme authority and more eminent principality of blessed Peter, Prince of the Apostles, and his successors in the Roman See is the principle, the root, and indefectible origin. She is no other than that Church which, built on Peter alone, grows up into one body knit together and compacted in unity of faith and charity; which blessed Cyprian in his 45th Epistle heartily acknowledged, where he addresses Pope Cornelius: 'that our colleagues may firmly approve and hold to thee and thy communion--that is, alike to the unity and charity of the Catholic Church.' It was the assertion of this same truth that Pope Hormisdas required of the bishops who abjured the schism of Acacius, in the formula approved by the suffrage of all Christian antiquity, in which they 'who agree not in all things with the Apostolic See' are said to be 'put forth from the communion of the Church Catholic.' So far from its being possible that communions separate from the Roman See can be rightly called or reputed Catholic, their very separation and disagreement is the mark by which to know those communities and Christians that hold neither the true faith, nor the true doctrine of Christ, as Irenæus (lib. iii. *contra Hæres.* c. 3) most clearly showed as early as the second century. Let the faithful, then, jealously beware of joining those societies to which they cannot unite themselves and yet keep their faith unimpaired; and listen to S. Augustine, who teaches that there can be neither truth nor piety where Christian unity and the charity of the Holy Spirit are absent.

A further reason why the faithful ought to keep themselves entirely apart from the London Society is this, that they who unite in it both favour *indifferentism* and introduce scandal. That Society, at least its founders and directors, assert that Photianism and Anglicanism are two forms of one true Christian religion, in which the same means of pleasing God are afforded as in the Catholic Church; and that the active dissensions in which these Christian communions exist, are short of any breach of the faith, inasmuch as their faith continues one and the same. Yet this is the very essence of that most baleful indifference in matters of religion, which is at this time especially spreading in secret with the greatest injury to souls. Hence no proof is needed that Catholics who join this Society are giving both to Catholics and non-Catholics an occasion of spiritual ruin: more especially because the Society, by holding out a vain expectation of those three communions, each in its integrity, and keeping each to its own persuasion, coalescing in one, leads the minds of non-Catholics away from conversion to the faith, and, by the journals it publishes, endeavours to prevent it.

The most anxious care, then, is to be exercised, that no Catholics may be deluded either by appearance of piety or by unsound opinions, to join or in any way favour the Society in question, or any

similar one; that they may not be carried away, by
a delusive yearning for such new-fangled Christian
unity, into a fall from that perfect unity which by a
wonderful gift of Divine grace stands on the firm
foundation of Peter.

C. CARD. PATRIZI.

Rome, this 16th day of September, 1864.

II.
ADDRESS FROM ANGLICAN CLERGY TO CARDINAL PATRIZI.

To the Most Eminent and Most Reverend Father in Christ, and Lord C. Cardinal Patrizi, Prefect of the Sacred Office.

MOST EMINENT LORD,

We the undersigned Deans, Canons, Parish Priests, and other Priests of the Anglo-Catholic Church, earnestly desiring the visible reunion, according to the will of our Lord, of the several parts of the Christian family, have read with great regret your Eminence's letter 'To all the English Bishops.'

In that letter, our Society, instituted to promote the Reunion of all Christendom, is charged with affirming in its prospectus, that 'the three Communions, the Roman Catholic, the Eastern, and the Anglican, have an equal claim to call themselves Catholic.'

On that question our prospectus gave no opinion whatever. What we said, treated of the question of *fact*, not of *right*. We merely affirmed that the Anglican Church claimed the name Catholic; as is abundantly plain to all, both from the Liturgy and the Articles of Religion.

Moreover, as to the intention of our Society, that letter asserts our especial aim to be, 'that the three Communions named, each in its integrity, and each maintaining still its own opinions, may coalesce into one.'

Far from us and from our Society be such an aim as this; from which were to be anticipated, not ecclesiastical unity, but merely a discord of brethren in personal conflict under one roof. What we beseech Almighty God to grant, and desire with all our hearts, is simply that œcumenical intercommunion which existed before the separation of East and West, founded and consolidated on the profession of one and the same Catholic faith.

Moreover, the Society aforesaid should all the less excite your jealousy, that it abstains from action,

and simply prays, in the words of Christ our Lord,
'May there be one Fold and one Shepherd.' This
alone finds place in our hearts' desire; and this is
the principle and the yearning we express to your
Eminence with the utmost earnestness, with sincere
heart and voice unfeigned.

As to the journal entitled 'The Union Review,'
the connection between it and the Society is purely
accidental, and we are therefore in no way pledged
to its *dicta*. In that little work various writers put
forth indeed their own opinions, but only to the
further elucidation of the truth of the Catholic Faith
by developing them. That such a mode of contributing papers should not be in use in Rome, where
the controversies of the day are seldom under discussion, is hardly to be wondered at; but in
England, where almost every question becomes public
property, none results in successful conviction without free discussion.

To hasten this event, we have now laboured during
many years. We have effected improvements, beyond
what could be hoped for, where the faith of the flock,
or divine worship, or clerical discipline, may have
been imperfect: and, not to be deemed forgetful of
others, we have cultivated a feeling of good will to-

wards the venerable Church of Rome, that has for a long time caused some to mistrust us.

We humbly profess ourselves your Eminence's servants, devoted to Catholic unity.

(This Address was signed by 198 Clergy of the Church of England.)

III.
ANSWER OF HIS EMINENCE CARDINAL PATRIZI TO THE FOREGOING LETTER.

Honoured and very dear Sirs,

In the letter you have sent me, you profess as your only desire, with sincere heart and voice unfeigned, that, in our Lord's words, there should be one fold and one shepherd. This gives the Sacred Congregation a pleasing hope of your finally attaining to true unity, through the Divine grace of our Lord Jesus Christ. But you must beware lest, in seeking it, you turn aside from the way. It causes the Sacred Congregation the most heartfelt sorrow that such has been your case; forasmuch as you imagine that those Christian communities which claim to have inherited the priesthood and the name

Catholic, constitute portions of the true Church of Jesus Christ, though divided and separated from the Apostolic See of Peter. Nothing is more contrary to the true idea of the Catholic Church than such a notion. For, as my letter to the English Bishops lays down, that is the Catholic Church which, built on Peter alone, grows up into one body, knit together and compacted in the unity of faith and charity.* If, indeed, you will examine the matter with care, and dispassionately consider it, evident proofs will show that this unity of faith and charity—that is, of communion—is, by the immutable institution of Christ, not only a chief and fundamental attribute of the Church, but a note, sure and ever visible, whereby the Church herself is securely and easily to be distinguished from all sects. Witness the express affirmations, the definite metaphors, the parables and similitudes of the sacred Scriptures, portraying, as it were, the Church in outline; then, the plain documents of the Holy Fathers and Councils; again, the uniform method which the Church has from the first adopted against heretics and schismatics of every kind, many of whom, all the while, arrogated to themselves the priesthood and the name Catholic. As, then, the Church of Christ is Catholic, and is called

* S. Ambros. de Offic. Ministr. lib. iii. c. 3, n. 19.

so, by virtue of that supreme unity of faith and communion which, diffused as she is through all nations and all time, she still firmly maintains; so, in virtue of that same unity, is she entitled Holy and Apostolic; and as without such unity she would cease, *de jure* and *de facto*, to be Catholic, so would she at once lose the attributes of sanctity and apostolical succession.

Its unity, however, the Church of Christ never has lost; never, for the briefest interval of time, will lose: forasmuch as, by the divine oracles, the Church is to endure for ever. But how can its perpetual duration be believed, if the succession of ages bring about new aspects and form in its essential condition, even as in the changeful things of this world; and if the Church itself could at any time lapse so far from that unity of faith and communion in which it was founded by Jesus Christ and then propagated by the Apostles? For therefore, says S. Ambrose, will the reign of the Church endure for ever, because the faith is undivided and the body one.* Now, if the Church of Christ be altogether indefectible, it follows at once that it is to be asserted and believed infallible also in propounding the doctrines of the

---

* In Luc. lib. vii. n. 91.

Gospel. And that Christ our Lord, by a wonderful gift, has bestowed on His Church, of which He is Himself the Head, the Bridegroom, and the Corner Stone, this prerogative of infallibility, is a fixed dogma of the Catholic faith. What man of sound mind, indeed, could persuade himself that error might lurk in the Church's public and authoritative office as teacher, instituted by Christ to this very end, that we should not now be children, tossed to and fro, and carried about with every wind of doctrine, in the wickedness of men, in craftiness by which they lie in wait to deceive;* which He promised should never be destitute of His own presence, and should be taught all truth by the Holy Ghost; through which He willed that all nations should be called to the obedience of faith, and be taught what to believe, and what to do; so that he should be condemned who would not believe the preaching of the Apostles and their lawful successors; and to which He gave the function and authority to prescribe the form of sound words, wherein all who are taught of God should unite? Hence S. Paul calls the Church the pillar and ground of the truth.† But how could the Church be the ground of the truth, unless they who

* Ephes. iv. 14. † 1 Timoth. iii. 15.

sought were secure of obtaining the truth at her hands? Moreover, the holy Fathers, speaking with one voice, proclaim that the unity of the faith and doctrine of Christ is so inherent in the unity of the Church that the one cannot be disjoined from the other; which is the meaning of that golden saying of S. Cyprian, that the Church is the home of unity and truth.* Nor has the Catholic Church been ever in doubt of this prerogative, promised and communicated to it by the continual presence of Christ and the assistance of the Holy Ghost, so often as it has applied itself to decide controversies arising on faith, to interpret the sacred Scriptures, or to overthrow such errors as oppose the deposit of revelation committed to it. It has ever put forth and proposed its definitions of dogma as a certain and immutable rule of faith, every one being bound to yield to them interior assent, without doubtfulness, uncertainty, or hesitation, as to a rule of faith. And such as contumaciously resist these definitions would, by the very fact, be judged to have made shipwreck of the faith necessary to salvation, and ceased to belong to Christ's flock. All which brings out more and more the absurdity of that figment of a Catholic Church

---

* Epist. viii. ad. Cornel. ap. Constant, n. 1.

as a coalition of three communions; a figment whose authors are of necessity driven to deny the Church's infallibility.

Quite as certain is the proof that Christ Jesus, in order to produce and ever preserve unity in His Church, and through the appointment of a head to remove occasion of schism,* has, by a special providence, chosen the most blessed Peter in preference to the other Apostles, to be their Prince, and the conspicuous centre and bond of that unity. On him He has built His Church; to him He has given supreme charge and authority to feed the entire flock, to confirm his brethren, to bind and to loose throughout the world; continuing it to his successors in every age. This is a Catholic dogma, coming from the lips of Christ, delivered and maintained by the perpetual teaching of the Fathers, religiously preserved by the universal Church through every age, and often confirmed against the errors of innovators, by decrees of supreme Pontiffs and Councils. Hence, that alone has ever been believed to be the Church Catholic which is united in faith and communion with the See of the Roman Pontiffs, successors of Peter; the See named, there-

* S. Hieronym. lib. i. adv. Jovin. n. 26.

fore, by S. Cyprian the root and matrix of the Catholic Church,* designated by Fathers and Councils, as its especial title, the Apostolic See; the See whence sacerdotal unity took its rise;† whence the laws of religious communion flow to all;‡ wherein Peter ever lives, presides, and holds out, to all who seek, the truths of faith.§ S. Augustine, as we know, when he would recall the Donatists, convicted of schism, to the root and the vine whence they had departed, uses an argument frequent with the earlier Fathers: 'Come, my brethren, if ye would be grafted into the Vine. It is grievous to see you cut off and lying there. Number up the priests from the See of Peter itself, and see who in that series of Fathers succeeded to whom. That is the Rock, against which the haughty gates of hell prevail not.'‖

No other proof is needed that he is not in the Catholic Church who is not joined to that Rock on which the foundation of Catholic unity is laid. In the same sense, S. Jerome held every one to be profane who was not united in communion with the

* Epist. iv. ad Cornel. ap. Constant, n. 3.
† S. Cypr. epist. xii. ad Cornel. ap. Constant, n. 11.
‡ Epist Conc. Aquil. ad Gratian. Imp. an. 381, inter epist. S. Ambrosii.
§ S. Pet. Chrysol. epist. ad Eutych. Act. iii. Concil. Ephes. ap. Harduin, i. 1478.
‖ Psalm. in part. Donati.

See of Peter and the Pontiff seated there. 'Following (he writes to Damasus) no Chief but Christ, I am joined in communion with your holiness, that is, with the chair of Peter. On that rock I know that the Church is built. Whosoever eateth the Lamb out of this house is profane. If any one be not in the ark of Noe he will perish when the flood prevails. Whosoever gathereth not with thee, scattereth; that is, he who is not of Christ is of Antichrist.'* In the same sense, S. Optatus of Milevis proclaims that chair to be one, known to all, set up in Rome, in which unity is so to be preserved by all, that he is a schismatic and heretic whosoever sets up any other chair against that one alone.† And rightly too; for, as S. Irenæus openly proclaims to all, in the ordination and succession of the Roman Pontiffs, the tradition and publication of truth in the Church, which began with the Apostles, has come down even to us; this being proof complete that one and the same life-giving faith in the Church is handed down and preserved in truth from the Apostles to this day.‡

If, then, it be a mark of Christ's Church, special and perpetual, that with perfect unity in faith and

* Epist. xiv. al. 57, ad Damas. n. 2.
† De Schism. Donatist. lib. ii. n. 2.
‡ Lib. iii. contra Hæres. c. 3, n. 3, ex vet. inter ret.

charity of communion, it coheres, flourishes, and, as a city set on a hill, is manifest to all men in all time; if, again, Christ has willed that of such unity the Apostolic See of Peter should be the source, the centre, and the bond, it follows that no congregation whatsoever, separated from the external visible communion and obedience of the Roman Pontiff, can be the Church of Christ, or can in any way whatsoever belong to the Church of Christ: to that Church which, after the Holy Trinity, is proposed to our belief in the Creed as a Church Holy, One, True, Catholic;* called Catholic not only by its children, but by all its enemies beside;† with such exclusive possession of the name that, whereas all heretics claim to be called Catholics, yet if a stranger should ask where the Catholic Church assembles, no heretic ventures to point out his own temple or place of meeting.‡ It cannot belong to that Church by means of which, as by a body in intimate union with Himself, Christ bestows the benefits of His redemption; severed from which, however much one may hold himself to be living blamelessly, yet for this sin alone, of being disjoined from the unity of Christ,

---

* S. Aug. de Symbol. ad Catech. c. vi.
† S. Aug. de Verâ Relig. c. vii.
‡ S. Aug. contra Epist. Fundam. c. iv. n. 5.

he shall not have life, but the wrath of God remaineth on him.* Wherefore, as the name Catholic can by no manner of right belong to such communions, so can it in no way be given to them without manifest heresy.

From all which, honoured and very dear Sirs, you will see why this Sacred Congregation has so carefully provided against the faithful of Christ being permitted to enrol themselves in, or in any way to favour the Society you have lately set on foot to promote (as you express it) the unity of Christendom. You will also see that every effort at reconciliation must needs be in vain, except on condition of those principles on which the Church was at first founded by Christ, and thenceforward in every succeeding age propagated one and the same throughout the world by the Apostles and their successors; principles clearly expressed in that well-known formula of Hormisdas, which has been approved beyond all question by the whole Catholic Church. Lastly, you will see that the universal intercommunion before the Photian schism, of which you speak, obtained because at that time the Eastern Churches had not fallen away from the submission due to the Apostolic See; and that to restore such intercommunion, so greatly to be desired, it will

* S. Aug. ep. cxli. al. 152, n. 5.

not suffice that ill-will and hatred to the Roman Church be laid aside, but, by the precept and appointment of Christ, and by an absolute necessity, that the faith and communion of the Roman Church be accepted; since, in the words of your illustrious countryman, Venerable Bede, 'Whosoever they be who in any way withdraw from the unity of the faith, or from communion with him (blessed Peter), these can neither be absolved from the bonds of their sins, nor enter the gate of the heavenly kingdom.'*

Seeing, then, honoured and very dear Sirs, that *the Catholic Church has been shown to be one, and incapable of partition or division,*† we would have you hesitate no longer to take refuge in the bosom of that Church, which, by acknowledgement of all mankind, holds the supreme authority by the succession of its Bishops from the Apostolic See; heretics contending against it in vain.‡ May the Holy Spirit vouchsafe to fulfil and perfect without delay what He has begun in you by that good will toward the Church which he has imparted to you. And this, in union with the Sacred Congregation, our most holy Lord Pope Pius IX. desires with all his heart; and

* Hom. in Nat. SS. Petri et Pauli.
† S. Cypr. ep. viii. ad Cornel. ap. Coustant, n. 2.
‡ S. Aug. de Utilit. Credendi, c. xvii. n. 35.

earnestly beseeches from the God of mercies and Father of lights that all of you at length, escaping from your severed, disinherited condition into the inheritance of Christ, the true Catholic Church, to which unquestionably your forefathers belonged before the deplorable separation of the sixteenth century, may happily attain the root of charity in the bond of peace and fellowship of unity.* Farewell.

C. CARD. PATRIZI.

Rome, this 8th November, 1865.

IV.

Supremae S. Romanae et Universalis Inquisitionis Epistola ad omnes Angliae Episcopos.

APOSTOLICAE Sedi nuntiatum est, catholicos nonnullos et ecclesiasticos quoque viros Societati *ad procurandam*, uti aiunt, *Christianitatis unitatem* Londini anno 1857 erectae, nomen dedisse, et jam plures evulgatos esse ephemeridum articulos, qui catholicorum huic Societati plaudentium nomine inscribuntur, vel ab ecclesiasticis viris eamdem Societatem commendantibus exarati perhibentur. Et sane quaenam

---

* S. Aug. ep. lxi. al. 223, n. 2; ep. lxix. al. 238, n. 1.

sit hujus Societatis indoles vel quo ea spectet, nedum ex articulis ephemeridis cui titulus '*The Union Review*,' sed ex ipso folio quo socii invitantur et adscribuntur, facile intelligitur. A protestantibus quippe efformata et directa eo excitata est spiritu, quem expresse profitetur, tres videlicet Christianas communiones Romano-catholicam, Graeco-schismaticam et Anglicanam, quamvis invicem separatas ac divisas, aequo tamen jure catholicum nomen sibi vindicare. Aditus igitur in illam patet omnibus ubique locorum degentibus tum Catholicis, tum Graeco-schismaticis, tum Anglicanis, ea tamen lege ut nemini liceat de variis doctrinae capitibus in quibus dissentiunt quaestionem movere, et singulis fas sit propriae religiosae confessionis placita tranquillo animo sectari. Sociis vero omnibus preces ipsa recitandas, et sacerdotibus sacrificia celebranda indicit juxta suam intentionem: ut nempe tres memoratae Christianae communiones, utpote quae, prout supponitur, Ecclesiam Catholicam omnes simul jam constituunt, ad unum corpus efformandum tandem aliquando coeant.

Suprema S. O. Congregatio, ad cujus examen hoc negotium de more delatum est, re mature perpensa, necessarium judicavit sedulam ponendam esse operam, ut edoceantur fideles ne haereticorum ductu hanc cum iisdem haereticis et schismaticis societatem ineant. Non dubitant profecto Emi Patres Cardinales una mecum praepositi Sacrae Inquisitioni, quin istius regionis Episcopi pro ea, qua eminent, caritate et doctrina omnem jam adhibeant diligentiam ad vitia demonstranda, quibus ista Societas scatet, et ad propulsanda quae secum affert pericula: nihilominus muneri suo deesse viderentur, si pastoralem eorumdem Episcoporum zelum in re adeo gravi vehementius non inflammarent: eo enim periculosior est haec novitas, quo ad speciem pia et de Christianae societatis unitate admodum sollicita videtur.

Fundamentum cui ipsa innititur hujusmodi est quod divinam Ecclesiae constitutionem susque deque vertit. Tota enim in eo est, ut supponat veram Jesu Christi Ecclesiam constare partim ex Romana Ecclesia per universum orbem diffusa et propagata, partim vero ex schismate Photiano et ex Anglicana haeresi, quibus aeque ac Ecclesiae Romanae unus sit Dominus, *una fides* et unum baptisma. Ad removendas vero dissensiones, quibus hae tres Christianae communiones cum gravi scandalo et cum veritatis et caritatis dispendio divexantur, preces et sacrificia indicit, ut a Deo gratia unitatis impetretur. Nihil certe viro Catholico potius esse debet, quam ut inter Christianos schismata et dissensiones a radice evellantur, et Christiani omnes sint *solliciti servare unitatem spiritus in vinculo pacis* (Ephes. iv.). Quapropter Ecclesia Catholica preces Deo O. M. fundit et Christifideles ad orandum excitat, ut ad veram fidem convertantur et in gratiam cum Sancta Romana Ecclesia, extra quam non est salus, ejuratis erroribus, restituantur quicumque omnes ab eadem Ecclesia recesserunt: imo ut omnes homines ad agnitionem veritatis, Deo bene juvante, perveniant. At quod Christifideles et ecclesiastici viri haereticorum ductu, et quod pejus est, juxta intentionem haeresi quammaxime pollutam et infectam pro Christiana unitate orent, tolerari nullo modo potest. Vera Jesu Christi Ecclesia quadruplici nota, quam in symbolo credendam asserimus, auctoritate divina constituitur et dignoscitur: et quaelibet ex hisce notis ita cum aliis cohaeret ut ab iis nequeat sejungi: hinc fit, ut quae vere est et dicitur Catholica, unitatis simul, sanctitatis et Apostolicae successionis praerogativa debeat effulgere. Ecclesia igitur Catholica una est unitate conspicua perfectaque orbis terrae et omnium gentium, ea profecto unitate, cujus principium, radix et origo indefectibilis est beati Petri Apostolorum Principis ejusque in Cathedra Romana Successorum suprema auctoritas et potior principalitas. Nec alia est Ecclesia Catholica nisi quae super unum Petrum aedificata in unum connexum corpus atque compactum unitate fidei et caritatis assurgit: quod beatus Cyprianus in ep. xlv. sincere professus est, dum Cornelium Papam in hunc modum alloquebatur: *ut te collegae nostri et communionem tuam, id est Catholicae Ecclesiae unitatem pariter et caritatem, probarent firmiter ac tenerent.* Et idipsum quoque Hormisdas Pontifex ab Episcopis Acacianum schisma ejurantibus assertum voluit in formula totius Christianae antiquitatis suffragio comprobata, ubi *sequestrati a communione Ecclesiae Catholicae* ii dicuntur, qui sunt *non consentientes in omnibus Sedi Apostolicae.* Et tantum abest quin communiones a Romana Sede separatae jure suo catholicae nominari et haberi possint, ut potius ex hac ipsa separatione et discordia dignoscatur quaenam societates et quinam Christiani nec veram fidem teneant nec veram Christi doctrinam: quemadmodum jam inde a secundo Ecclesiae saeculo luculentissime demonstrabat S. Irenaeus lib. iii. contra Haeres. c. iii. Caveant igitur summo studio Christifideles ne hisce societatibus conjungantur, quibus salva fidei integritate nequeunt adhaerere; et audiant sanctum Augustinum docentem, nec veritatem nec pietatem esse posse ubi Christiana unitas et Sancti Spiritus caritas deest.

Praeterea inde quoque a Londinensi Societate fideles abhorrere summopere debent, quod conspirantes in eam et *indifferentismo* favent et scandalum ingerunt. Societas illa, vel saltem ejusdem conditores et rectores profitentur, Photianismum et Anglicanismum duas esse ejusdem verae Christianae religionis formas, in quibus aeque ac in Ecclesia Catholica Deo placere datum sit : et dissensionibus utique Christianas hujusmodi communiones invicem urgeri, sed citra fidei violationem, propterea quia una eademque manet earumdem fides. Haec tamen est summa pestilentissimae indifferentiae in negotio religionis, quae hac potissimum aetate in maximam serpit animarum perniciem. Quare non est cur demonstretur Catholicos huic Societati adhaerentes spiritualis ruinae catholicis juxta atque acatholicis occasionem praebere, praesertim quum ex vana expectatione ut tres memoratae communiones integrae et in sua quaeque persuasione persistentes simul in unum coeant, Societas illa acatholicorum conversiones ad fidem aversetur et per ephemerides a se evulgatas impedire conetur.

Maxima igitur sollicitudine curandum est, ne Catholici vel specie pietatis vel mala sententia decepti Societati, de qua hic habitus est sermo, aliisque similibus adscribantur vel quoquomodo faveant, et ne fallaci novae Christianae unitatis desiderio abrepti ab ea desciscant unitate perfecta, quae mirabili munere gratiae Dei in Petri soliditate consistit.

C. CARD. PATRIZI.

Romae, hac die 16 Septembris, 1864.

V.

Eminentissimo et Reverendissimo in Christo Patri et Domino C. Cardinali Patrizi, S. Officii Praeposito.

EMINENTISSIME DOMINE,—

Nos infrascripti Decani, Canonici, Parochi, aliique Sacerdotes, Ecclesiae Anglo-Catholicae, Reunionem, juxta Christi voluntatem, visibilem inter omnes partes familiae Christianae vehementer desiderantes, Litteras ab Eminentiâ Tuâ 'Ad omnes Angliae Episcopos' emissas magno moerore perlegimus.

In his litteris Societas nostra, ad Reunionem totius Christianitatis promovendam instituta, inculpatur, quod in programmate suo 'Tres communiones, scilicet Romano-Catholicam, Orientalem atque Anglicanam, *aequo jure* Catholicum nomen sibi vindicare' affirmet.

De quâ quaestione nullam prorsus programma

nostrum tulit sententiam. Quod diximus quaestionem *facti* non *juris* tractavit, affirmavimus solummodo, Ecclesiam Anglicanam nomen sibi Catholicum vindicare; quod omnibus, tam a Liturgiâ quam ab Articulis Religionis, abunde patet.

Quin etiam, quod ad Societatis nostrae intentionem attinet, in hisce litteris asseritur, nos hoc potissimum agere, 'ut tres memoratae communiones integrae, et in suâ quaeque persuasione persistentes, simul in unum coeant.'

Longe a nobis et a Societate nostrâ tale propositum absit, ex quo non unitas ecclesiastica, sed discordia fratrum sub eodem tecto comminus pugnantium, foret speranda.

Id quod a Deo O. M. enixe rogamus, quod toto corde desideramus, non aliud est, quam illa, quae ante Orientis et Occidentis scissionem, intercommunio oecumenica extitit, unius ejusdemque Fidei Catholicae professione stabilita atque compacta. Societas immo illa supra dicta eo minorem invidiam apud vos movere debet, quod, ab agendo abstinens, solummodo oret, ut, secundum Domini nostri Christi verba, 'Unus Pastor fiat, et unum Ovile.' Hoc tantum in votis nostris collocatur, et hanc sententiam et desiderium Eminentiae Tuae corde sincero et voce non fictâ pro virili parte profitemur.

Quod ad ephemeridem, cui titulus 'The Union Review' attinet, inter eam et Societatem nostram non nisi fortuita conjunctio exstat, ideoque nullo modo ejus dictis obligamur. In isto quidem opusculo varii scriptores opiniones proprias emittunt, ita tamen ut ex illorum sententiis evolvendis veritas Fidei Catholicae magis eluceat. Talem conscribendi rationem Romae, ubi controversiae hodiernae raro agitantur, in usu non esse vix mirandum est; at in Angliâ, ubi omnis fere quaestio fit publici juris, nulla sine liberâ disputatione in convictionem feliciter evadit.

Nos, ut in hunc eventum festinetur, multos jam annos laboravimus. Si quid minus perfectum fuerit in fide gregis, in cultu, et in disciplina cleri, nos ultra spem in melius redegimus; et, ne aliorum obliti haberemur, erga venerabilem Romae ecclesiam eâ benevolentiâ, quae apud nonnullos olim nos suspectos fecit, usi sumus.

Eminentiae tuae nos servos, Catholicae Unitatis studiosos, humiliter profitemur.

VI.

HONORABILES ET DILECTISSIMI DOMINI,

Quod vos, litteris ad me datis, *corde sincero et voce non ficta* hoc tantum optare profiteamini, ut secundum Domini Nostri Jesu Christi verba unum ovile fiat et unus pastor, id spem affert huic Sacrae Congregationi jucundissimam, vos tandem divina ejusdem Jesu Christi gratia ad veram unitatem esse perventuros. Cavendum tamen vobis est, ne ipsam quaerentes deflectatis a via. Id porro Sacra Congregatio vobis contigisse vehementer dolet existimantibus, ad veram Jesu Christi Ecclesiam pertinere, tamquam partes, Christianos illos coetus, qui *sacerdotii et catholici nominis haereditatem* habere se jactant, licet sint ab Apostolica Petri Sede divisi ac separati. Qua opinione nihil est, quod magis a genuina catholicae Ecclesiae notione abhorreat. Catholica enim Ecclesia, ut in meis ad Episcopos Angliae litteris monetur, ea est quae super unum Petrum aedificata in unum connexum corpus atque compactum unitate fidei et caritatis assurgit.* Equidem hanc fidei et caritatis seu communionis unitatem, ex irreformabili

* S. Ambros. de Offic. Ministr. lib. iii. c. 3, n. 19.

Christi institutione, non modo praecipuam esse ac fundamentalem verae Ecclesiae proprietatem, sed certissimam quoque semperque visibilem notam, qua ipsa Ecclesia ab omnibus sectis tuto ac facile distinguatur, evidentissime vobis, si rem sedulo inspicere pacatoque animo considerare volueritis, demonstrabunt tum Sacrarum Scripturarum diserta testimonia insignesque metaphorae, parabolae et imagines, quibus delineatur ac veluti repraesentatur Ecclesia, tum praeclarissima sanctorum Patrum antiquissimarumque synodorum documenta, tum constans agendi ratio, quam Ecclesia a suis usque primordiis sequi consuevit adversus cujusque generis haereticos et schismaticos, tametsi ex iis complures sacerdotii et catholici nominis haereditatem sibi arrogarent. Quemadmodum igitur Ecclesia Christi propter summam, quam per omnes gentes et in omne tempus diffusa firmissime retinet, fidei communionisque unitatem, catholica est et dicitur, ita propter unitatem eamdem sancta et apostolica praedicatur; et quemadmodum absque tali unitate desineret et jure et facto esse catholica, ita sanctitatis etiam et apostolicae successionis insignibus continuo privaretur.

At Christi Ecclesia suam unitatem nunquam amisit, nunquam ne brevissimo quidem temporis intervallo amittet; quippe quae perenniter, juxta divina oracula, fidei regulae, intimum quisque assensum sine ulla duratura sit. Quomodo vero Ecclesia perenniter duratura credatur, si in essentialem ejus statum aetas aetati succedens, non secus atque fit in mundanarum rerum mutabilitate, novam induceret speciem et formam, et ipsa adeo Ecclesia ab illa fidei et communionis unitate desciscere aliquando posset, qua et a Jesu Christo fundata est et ab Apostolis deinde propagata? Ideo enim, ait S. Ambrosius, regnum Ecclesiae manebit in aeternum, quia individua fides, corpus est unum.* Quod si Ecclesia Christi indefectibilis prorsus est, sponte sequitur, eam infallibilem quoque dici et credi debere in evangelica doctrina tradenda; quam infallibilitatis praerogativam Christum Dominum Ecclesiae suae, cujus ipse est caput, sponsus et lapis angularis, mirabili munere contulisse, inconcussum est catholicae fidei dogma. Et profecto quis sanus sibi persuadeat, errorem subesse posse publico ac sollemni Ecclesiae magisterio, quod Christus eo consilio instituit, ut jam non simus parvuli fluctuantes et circumferamur omni vento doctrinae in nequitia hominum, in astutia ad circumventionem erroris;† quod sui praesentia nunquam deserendum, atque a Spiritu Sancto de omni veritate edocendum pollicitus est; a quo voluit universas

---

* In Luc. lib. vii. n. 91.   † Ephes. iv. 14.

gentes ad obedientiam fidei vocari, et rerum credendarum agendarumque doctrinam ita accipere, ut qui Apostolis legitimisque eorum successoribus praedicantibus non credidisset, condemnaretur; cui munus auctoritatemque attribuit sanorum verborum formae praescribendae, in qua omnes docibiles Dei convenirent? Hinc Paulus Ecclesiam appellat columnam et firmamentum veritatis.* Sed quo pacto Ecclesia esset firmamentum veritatis, nisi tuto ab ea veritas peteretur? Sanctissimi quoque Patres una voce loquuntur ac praedicant, in unitate Ecclesiae unitatem fidei ac doctrinae Christi sic defixam esse ut una disjungi ab alia non valeat; quo spectat aurea illa S. Cypriani sententia, Ecclesiam esse unitatis ac veritatis domicilium.† Neque Catholica Ecclesia dubitavit unquam de hac praerogativa sibi promissa et per jugem Christi praesentiam Sanctique Spiritus afflatum communicata, quoties subortas fidei controversias dirimere, sacrarum Scripturarum sensum interpretari, erroresque commisso revelationis deposito adversos profligare aggressa est; suas enim dogmaticas definitiones edidit semper ac proposuit tamquam certam et immutabilem fidei regulam; quibus, ut

* 1 Timoth. iii. 15.
† Epist. viii. ad Corn. ap. Coustant, n. 1.

dubitatione, suspicione, haesitatione praestare deberet; qui vero iisdem definitionibus contumaciter obsisterent, hoc ipso circa fidem saluti consequendae necessariam naufragavisse nec amplius ad Christi ovile pertinere censerentur. Atque haec magis magisque absurditatem produnt illius commenti de Catholica Ecclesia ex tribus communionibus coalescente, cujus commenti fautores infallibilitatem Ecclesiae necessario inficiari coguntur.

Jam non minus certum atque exploratum est, Christum Jesum, ut fidei communionisque unitas in Ecclesia gigneretur ac perpetuo servaretur, utque capite constituto schismatis tolleretur occasio,* beatissimum Petrum prae caeteris Apostolis, tamquam illorum principem et ejusdem unitatis centrum et vinculum conspicuum, singulari providentia elegisse: super quem Ecclesiam suam aedificavit, et cui totius gregis pascendi, fratres confirmandi, totoque orbe ligandi ac solvendi summam curam auctoritatemque contulit in successores omni aevo prorogandam. Catholicum dogma hoc est, quod ore Christi acceptum, perenni Patrum praedicatione traditum ac defensum Ecclesia universa omni aetate sanctissime retinuit, saepiusque adversus Novatorum errores

---

* S. Hieronym. lib. i. adv. Jovin. n. 26.

Summorum Pontificum Conciliorumque decretis confirmavit. Quare Catholica Ecclesia illa solum semper credita est, quae fide et communione cum Sede Romanorum Pontificum Petri successorum cohaeret, quam propterea Sedem S. Cyprianus nuncupat Catholicae Ecclesiae radicem et matricem; * quam unam Patres et Concilia per antonomasticam appellationem Apostolicae Sedis nomine designant; e qua sacerdotalis unitas exorta est † et in omnes venerandae communionis jura dimanant; ‡ in qua Petrus jugiter vivit et praesidet et praestat quaerentibus fidei veritatem.§ Certe S. Augustinus, ut schismatis convictos Donatistas ad radicem et vitem, unde discesserant, revocaret, argumento utitur ab antiquioribus Patribus frequentato: Venite, fratres, si vultis ut inseramini in vite. Dolor est, cum vos videmus praecisos ita jacere. Numerate sacerdotes vel ab ipsa Petri Sede, et in ordine illo patrum, quis cui successit, videte. Ipsa est petra, quam non vincunt superbae inferorum portae.‖ Quo uno satis ostendit, in Ca-

---

* Epist. iv. ad Cornelium ap. Constant, n. 3.
† S. Cypr. epist. xii. ad Corn. ap. Constant, n. 14.
‡ Epist. Concilii Aquileiensis ad Gratianum Imp. an. 381, inter Epistolas S. Ambrosii.
§ S. Petrus Chrysol. Epist. ad Eutych. Act. iii. Concilii Ephes. ap. Harduin, i. 1478.
‖ Psalm. in part. Donati.

tholica Ecclesia cum non esse qui non inhaereat illi Petrae, in qua fundamentum positum est unitatis catholicae. Neque aliter sensit S. Hieronymus, cui profanus erat quisquis non Cathedrae Petri et Pontifici in ea sedenti communione consociaretur : Nullum primum (sic ille ad Damasum) nisi Christum sequens, beatitudini tuae, id est cathedrae Petri communione consocior ; super illam petram aedificatam esse Ecclesiam scio. Quicumque extra hanc domum agnum comederit, profanus est. Si quis in Noe arca non fuerit, peribit regnante diluvio. Quicumque tecum non colligit, spargit, hoc est, qui Christi non est, Antichristi est.* Neque aliter S. Optatus Milevitanus, qui singularem illam cathedram celebrat, omnibus notam, Romae constitutam, in qua unitas ab omnibus ita servari debet, ut schismaticus et haereticus sit, qui contra illam singularem cathedram aliam collocet.† Et merito quidem ; in Romanorum enim Pontificum ordinatione et successione, uti denunciat aperte omnibus S. Irenaeus, ea quae est ab Apostolis in Ecclesia traditio et veritatis praeconatio pervenit usque ad nos ; et est plenissima haec ostensio, unam et eamdem vivificatricem fidem

---

* Epist. xiv. al. 57, ad Damas. n. 2.
† De Schism. Donatist. lib. ii. n. 2.

esse quae in Ecclesia ab Apostolis usque nunc sit conservata et tradita in veritate.*

Itaque si proprium est ac perpetuum verae Christi Ecclesiae insigne, ut summa fidei caritatisque socialis unitate contineatur, efflorescat ac veluti civitas supra montem posita omnibus hominibus omni tempore patefiat; et si, alia ex parte, ejusdem unitatis originem, centrum ac vinculum Christus esse voluit Apostolicam Petri Sedem, consequens fit, coetus prorsus omnes ab externa visibilique communione et obedientia Romani Pontificis separatos, esse non posse Ecclesiam Christi, neque ad Ecclesiam Christi quomodolibet pertinere, ad illam scilicet Ecclesiam, quae in symbolo post Trinitatis commendationem credenda proponitur Ecclesia sancta, Ecclesia una, Ecclesia vera, Ecclesia catholica; † quae catholica nominatur non solum a suis, verum etiam ab omnibus inimicis,‡ sicque ipsum catholicae nomen sola obtinuit, ut cum omnes haeretici se catholicos dici velint, quaerenti tamen peregrino alicui, ubi ad catholicam conveniatur, nullus haereticorum vel basilicam suam vel domum audeat ostendere :§ per quam Christus veluti per corpus sibi penitissime conjunctum beneficia re-

* Lib. iii. contra Haeres. cap. iii. n. 3, ex vet. interpr.
† S. Aug. de Symb. ad Catech. cap. vi.
‡ S. Aug. de Vera Relig. cap. vii.
§ S. Aug. contr. Epist. Fundam. cap. iv. n. 5.

demptionis impertit, et a qua quisque fuerit separatus, quantumlibet laudabiliter se vivere existimet, hoc solo scelere quod a Christi unitate disjunctus est, non habebit vitam, sed ira Dei manet super eum : * ejusmodi proinde coetibus catholicum nomen tum jure minime competere, tum facto attribui nullatenus posse citra manifestam haeresim. Iude autem perspicietis, honorabiles ac dilectissimi Domini, quare sacra haec Congregatio tanta sollicitudine caverit, ne Christifideles societati a vobis recens institutae ad promovendam, ut dicitis, Christianitatis unitatem cooptari paterentur aut quoquomodo faverent. Perspicietis etiam in irritum necessario cadere quamcumque conciliandae concordiae molitionem, nisi ad ea principia exigatur, quibus Ecclesia et ab initio est a Christo stabilita et deinceps omni consequenti aetate per Apostolos eorumque successores una eademque in universum orbem propagata ; quaeque in celeberrima Hormisdae formula, quam certum est a tota catholica Ecclesia comprobatam esse, dilucide exponuntur. Perspicietis denique, oecumenicam illam quam memoratis, *intercommunionem* ante schisma Photianum, ideo viguisse quia orientales ecclesiae nondum a debito Apostolicae Cathedrae obsequio

---

* S. Aug. ep. cxli. al. 152, n. 5.

desciverant; neque ad optatissimam hanc intercommunionem restaurandam satis esse, simultates et odia in Romanam Ecclesiam deponere, sed omnino, ex praecepto et instituto Christi, oportere Romanae Ecclesiae fidem et communionem amplecti; quandoquidem, ut ait venerabilis Beda splendidissimum vestrae gentis ornamentum: Quicumque ab unitate fidei vel societate illius (beati Petri) quolibet modo semetipsos segregant, tales nec vinculis peccatorum absolvi nec januam possint regni coelestis ingredi.*

Atque utinam, honorabiles et dilectissimi Domini, quoniam *Ecclesia catholica una esse nec scindi nec dividi posse monstrata est*,† non amplius dubitetis, vos ejusdem Ecclesiae condere gremio, quae usque ad confessionem generis humani ab Apostolica Sede per successiones episcoporum, frustra haereticis circumlatrantibus, culmen auctoritatis obtinuit.‡ Utinam quod in vobis per inditam benevolentiam erga hanc Ecclesiam Spiritus Sanctus coepit, ipse complere et perficere sine mora dignetur. Id vobis una cum hac Sacra Congregatione toto ominatur animo et a Deo misericordiarum et luminum Patre enixe adprecatur sanctissimus Dominus Noster Pius Papa IX., ut vos

---

* Hom. in Nat. SS. Petri et Pauli.
† S. Cypr. ep. viii. ad Corn. apud Coustant, n. 2.
‡ S. Aug. de Util. Credendi, c. xvii. n. 35.

tandem omnes ab exhaeredata praecisione fugientes in haereditatem Christi, in veram Catholicam Ecclesiam, ad quam certe spectarunt majores vestri ante lugendam saeculi sextideeimi separationem, accipere feliciter mercamini radicem caritatis in vinculo pacis et in societate unitatis.* Valete.

C. CARD. PATRIZI.

Romae, hac die 8 Novembris, 1865.

VII.

THE Catholic Church has no need of any new association of prayer for the reunion of Christendom. Every morning, at every altar, offered by the whole Catholic priesthood throughout the world, in the beginning of the Canon of the Holy Mass, we intercede, both priests and people, first of all, for the Holy Church, that God may ' grant peace to it, and preserve and unite it and govern it throughout all the world.'

The Catholic Church directs all its members to pray in private also for the same intention. In the

---

* S. Aug. ep. lxi. al. 223, n. 2 ; ep. lxix. al. 238, n. 1.

'Raccolta' of Prayers to which Indulgences are attached—a volume of 300 pages—explicit directions are given that they who use them shall pray 'for the rooting out of heresies and the healing of schisms, for the extension of the Faith, for peace and concord among Christian princes.'

The Reunion of Christendom can hardly be more precisely described.

Gregory XVI., on the 26th January, 1840, granted to all who should daily repeat certain prayers for the conversion of England to the Catholic faith, an indulgence of three hundred days: and to all who should persevere in the same for a whole month, a plenary indulgence, every month, on the usual conditions.

By a rescript, dated March 12, 1857, Pius IX. granted an indulgence of seven days to whomsoever should recite the *Gloria* seven times with the intention of obtaining from the Holy Spirit, the Fountain of Light and of infallible Truth, His seven gifts for the diffusion of the Faith.

This indulgence was asked with the intention of promoting a special devotion to the Holy Ghost and a spread of the Faith in England.

His Eminence the late Cardinal drew up a form of intercession for the conversion of England, which was daily used by the students in the chapel of the English College in Rome.

The following are some of the prayers :—

Lord God Almighty, who hast vouchsafed to build Thy Church on the foundation of the Apostles, and hast delivered the plenitude of authority in teaching and ruling to their successors alone, mercifully look upon our beloved country, now for a long time torn from the foundation ; and mercifully gather together the people who are wandering as sheep without shepherds, that the multitude of the nations may come to Thy holy temple, and that our hearts may be enlarged with joy and charity. Through Christ our Lord.

Merciful and pitiful Lord, who in bestowing on Blessed Peter the keys of the kingdom of heaven, hast so made his chair to be the centre of unity and communion, that whosoever is not within this ark is shipwrecked, graciously look upon our beloved country, for the most part separated from the fellowship of the Apostolic See, and grant that though it be wasted by the manifold frauds of the enemy, it may hereafter attain, under the rule of the Chief Shepherd, whom Thou hast mercifully set over Thy flock, the food of life and the hope of eternal bliss. Who livest and reignest for ever and ever.

O most loving Lord Jesus, who whilst hanging on the Cross didst commend us all in Thy disciple John to Thy most sweet Mother, that in her we might find shelter, solace, and hope ; graciously look upon our beloved country, robbed of so high a protection ; that it may now at length acknowledge the dignity of the Most Holy Virgin, and venerate her with all-loving devotion. May it call her Queen and Mother: may her sweet name be heard in the mouth of little ones; let it be ever on the lips of the aged and the dying; let the afflicted call upon her, and the joyful give thanks to her; that by the favour and leading of this Star of the Sea all may attain to the haven of eternal salvation. Who livest and reignest for ever and ever.

Merciful God, may the glorious intercession of Thy Saints be our help; above all, of the most Blessed Virgin Mary, Mother of Thy only begotten Son, and of Thy holy Apostles, Peter and Paul, to whose protection we humbly commend our country, which is most dear to us. Remember our fathers, Gregory, Bishop of Rome, which is our Mother, and Augustine, who delivered to us the inviolate faith of the Holy Roman Church. Remember our holy Martyrs, who shed their blood for Christ; above all, Thy most glorious prelate Thomas. Remember the many holy confessors, pontiffs and kings, monks and hermits, virgins and widows, who illuminated by their glorious merits and virtues this island, once of Saints. Let not their memory perish before Thee, O Lord : but let their supplication enter daily into Thy presence; and as Thou didst spare so often Thy people who sinned, for the sake of Abraham, Isaac, and Jacob, so now, for the prayers of our fathers who are reigning with Thee, have mercy upon us : save Thy people, and bless Thine inheritance : and suffer not the souls to perish which Thy Son hath redeemed with His precious Blood. Who livest and reignest for ever and ever. Amen.

We must not here forget the labours of Father Spencer, who was consumed by a zeal for the conversion of England, and spent the last years of his innocent and guileless life in asking prayers for the restoration of our country to Catholic faith and unity. Through evil report and good report he persevered, exposing himself to all kinds of humiliation for the object so dear to his heart. To him we owe much of the spirit of hope and prayer, which has made the thought of a better future for England a calm and confident expectation.

So much for England. Now for the East. It seems as if God were raising up the hearts of men by the inspiration of a longing desire for unity. F. Toudini, of the Congregation of Barnabites, has obtained the blessing of the Holy Father on an 'Association of prayer for the honour of the Most Blessed and Immaculate Virgin, by the conversion of the Oriental schismatics, and especially of the Russians, to the Catholic Faith.' The following extract from his circular will explain the motives and intentions of this association :—

'The triumph of the Most Blessed and Immaculate Virgin by the conversion of Russia;' such will be the glorious result of the battle; this will be the reward of our sorrows, this the answer to the prayers which are ascending to her throne. 'It will not be without a result that Russians have preserved amongst the treasures of their faith an intense devotion to Mary ; that they invoke her and believe (perhaps without knowing it) in her Immaculate Conception, ... Mary will be the bond which shall unite the two Churches, and she will make of all those who love her a family of brothers, under the common Father—the Vicar of Jesus Christ.' This is the joyful hope of a vast number of holy souls, who now, for a very long time, have been offering frequent and fervent prayers and generous sacrifices in behalf of the great triumph of Mary.

The people of Russia are most devout towards Mary, and most reverently and warmly honour her. This consideration alone avails more with Catholic souls than any human motive whatever: indeed, the object which is now put forward for the prayers of the faithful is, of necessity, not a human, but a heavenly object—it is work for the kingdom of God. But yet there are considerations which will tend to stimulate the fervour of their prayers; and the chief among these is the knowledge of what has, for some time past, been going on amongst the members of the Greek Church in the Ottoman Empire, and notably in Bulgaria. The continual petitions presented to the Czar from all parts of Russia, with the object of obtaining liberty of conscience, leave no room to doubt that it will, sooner or later, be proclaimed in that Empire, and the Catholics are well aware of this; and they know, also, that as surely as the true Faith is permitted the means of manifesting itself, so surely does it gain souls to itself—souls that are seeking for nought but the truth. The Bulgarians have sought it, and, thank God and our dear Lady, they have found and ardently embraced it.

It is well known that to the heart of our Holy Father, Pius IX., the conversion of the Schismatical Greeks has long been an object of the warmest interest and the most anxious solicitude. And there are numbers of pious souls who, by their prayers, are seconding his wishes and hopes. The good Barnabite, Father Schouvaloff, from whose wonderfully interesting work a quotation is given above, was in the habit of offering three times daily his life to Almighty God for this object; and this devotion he practised in accordance with the recommendation of the Holy Father. Hardly had he completed the publication of his work than he was called to give up the life he had so generously offered. There is good reason to believe that his influence is still living, and bearing good fruit.

To the Catholics of England little need be said to induce them to second by their prayers this great work. 'Freely you have received; freely give.' We have had the prayers of the faithful throughout Europe in behalf of the conversion of our country. Let our gratitude, then, move our hearts, and induce us to help others towards the same blessings we have received.

This work has received the blessing of His Holiness (Brief, dated Sept. 2, 1862); it has been greatly encouraged and promoted by the Bishops of Italy, France, and Germany; and has the cordial approbation of the Archbishop of Westminster.

PRAYER.

O Mary, Immaculate Virgin, we, who are thy servants and children of the Holy Roman Catholic Church, humbly pray thee to use thy powerful influence with the Holy Ghost to obtain, for the honour and glory of His eternal Procession from the Father and the Son, the abundance of His gifts for our brethren, the Schismatic Greeks, to the end that, enlightened by His holy and quickening grace, they may return to the bosom of Catholic faith, under the infallible guidance of its Supreme Pastor and Teacher, the Sovereign Pontiff; and that, thus truly reunited to us by the indissoluble bonds of one Faith and one Charity, they may with us, by the practice of good works, render glory to the Most Holy Trinity, and likewise honour thee, O Virgin, Mother of God, full of grace, now and for ever. Amen.

His Holiness Pope Pius IX., ' with the intention of encouraging this work, which is so dear' to his paternal heart, deigned, by a brief, dated September 2, 1862, to grant to every faithful translation of the above prayer the same indulgences which had been granted to the original Italian. These are—1. An indulgence of 300 days for every time the said prayer is recited. 2. A plenary indulgence to those who, having recited it for a whole month, and having confessed and received Holy Communion, shall pray for the intention of the Sovereign Pontiff. These indulgences are applicable to the holy souls in Purgatory.

Besides the daily recital of the above prayer, the following practices are recommended:

1. The frequent use of the following ejaculatory prayer, and the special application of it for the conversion of the Russian Schismatics.

EJACULATION.—Eternal Father, I offer to Thee the most Precious Blood of Jesus Christ, in expiation of my sins, and as a suffrage for the wants of Holy Church. [To this Ejaculation was granted an indulgence of 100 days for each recital, by a brief of Pius VII., November 29, 1817.]

2. The invocation of the Saints who are the patrons of this work; S. Joseph, the Archangel S. Michael, the Apostles SS. Peter and Paul, and the Apostles of the Sclavonians, SS. Cyril and Methodius, whose feast is kept on the 8th of July.

3. The daily offering of our suffrages, prayers, and good works, for the conversion of these people, and a particular memento in hearing or saying Mass, or at Communion.

4. A communion, by way of reparation for Russia, on May 8th—the feast of the Archangel St. Michael. This devotion has been practised widely by good people for many years past.

Finally, persons, both priests and laymen, who are associated in other confraternities, are besought to add to their other intentions that of praying for the conversion of Russia.

'8, York Place, Portman Square, London, W.,
Nov. 7, 1866.

'Rev. and dear Father,—I have the greatest pleasure in giving my approbation to the Association of Prayers for the Conversion of the Oriental Schismatics, and especially of the Russians and Greeks, to the Catholic Faith and Unity, and in granting forty days' indulgence to all who shall co-operate with you in spreading the Association in the Diocese of Westminster, by reciting the prayer to our Immaculate Mother with that intention.

'Be so good as to enrol my name in the Association. At this time, when the thought and desire of union is so active in the minds of men, I rejoice to see so truly and purely Catholic an association extending in the midst of us. I am glad, also, to see it introduced among us by a spiritual son of the B. Alessandro Sauli, the friend of S. Charles; this gives us the true reunion of Christendom on the basis of Trent, in submission to the Sovereign Pontiff, and under the intercession of the most Blessed and Immaculate Mother of God. I heartily pray that God may bless you and your work; and remain, Rev. and dear Father, your affectionate servant in Christ,

✠ 'HENRY EDWARD, Archbishop of Westminster.

'The Rev. F. Tondini, of the Congregation of the Fathers Barnabites.'

The Bishop of Southwark has decreed an indulgence of forty days to any of the faithful who shall recite an Ave for the object of the Association.

VIII.

The Injunctions by which the Pope notified to the Legates what he would have to be observed before the Protestants were admitted to be heard.

Before any question is treated or discussed with heretics, one thing, which is a matter both of divine and human law, must be strictly observed: that they should first give in their adhesion as to the tribunal and the judge, and acknowledge that the Church of Christ is one, spread throughout the world; and that that Church's one head is the Vicar of Christ, appointed by the word of Christ Himself; and that a lawful General Council, that is, one summoned and approved by that same head of the Church, represents the entire Church; and that they submit themselves, and will and consent to submit, to the decrees, determinations, and declarations of the said Council.

But if they decline this, they ought in nowise to be heard, on whatsoever point contending; since they openly proclaim themselves schismatics and heretics: for he who doubts, holds not the principles of faith, and is convicted of not receiving the article of 'the Catholic Church.' Wherefore in that case they are to be dealt with as condemned schismatics and heretics, not as equals, having equal rights with us; according to those words, Psalm xxv., 'I have not sat with the council of vanity: neither will I go in with the doers of unjust things. I have hated the assembly of the malignant; and with the wicked I will not sit.'

But if they admit as aforesaid, let their complaints and statements be listened to and discussed with all gentleness and deliberation, and be carried to the head himself, the Supreme Pontiff, for his final determination, together with the approval of the Council.

Monita quibus Pontifex legatos instruxit de iis quæ servari voluit antequam Protestantes audirentur.

Antequam quidquam cum hæreticis tractetur aut disputetur, illud omnino servandum (quod et divini et humani juris est) ut primum conveniant de judicio ac judice, et confiteantur unam esse ecclesiam Christi toto terrarum orbe diffusam, unumque esse ipsius ecclesiae caput Christi vicarium, ipsiusque Christi verbo constitutum ; et quod concilium generale legitimum, id est ab eodem ipso ecclesiae capite indictum ac probatum, repraesentet universam ecclesiam; cujus quidem concilii decretis, determinationibus ac declarationibus se subdere subditosque esse volunt atque consentiunt.

Quod si haec inficientur, non debent quovis modo audiri super quoquam contendentes, cum se declarent apertissime schismaticos et haereticos; nam is qui dubitat, non habet principia fidei, et articulum Catholicae ecclesiae convincitur non recipere ; et ideo hoc casu cum illis agendum est, quasi cum schismaticis et haereticis damnatis, non quasi cum paribus paremque nobiscum causam habentibus, juxta illud Psalm xxv.: *Non sedi cum concilio vanitatis, et cum iniqua gerentibus non introibo. Odivi ecclesiam malignantium, et cum impiis non sedebo.*

Si autem supradicta admiserint, audiantur et discutiantur eorum querelae et positiones cum omni mansuetudine et maturitate, et ad ipsum caput summum pontificem, ab eo deinceps cum approbatione concilii determinandae, deferantur.—LE PLAT, *Monumentorum ad Hist. Conc. Trid. etc. Collectio*, tom. iv. p. 417. Anno 1552. LOV. MDCCLXXXIV.

IX.

The following Resolutions are added as a striking confirmation of the description given in the Introduction to this volume of the present state and tendency of religious thought in England, viewed from an opposite side.

Resolutions of the general body of Protestant Dissenting Ministers of the three denominations in and about London, concerning the present state of the Church of England, and the duty of Protestant Churches in relation to it :—

RESOLVED,

1. That, as the Church of England claims the privilege of being national, and as all national institutions are responsible to the nations sustaining them, we feel, that while as Nonconformists we regard all secular legislation concerning religion as an error, it becomes us as Englishmen to see, as far as we may, that so long as a Church Establishment shall exist in this kingdom, it shall exist to such ends only as have been determined by public law.

2. That we have seen with deep regret that over the space of a generation the English Church has been passing more and more into the hands of clergymen who have ceased to be Protestants; men whose exposition of the doctrine of the Eucharist, if it does not include the doctrine of Transubstantiation, is hard to be distinguished from it, and

is fully as much open to superstitious abuses; men whose teaching in regard to the Confessional is pregnant with all the mischiefs—secret, social, and religious—which have resulted from that institute in Catholic countries; and whose assumption as priests, based on the fiction of Apostolical Succession, has wedded them to sacramental theories opposed both to the letter and spirit of Christianity, and necessarily hostile to the civil and religious liberties of Englishmen; the recent progress of Ritualism being only the natural and stronger manifestation of this wide declension from the principles of the Reformation.

3. That, while we are of opinion that neither the formularies nor the past usages of the Church of England sanction all the Romanist dogmas and practices which Anglo-Catholics would found on them, we feel bound to say that these distractions in that Church would not have arisen had the wisdom of our Puritan and Nonconformist forefathers been heeded, who knowing it to be in the nature of seed that it should bear fruit after its kind, never failed to protest against the latent Romanism allowed to remain in the services of the Established Church.

4. That we see, moreover, and with no less regret, that Rationalism may proclaim itself in strange developments in the English Church side by side with Romanism; so that while one portion of our clergy may teach that the difference between Canterbury and Rome is no more than a little mutual explanation might suffice to remove, others may seem wholly to exclude the supernatural from Revelation, and may bid us regard Moses as little better than a myth.

5. That, in our judgment, the present tendency to stretch the existing articles and formularies so as to include all these differences, is a virtual establishment of all religions,

and that, too, by means which cannot fail to convert an institution professedly religious, into an offence against all natural truthfulness and honour ; while to establish a more definite creed, to be guarded by more stringent laws, would of necessity be to show favour to a sect, at the cost of wrong to the nation.

6. That to us the weighty conclusion from these facts is, that modern thought has outgrown the Church Establishment principle ; that these events show, in a signal manner, the soundness of the principle derived by Nonconformists from the New Testament, which requires that the action of the civil power should be restricted to purely civil affairs ; and that Providence seems to be summoning all good men, who may have rejected that principle, to consider it anew, and to prepare themselves for demanding that men of all opinions shall be left to support their own creeds and observances.

7. That our experience as Nonconformists enables us to look on the shadows of such coming events without fear as to the future of religion, remembering, as we do, with devout thankfulness, that the churches of our three denominations in England and Wales—Presbyterians, Independents, and Baptists—number some 5,000; that these organisations have all originated in individual conviction ; that their large property as churches has come from the same source; that their creed is substantially one orthodox and evangelical creed; and their worship is everywhere the same simple service: while Methodism shows no less conspicuously how the aid of the State may be dispensed with in this field—facts which, taken alone, warrant the conclusion that Episcopalianism, were it dis-established to-morrow, might do much greater things in its freedom than

it has ever done while subject to the restraints of secular authority.

8. That we congratulate our Churches that, in these new circumstances, they have not to take new ground; that the changes which are inevitable will be changes in the direction of their principles; and we earnestly counsel them to hold fast to their present liberty, and, while ceding to others all the freedom they claim, that they avail themselves to the utmost of every legitimate means in resisting all action menacing to the interests of truth and liberty.

ROBERT VAUGHAN, *Chairman.*
WILLIAM BROCK, *Secretary.*

The Times, February 18, 1867.

By the same Author.

THE TEMPORAL MISSION OF THE HOLY GHOST; or, Reason and Revelation. 8s. 6d. (Longmans.)

SERMONS ON ECCLESIASTICAL SUBJECTS. 6s. (Duffy.)

THE TEMPORAL POWER OF THE POPE. Second Edition. 5s. (Burns.)

THE LOVE OF JESUS TO PENITENTS. 2s. 6d. (Duffy.)

THE GROUNDS OF FAITH: Four Lectures. Fifth Edition. 1s. (Burns.)

THE BLESSED SACRAMENT THE CENTRE OF IMMUTABLE TRUTH. 1s.

THE TEMPORAL POWER IN ITS POLITICAL ASPECT. 1s. (Burns.)

THE MISSION OF S. ALPHONSUS. 1s. (Duffy.)

TRUTH BEFORE PEACE. 1s. (Duffy.)

Edited by the same Author.

ESSAYS ON RELIGION AND LITERATURE. 10s. 6d. (Longmans.) *The Second Volume in the Press.*

MARCH 1882.

GENERAL LISTS OF NEW WORKS

PUBLISHED BY

MESSRS. LONGMANS, GREEN & CO.

PATERNOSTER ROW, LONDON.

HISTORY, POLITICS, HISTORICAL MEMOIRS, &c.

Armitage's Childhood of the English Nation. Fcp. 8vo. 2s. 6d.
Arnold's Lectures on Modern History. 8vo. 7s. 6d.
Bagehot's Literary Studies, edited by Hutton. 2 vols. 8vo. 28s.
Beaconsfield's (Lord) Speeches, by Kebbel. 2 vols. 8vo. 32s.
Bingham's Marriages of the Bonapartes. 2 vols. crown 8vo. 21s.
Bosco's Italian History, by Morell. Royal 8vo. 7s. 6d.
Browning's Modern France, 1814–1879. Fcp. 8vo. 1s.
Buckle's History of Civilisation. 3 vols. crown 8vo. 24s.
Chesney's Waterloo Lectures. 8vo. 10s. 6d.
Davis's Rise and Fall of the Confederate Government. 2 vols. 8vo. 42s.
Dun's Landlord and Tenant in Ireland. Crown 8vo. 6s.
Dun's American Food and Farming. Crown 8vo. 10s. 6d.
Epochs of Ancient History :—
    Beesly's Gracchi, Marius, and Sulla, 2s. 6d.
    Capes's Age of the Antonines, 2s. 6d.
    — Early Roman Empire, 2s. 6d.
    Cox's Athenian Empire, 2s. 6d.
    — Greeks and Persians, 2s. 6d.
    Curteis's Rise of the Macedonian Empire, 2s. 6d.
    Ihne's Rome to its Capture by the Gauls, 2s. 6d.
    Merivale's Roman Triumvirates, 2s. 6d.
    Sankey's Spartan and Theban Supremacies, 2s. 6d.
    Smith's Rome and Carthage, the Punic Wars, 2s. 6d.
Epochs of English History, complete in One Volume. Fcp. 8vo. 5s.
    Creighton's Shilling History of England (Introductory Volume) Fcp. 8vo. 1s.
    Browning's Modern England, 1820–1875, 9d.
    Cordery's Struggle against Absolute Monarchy, 1603–1688, 9d.
    Creighton's (Mrs.) England a Continental Power, 1066–1216, 9d.
    Creighton's (Rev. M.) Tudors and the Reformation, 1485–1603, 9d.
    Rowley's Rise of the People, 1215–1485, 9d.
    Rowley's Settlement of the Constitution, 1689–1784, 9d.
    Tancock's England during the American & European Wars, 1765–1820, 9d.
    York-Powell's Early England to the Conquest, 1s.
Epochs of Modern History :—
    Church's Beginning of the Middle Ages, 2s. 6d.
    Cox's Crusades, 2s. 6d.
    Creighton's Age of Elizabeth, 2s. 6d.

London, LONGMANS & CO.

Epochs of Modern History—*continued.*
- Gairdner's Houses of Lancaster and York, 2*s.* 6*d.*
- Gardiner's Puritan Revolution, 2*s.* 6*d.*
- — Thirty Years' War, 2*s.* 6*d.*
- Hale's Fall of the Stuarts, 2*s.* 6*d.*
- Johnson's Normans in Europe, 2*s.* 6*d.*
- Longman's Frederick the Great and the Seven Years' War, 2*s.* 6*d.*
- Ludlow's War of American Independence, 2*s.* 6*d.*
- M'Carthy's Epoch of Reform, 1830-1850, 2*s.* 6*d.*
- Morris's Age of Queen Anne, 2*s.* 6*d.*
- Seebohm's Protestant Revolution, 2*s.* 6*d.*
- Stubbs's Early Plantagenets, 2*s.* 6*d.*
- Warburton's Edward III., 2*s.* 6*d.*

Froude's English in Ireland in the 18th Century. 3 vols. crown 8vo. 18*s.*
- — History of England. Popular Edition. 12 vols. crown 8vo. 3*s.* 6*d.* each.
- — Julius Cæsar, a Sketch. 8vo. 16*s.*

Gardiner's England under Buckingham and Charles I., 1624-1628. 2 vols. 8vo. 24*s.*
- — Personal Government of Charles I., 1628-1637. 2 vols. 8vo. 24*s.*
- — Fall of the Monarchy of Charles I. 8vo. Vols. I. & II. 1637-1642. 28*s.*
- — Outline of English History, B.C. 55-A.D. 1880. Fcp. 8vo. 2*s.* 6*d.*

Greville's Journal of the Reigns of George IV. & William IV. 3 vols. 8vo. 36*s.*
Hayward's Selected Essays. 2 vols. crown 8vo. 12*s.*
Ihne's History of Rome. 3 vols. 8vo. 45s.
Lecky's History of England. Vols. I. & II. 1700-1760. 8vo. 36*s.* Vols. III. & IV. 1760-1780, in the press.
Lecky's History of European Morals. 2 vols. crown 8vo. 16*s.*
- — — Rationalism in Europe. 2 vols. crown 8vo. 16*s.*

Lewes's History of Philosophy. 2 vols. 8vo. 32*s.*
Longman's Lectures on the History of England. 8vo. 15*s.*
- — Life and Times of Edward III. 2 vols. 8vo. 28*s.*

Macaulay's Complete Works. Library Edition. 8 vols. 8vo. £5. 5*s.*
- — — — Cabinet Edition. 16 vols. crown 8vo. £4. 16*s.*
- — History of England :—
  - Student's Edition. 2 vols. cr. 8vo. 12*s.* | Cabinet Edition. 8 vols. post 8vo. 48*s.*
  - People's Edition. 4 vols. cr. 8vo. 16*s.* | Library Edition. 5 vols. 8vo. £4.

Macaulay's Critical and Historical Essays. Cheap Edition. Crown 8vo. 3*s.* 6*d.*
- Student's Edition. 1 vol. cr. 8vo. 6*s.* | Cabinet Edition. 4 vols. post 8vo. 24*s.*
- People's Edition. 2 vols. cr. 8vo. 8*s.* | Library Edition. 3 vols. 8vo. 36*s.*

May's Constitutional History of England, 1760-1870. 3 vols. crown 8vo. 18*s.*
- — Democracy in Europe. 2 vols. 8vo. 32*s.*

Merivale's Fall of the Roman Republic. 12mo. 7*s.* 6*d.*
- — General History of Rome, B.C. 753-A.D. 476. Crown 8vo. 7*s.* 6*d.*
- — History of the Romans under the Empire. 8 vols. post 8vo. 48*s.*

Orsi's Recollections of the last Half-Century. Crown 8vo. 7*s.* 6*d.*
Rawlinson's Ancient Egypt. 2 vols. 8vo. 63*s.*
- — Seventh Great Oriental Monarchy—The Sassanians. 8vo. 28*s.*

Seebohm's Oxford Reformers—Colet, Erasmus, & More. 8vo. 14*s.*
Sewell's Popular History of France to the Death of Louis XIV. Crown 8vo. 7*s.* 6*d.*
Short's History of the Church of England. Crown 8vo. 7*s.* 6*d.*
Smith's Carthage and the Carthaginians. Crown 8vo. 10*s.* 6*d.*
Taylor's Manual of the History of India. Crown 8vo. 7*s.* 6*d.*

London, LONGMANS & CO.

Todd's Parliamentary Government in England. 2 vols. 8vo. 37s.
— — — — the British Colonies. 8vo. 21s.
Trench's Realities of Irish Life. Crown 8vo. 2s. 6d.
Trevelyan's Early History of Charles James Fox. Crown 8vo. 6s.
Walpole's History of England, 1815–1841. Vols. I. & II. 8vo. 36s. Vol. III. 18s.

BIOGRAPHICAL WORKS.

Bagehot's Biographical Studies. 1 vol. 8vo. 12s.
Bain's Biography of James Mill. Crown 8vo. Portrait, 5s.
— Criticism and Recollections of J. S. Mill. Crown 8vo. 2s. 6d.
Burke's Vicissitudes of Families. 2 vols. crown 8vo. 21s.
Carlyle's Reminiscences, edited by J. A. Froude. 2 vols. crown 8vo. 18s.
Cates's Dictionary of General Biography. Medium 8vo. 28s.
Froude's Thomas Carlyle, 1795–1835. 2 vols. 8vo. with Portraits and Plates, 32s.
Gleig's Life of the Duke of Wellington. Crown 8vo. 6s.
Jerrold's Life of Napoleon the Third. 4 vols. 8vo. £3. 18s.
Lecky's Leaders of Public Opinion in Ireland. Crown 8vo. 7s. 6d.
Life (The) and Letters of Lord Macaulay. By his Nephew, G. Otto Trevelyan, M.P. Popular Edition, 1 vol. crown 8vo. 6s. Cabinet Edition, 2 vols. post 8vo. 12s. Library Edition, 2 vols. 8vo. 36s.
Marshman's Memoirs of Havelock. Crown 8vo. 3s. 6d.
Memoir of Augustus De Morgan, By his Wife. 8vo.
Mendelssohn's Letters. Translated by Lady Wallace. 2 vols. cr. 8vo. 5s. each.
Mill's (John Stuart) Autobiography. 8vo. 7s. 6d.
Newman's Apologia pro Vitâ Suâ. Crown 8vo. 6s.
Nohl's Life of Mozart. Translated by Lady Wallace. 2 vols. crown 8vo. 21s.
Overton's Life &c. of William Law. 8vo. 15s.
Southey's Correspondence with Caroline Bowles. 8vo. 14s.
Spedding's Letters and Life of Francis Bacon. 7 vols. 8vo. £4. 4s.
Stephen's Essays in Ecclesiastical Biography. Crown 8vo. 7s. 6d.

MENTAL AND POLITICAL PHILOSOPHY.

Amos's View of the Science of Jurisprudence. 8vo. 18s.
— Fifty Years of the English Constitution, 1830–1880. Crown 8vo. 10s. 6d.
— Primer of the English Constitution. Crown 8vo. 6s.
Bacon's Essays, with Annotations by Whately. 8vo. 10s. 6d.
— Works, edited by Spedding. 7 vols. 8vo. 73s. 6d.
Bagehot's Economic Studies, edited by Hutton. 8vo. 10s. 6d.
Bain's Logic, Deductive and Inductive. Crown 8vo. 10s. 6d.
    PART I. Deduction, 4s. | PART II. Induction, 6s. 6d.
Bolland & Lang's Aristotle's Politics. Crown 8vo. 7s. 6d.
Comte's System of Positive Polity, or Treatise upon Sociology. 4 vols. 8vo. £4.
Grant's Ethics of Aristotle; Greek Text, English Notes. 2 vols. 8vo. 32s.
Hodgson's Philosophy of Reflection. 2 vols. 8vo. 21s.
Kalisch's Path and Goal. 8vo. 12s. 6d.
Lewis on Authority in Matters of Opinion. 8vo. 14s.
Leslie's Essays in Political and Moral Philosophy. 8vo. 10s. 6d.
Macaulay's Speeches corrected by Himself. Crown 8vo. 3s. 6d.
Macleod's Economical Philosophy. Vol. I. 8vo. 15s. Vol. II. Part I. 12s.
Mill on Representative Government. Crown 8vo. 2s.

London, LONGMANS & CO.

4 General Lists of New Works.

Mill on Liberty. Post 8vo. 7*s.* 6*d.* Crown 8vo. 1*s.* 4*d.*
Mill's Analysis of the Phenomena of the Human Mind. 2 vols. 8vo. 28*s.*
— Dissertations and Discussions. 4 vols. 8vo. 47*s.*
— Essays on Unsettled Questions of Political Economy. 8vo. 6*s.* 6*d.*
— Examination of Hamilton's Philosophy. 8vo. 16*s.*
— Logic, Ratiocinative and Inductive. 2 vols. 8vo. 25*s.*
— Principles of Political Economy. 2 vols. 8vo. 30*s.* 1 vol. crown 8vo. 5*s.*
— Subjection of Women. Crown 8vo. 6*s.*
— Utilitarianism. 8vo. 5*s.*
Müller's (Max) Chips from a German Workshop. 4 vols. 8vo. 36*s.*
— — Hibbert Lectures on Origin and Growth of Religion. 8vo. 10*s.* 6*d.*
— — Selected Essays on Language, Mythology, and Religion. 2 vols. crown 8vo. 16*s.*
Sandars's Institutes of Justinian, with English Notes. 8vo. 18*s.*
Swinburne's Picture Logic. Post 8vo. 5*s.*
Thomson's Outline of Necessary Laws of Thought. Crown 8vo. 6*s.*
Tocqueville's Democracy in America, translated by Reeve. 2 vols. crown 8vo. 16*s.*
Twiss's Law of Nations, 8vo. in Time of Peace, 12*s.* in Time of War, 21*s.*
Whately's Elements of Logic. 8vo. 10*s.* 6*d.* Crown 8vo. 4*s.* 6*d.*
— — — Rhetoric. 8vo. 10*s.* 6*d.* Crown 8vo. 4*s.* 6*d.*
— English Synonymes. Fcp. 8vo. 3*s.*
Williams's Nicomachean Ethics of Aristotle translated. Crown 8vo. 7*s.* 6*d.*
Zeller's Socrates and the Socratic Schools. Crown 8vo. 10*s.* 6*d.*
— Stoics, Epicureans, and Sceptics. Crown 8vo. 15*s.*
— Plato and the Older Academy. Crown 8vo. 18*s.*
— Pre-Socratic Schools. 2 vols. crown 8vo. 30*s.*

MISCELLANEOUS AND CRITICAL WORKS.

Arnold's (Dr. Thomas) Miscellaneous Works. 8vo. 7*s.* 6*d.*
— (T.) Manual of English Literature. Crown 8vo. 7*s.* 6*d.*
— English Poetry and Prose. Crown 8vo. 7*s.* 6*d.*
Bain's Emotions and the Will. 8vo. 15*s.*
— Mental and Moral Science. Crown 8vo. 10*s.* 6*d.*
— Senses and the Intellect. 8vo. 15*s.*
Beaconsfield (Lord), The Wit and Wisdom of. Crown 8vo. 6*s.*
Becker's *Charicles* and *Gallus*, by Metcalfe. Post 8vo. 7*s.* 6*d.* each.
Brown on the Unicorn. 8vo. 3*s.*
Blackley's German and English Dictionary. Post 8vo. 7*s.* 6*d.*
Contanseau's Practical French & English Dictionary. Post 8vo. 7*s.* 6*d.*
— Pocket French and English Dictionary. Square 18mo. 3*s.* 6*d.*
Farrar's Language and Languages. Crown 8vo. 6*s.*
Froude's Short Studies on Great Subjects. 3 vols. crown 8vo. 18*s.*
German Home Life, reprinted from *Fraser's Magazine.* Crown 8vo. 6*s.*
Hodgson's Outcast Essays and Verse Translations. Crown 8vo. 8*s.* 6*d.*
Hume's Essays, edited by Green & Grose. 2 vols. 8vo. 28*s.*
— Treatise on Human Nature, edited by Green & Grose. 2 vols. 8vo. 28*s.*
Latham's Handbook of the English Language. Crown 8vo. 6*s.*
— English Dictionary. 1 vol. medium 8vo. 14*s.* 4 vols. 4to. £7.
Liddell & Scott's Greek-English Lexicon. Crown 4to. 36*s.*

London, LONGMANS & CO.

Liddell & Scott's Abridged Greek-English Lexicon. Square 12mo. 7*s.* 6*d.*
Longman's Pocket German and English Dictionary. 18mo. 5*s.*
Macaulay's Miscellaneous Writings. 2 vols. 8vo. 21*s.* 1 vol. crown 8vo. 4*s.* 6*d.*
— Miscellaneous Writings and Speeches. Crown 8vo. 6*s.*
— Miscellaneous Writings, Speeches, Lays of Ancient Rome, &c. Cabinet Edition. 4 vols. crown 8vo. 24*s.*
Mahaffy's Classical Greek Literature. Crown 8vo. Vol. I. the Poets, 7*s.* 6*d.* Vol. II. the Prose Writers, 7*s.* 6*d.*
Milner's Country Pleasures. Crown 8vo. 6*s.*
Müller's (Max) Lectures on the Science of Language. 2 vols. crown 8vo. 16*s.*
Owen's Evenings with the Skeptics. 2 vols. 8vo. 32*s.*
Rich's Dictionary of Roman and Greek Antiquities. Crown 8vo. 7*s.* 6*d.*
Rogers's Eclipse of Faith. Fcp. 8vo. 5*s.*
— Defence of the Eclipse of Faith Fcp. 8vo. 3*s.* 6*d.*
Roget's Thesaurus of English Words and Phrases. Crown 8vo. 10*s.* 6*d.*
Savile's Apparitions, a Narrative of Facts. Crown 8vo. 5*s.*
Selections from the Writings of Lord Macaulay. Crown 8vo. 6*s.*
Simcox's Latin Classical Literature. 2 vols. 8vo.
White & Riddle's Large Latin-English Dictionary. 4to. 21*s.*
White's Concise Latin-English Dictionary. Royal 8vo. 12*s.*
— Junior Student's Lat.-Eng. and Eng.-Lat. Dictionary. Square 12mo. 12*s.*
Separately { The English-Latin Dictionary, 5*s.* 6*d.* The Latin-English Dictionary, 7*s.* 6*d.*
Wilson's Studies of Modern Mind &c. 8vo. 12*s.*
Wit and Wisdom of the Rev. Sydney Smith. 16mo. 3*s.* 6*d.*
Yonge's English-Greek Lexicon. Square 12mo. 8*s.* 6*d.* 4to. 21*s.*
The Essays and Contributions of A. K. H. B. Crown 8vo.
    Autumn Holidays of a Country Parson. 3*s.* 6*d.*
    Changed Aspects of Unchanged Truths. 3*s.* 6*d.*
    Common-place Philosopher in Town and Country. 3*s.* 6*d.*
    Counsel and Comfort spoken from a City Pulpit. 3*s.* 6*d.*
    Critical Essays of a Country Parson. 3*s.* 6*d.*
    Graver Thoughts of a Country Parson. Three Series, 3*s.* 6*d.* each.
    Landscapes, Churches, and Moralities. 3*s.* 6*d.*
    Leisure Hours in Town. 3*s.* 6*d.* Lessons of Middle Age. 3*s.* 6*d.*
    Our Little Life. Essays Consolatory and Domestic. 3*s.* 6*d.*
    Present-day Thoughts. 3*s.* 6*d.*
    Recreations of a Country Parson. Three Series, 3*s.* 6*d.* each.
    Seaside Musings on Sundays and Week-Days. 3*s.* 6*d.*
    Sunday Afternoons in the Parish Church of a University City. 3*s.* 6*d.*

ASTRONOMY, METEOROLOGY, GEOGRAPHY &c.

Freeman's Historical Geography of Europe. 2 vols. 8vo. 31*s.* 6*d.*
Herschel's Outlines of Astronomy. Square crown 8vo. 12*s.*
Keith Johnston's Dictionary of Geography, or General Gazetteer. 8vo. 42*s.*
Nelson's Work on the Moon. Medium 8vo. 31*s.* 6*d.*
Proctor's Essays on Astronomy. 8vo. 12*s.* Proctor's Moon. Crown 8vo. 10*s.* 6*d.*
— Larger Star Atlas. Folio, 15*s.* or Maps only, 12*s.* 6*d.*
— New Star Atlas. Crown 8vo. 5*s.* Orbs Around Us. Crown 8vo. 7*s.* 6*d.*
— Other Worlds than Ours. Crown 8vo. 10*s.* 6*d.*
— Sun. Crown 8vo. 14*s.* Universe of Stars. 8vo. 10*s.* 6*d.*
Smith's Air and Rain. 8vo. 24*s.*

London, LONGMANS & CO.

The Public Schools Atlas of Ancient Geography. Imperial 8vo. 7s. 6d.
— — — Atlas of Modern Geography. Imperial 8vo. 5s.
Webb's Celestial Objects for Common Telescopes. Crown 8vo. 9s.

NATURAL HISTORY & POPULAR SCIENCE.

Arnott's Elements of Physics or Natural Philosophy. Crown 8vo. 12s. 6d.
Brande's Dictionary of Science, Literature, and Art. 3 vols. medium 8vo. 63s.
Decaisne and Le Maout's General System of Botany. Imperial 8vo. 31s. 6d.
Dixon's Rural Bird Life. Crown 8vo. Illustrations, 7s. 6d.
Evans's Bronze Implements &c. of Great Britain. 8vo. 25s.
Ganot's Elementary Treatise on Physics, by Atkinson. Large crown 8vo. 15s.
— Natural Philosophy, by Atkinson. Crown 8vo. 7s. 6d.
Goodeve's Elements of Mechanism. Crown 8vo. 6s.
Grove's Correlation of Physical Forces. 8vo. 15s.
Hartwig's Aerial World. 8vo. 10s. 6d. Polar World. 8vo. 10s. 6d.
— Sea and its Living Wonders. 8vo. 10s. 6d.
— Subterranean World. 8vo. 10s. 6d. Tropical World. 8vo. 10s. 6d.
Haughton's Six Lectures on Physical Geography. 8vo. 15s.
Heer's Primæval World of Switzerland. 2 vols. 8vo. 12s.
Helmholtz's Lectures on Scientific Subjects. 2 vols. cr. 8vo. 7s. 6d. each.
Hullah's Lectures on the History of Modern Music. 8vo. 8s. 6d.
— Transition Period of Musical History. 8vo. 10s. 6d.
Keller's Lake Dwellings of Switzerland, by Lee. 2 vols. royal 8vo. 42s.
Lee's Note Book of an Amateur Geologist. 8vo. 21s.
Lloyd's Treatise on Magnetism. 8vo. 10s. 6d.
— — on the Wave-Theory of Light. 8vo. 10s. 6d.
Loudon's Encyclopædia of Plants. 8vo. 42s.
Lubbock on the Origin of Civilisation & Primitive Condition of Man. 8vo. 18s.
Macalister's Zoology and Morphology of Vertebrate Animals. 8vo. 10s. 6d.
Nicols' Puzzle of Life. Crown 8vo. 3s. 6d.
Owen's Comparative Anatomy and Physiology of the Vertebrate Animals. 3 vols. 8vo. 73s. 6d.
Proctor's Light Science for Leisure Hours. 2 vols. crown 8vo. 7s. 6d. each.
Rivers's Orchard House. Sixteenth Edition. Crown 8vo. 5s.
— Rose Amateur's Guide. Fcp. 8vo. 4s. 6d.
Stanley's Familiar History of British Birds. Crown 8vo. 6s.
Text-Books of Science, Mechanical and Physical.
  Abney's Photography, 3s. 6d.
  Anderson's (Sir John) Strength of Materials, 3s. 6d.
  Armstrong's Organic Chemistry, 3s. 6d.
  Ball's Astronomy, 6s.
  Barry's Railway Appliances, 3s. 6d. Bloxam's Metals, 3s. 6d.
  Bauerman's Systematic Mineralogy, 6s.
  Goodeve's Principles of Mechanics, 3s. 6d.
  Gore's Electro-Metallurgy, 6s.
  Griffin's Algebra and Trigonometry, 3s. 6d.
  Jenkin's Electricity and Magnetism, 3s. 6d.
  Maxwell's Theory of Heat, 3s. 6d.
  Merrifield's Technical Arithmetic and Mensuration, 3s. 6d.
  Miller's Inorganic Chemistry, 3s. 6d.
  Preece & Sivewright's Telegraphy, 3s. 6d.

London, LONGMANS & CO.

Text-Books of Science, Mechanical and Physical—*continued.*
Rutley's Study of Rocks, 4*s.* 6*d.*
Shelley's Workshop Appliances, 3*s.* 6*d.*
Thomé's Structural and Physiological Botany, 6*s.*
Thorpe's Quantitative Chemical Analysis, 4*s.* 6*d.*
Thorpe & Muir's Qualitative Analysis, 3*s.* 6*d.*
Tilden's Chemical Philosophy, 3*s.* 6*d.*
Unwin's Machine Design, 3*s.* 6*d.*
Watson's Plane and Solid Geometry, 3*s.* 6*d.*
Tyndall on Sound. New Edition in the press.
Tyndall's Floating Matter of the Air. Crown 8vo. 7*s.* 6*d.*
— Fragments of Science. 2 vols. post 8vo. 16*s.*
— Heat a Mode of Motion. Crown 8vo. 12*s.*
— Notes on Electrical Phenomena. Crown 8vo. 1*s.* sewed, 1*s.* 6*d.* cloth.
— Notes of Lectures on Light. Crown 8vo. 1*s.* sewed, 1*s.* 6*d.* cloth.
— Lectures on Light delivered in America. Crown 8vo. 7*s.* 6*d.*
— Lessons in Electricity. Crown 8vo. 2*s.* 6*d.*
Von Cotta on Rocks, by Lawrence. Post 8vo. 14*s.*
Woodward's Geology of England and Wales. Crown 8vo. 14*s.*
Wood's Bible Animals. With 112 Vignettes. 8vo. 14*s.*
— Homes Without Hands. 8vo. 14*s.* Insects Abroad. 8vo. 14*s.*
— Insects at Home. With 700 Illustrations. 8vo. 14*s.*
— Out of Doors. Crown 8vo. 7*s.* 6*d.*
— Strange Dwellings. Crown 8vo. 7*s.* 6*d.* Popular Edition, 4to. 6*d.*

CHEMISTRY & PHYSIOLOGY.

Buckton's Health in the House, Lectures on Elementary Physiology. Cr. 8vo. 2*s.*
Jago's Practical Inorganic Chemistry. Fcp. 8vo. 2*s.*
Miller's Elements of Chemistry, Theoretical and Practical. 3 vols. 8vo. Part I. Chemical Physics, 16*s.* Part II. Inorganic Chemistry, 24*s.* Part III. Organic Chemistry, price 31*s.* 6*d.*
Reynolds's Experimental Chemistry, Part I. fcp. 8vo. 1*s.* 6*d.* Part II. 2*s.* 6*d.*
Thudichum's Annals of Chemical Medicine. Vols. I. & II. 8vo. 14*s.* each.
Tilden's Practical Chemistry. Fcp. 8vo. 1*s.* 6*d.*
Watts's Dictionary of Chemistry. 7 vols. medium 8vo. £10. 16*s.* 6*d.*
— Third Supplementary Volume, in Two Parts. PART I. 36*s.* PART II. 50*s.*

THE FINE ARTS & ILLUSTRATED EDITIONS.

Dresser's Arts and Art Industries of Japan. [*In preparation.*
Jameson's Sacred and Legendary Art. 6 vols. square crown 8vo.
Legends of the Madonna. 1 vol. 21*s.*
— — — Monastic Orders. 1 vol. 21*s.*
— — — Saints and Martyrs. 2 vols. 31*s.* 6*d.*
— — — Saviour. Completed by Lady Eastlake. 2 vols. 42*s.*
Longman's Three Cathedrals Dedicated to St. Paul. Square crown 8vo. 21*s.*
Macaulay's Lays of Ancient Rome, illustrated by Scharf. Fcp. 4to. 21*s.* imp. 16mo. 10*s.* 6*d.*
— — — illustrated by Weguelin. Crown 8vo. 6*s.*
Macfarren's Lectures on Harmony. 8vo. 12*s.*
Moore's Irish Melodies. With 161 Plates by D. Maclise, R.A. Super-royal 8vo. 21*s.*
— Lalla Rookh, illustrated by Tenniel. Square crown 8vo. 10*s.* 6*d.*
Perry on Greek and Roman Sculpture. With 280 Illustrations engraved on Wood. Square crown 8vo. 31*s.* 6*d.*

London, LONGMANS & CO.

THE USEFUL ARTS, MANUFACTURES, &c.

Barry & Bramwell's Railways and Locomotives. 8vo. 21s.
Bourne's Catechism of the Steam Engine. Fcp. 8vo. 6s.
— Examples of Steam, Air, and Gas Engines. 4to. 70s.
— Handbook of the Steam Engine. Fcp. 8vo. 9s.
— Recent Improvements in the Steam Engine. Fcp. 8vo. 6s.
— Treatise on the Steam Engine. 4to. 42s.
Brassey's British Navy, in 6 vols. 8vo. with many Illustrations. Vol. I. Shipbuilding for the Purposes of War, 10s. 6d. Vol. II. Miscellaneous Papers on the same subject, 3s. 6d.
Cresy's Encyclopædia of Civil Engineering. 8vo. 25s.
Culley's Handbook of Practical Telegraphy. 8vo. 16s.
Eastlake's Household Taste in Furniture, &c. Square crown 8vo. 14s.
Fairbairn's Useful Information for Engineers. 3 vols. crown 8vo. 31s. 6d.
— Applications of Cast and Wrought Iron. 8vo. 16s.
— Mills and Millwork. 1 vol. 8vo. 25s.
Gwilt's Encyclopædia of Architecture. 8vo. 52s. 6d.
Hoskold's Engineer's Valuing Assistant. 8vo. 31s. 6d.
Kerl's Metallurgy, adapted by Crookes and Röhrig. 3 vols. 8vo. £4. 19s.
Loudon's Encyclopædia of Agriculture. 8vo. 21s.
— — — Gardening. 8vo. 21s.
Mitchell's Manual of Practical Assaying. 8vo. 31s. 6d.
Northcott's Lathes and Turning. 8vo. 18s.
Payen's Industrial Chemistry Edited by B. H. Paul, Ph.D. 8vo. 42s.
Piesse's Art of Perfumery. Fourth Edition. Square crown 8vo. 21s.
Sennett's Treatise on the Marine Steam Engine. 8vo. 21s.
Stoney's Theory of Strains in Girders. Royal 8vo. 36s.
Ure's Dictionary of Arts, Manufactures, & Mines. 4 vols. medium 8vo. £7. 7s.
Ville on Artificial Manures. By Crookes. 8vo. 21s.

RELIGIOUS & MORAL WORKS.

Abbey & Overton's English Church in the Eighteenth Century. 2 vols. 8vo. 36s.
Arnold's (Rev. Dr. Thomas) Sermons. 6 vols. crown 8vo. 5s. each.
Bishop Jeremy Taylor's Entire Works. With Life by Bishop Heber. Edited by the Rev. C. P. Eden. 10 vols. 8vo. £5. 5s.
Boultbee's Commentary on the 39 Articles. Crown 8vo. 6s.
— History of the Church of England, Pre-Reformation Period. 8vo. 15s.
Browne's (Bishop) Exposition of the 39 Articles. 8vo. 16s.
Colenso's Lectures on the Pentateuch and the Moabite Stone. 8vo. 12s.
Colenso on the Pentateuch and Book of Joshua. Crown 8vo. 6s.
— — Part VII. completion of the larger Work. 8vo. 24s.
Conder's Handbook of the Bible. Post 8vo. 7s. 6d.
Conybeare & Howson's Life and Letters of St. Paul :—
   Library Edition, with all the Original Illustrations, Maps, Landscapes on Steel, Woodcuts, &c. 2 vols. 4to. 42s.
   Intermediate Edition, with a Selection of Maps, Plates, and Woodcuts. 2 vols. square crown 8vo. 21s.
   Student's Edition, revised and condensed, with 46 Illustrations and Maps. 1 vol. crown 8vo. 7s. 6d.
Creighton's History of the Papacy during the Reformation. 2 vols. 8vo.

London, LONGMANS & CO.

Davidson's Introduction to the Study of the New Testament. 2 vols. 8vo. 30s.
Ellicott's (Bishop) Commentary on St. Paul's Epistles. 8vo. Galatians, 8s. 6d.
Ephesians, 8s. 6d. Pastoral Epistles, 10s. 6d. Philippians, Colossians, and
Philemon, 10s. 6d. Thessalonians, 7s. 6d.
Ellicott's Lectures on the Life of our Lord. 8vo. 12s.
Ewald's History of Israel, translated by Carpenter. 5 vols. 8vo. 63s.
— Antiquities of Israel, translated by Solly. 8vo. 12s. 6d.
Gospel (The) for the Nineteenth Century. 4th Edition. 8vo. 10s. 6d.
Hopkins's Christ the Consoler. Fcp. 8vo. 2s. 6d.
Jukes's New Man and the Eternal Life. Crown 8vo. 6s.
— Second Death and the Restitution of all Things. Crown 8vo. 3s. 6d.
— Types of Genesis. Crown 8vo. 7s. 6d.
Kalisch's Bible Studies. PART I. the Prophecies of Balaam. 8vo. 10s. 6d.
— — — PART II. the Book of Jonah. 8vo. 10s. 6d.
— Historical and Critical Commentary on the Old Testament; with a
New Translation. Vol. I. *Genesis*, 8vo. 18s. or adapted for the General
Reader, 12s. Vol. II. *Exodus*, 15s. or adapted for the General Reader, 12s.
Vol. III. *Leviticus*, Part I. 15s. or adapted for the General Reader, 8s.
Vol. IV. *Leviticus*, Part II. 15s. or adapted for the General Reader, 8s.
Lyra Germanica: Hymns translated by Miss Winkworth. Fcp. 8vo. 5s.
Martineau's Endeavours after the Christian Life. Crown 8vo. 7s. 6d.
— Hymns of Praise and Prayer. Crown 8vo. 4s. 6d. 32mo. 1s. 6d.
— Sermons, Hours of Thought on Sacred Things. 2 vols. 7s. 6d. each.
Mill's Three Essays on Religion. 8vo. 10s. 6d.
Monsell's Spiritual Songs for Sundays and Holidays. Fcp. 8vo. 5s. 18mo. 2s.
Müller's (Max) Lectures on the Science of Religion. Crown 8vo. 10s. 6d.
Newman's Apologia pro Vitâ Suâ. Crown 8vo. 6s.
Passing Thoughts on Religion. By Miss Sewell. Fcp. 8vo. 3s. 6d.
Sewell's (Miss) Preparation for the Holy Communion. 32mo. 3s.
— — Private Devotions for Young Persons. 18mo. 2s.
Smith's Voyage and Shipwreck of St. Paul. Crown 8vo. 7s. 6d.
Supernatural Religion. Complete Edition. 3 vols. 8vo. 36s.
Thoughts for the Age. By Miss Sewell. Fcp. 8vo. 3s. 6d.
Whately's Lessons on the Christian Evidences. 18mo. 6d.
White's Four Gospels in Greek, with Greek-English Lexicon. 32mo. 5s.

TRAVELS, VOYAGES, &c.

Baker's Rifle and Hound in Ceylon. Crown 8vo. 7s. 6d.
— Eight Years in Ceylon. Crown 8vo. 7s. 6d.
Ball's Alpine Guide. 3 vols. post 8vo. with Maps and Illustrations:—I. Western
Alps, 6s. 6d. II. Central Alps, 7s. 6d. III. Eastern Alps, 10s. 6d.
Ball on Alpine Travelling, and on the Geology of the Alps, 1s.
Brassey's Sunshine and Storm in the East. Crown 8vo. 7s. 6d.
— Voyage in the Yacht 'Sunbeam.' Crown 8vo. 7s. 6d. School Edition,
fcp. 8vo. 2s. Popular Edition, 4to. 6d.
Hassall's San Remo and the Western Riviera. Crown 8vo. 10s. 6d.
Macnamara's Medical Geography of India. 8vo. 21s.
Miller's Wintering in the Riviera. Post 8vo. Illustrations, 7s. 6d.

London, LONGMANS & CO.

Packe's Guide to the Pyrenees, for Mountaineers. Crown 8vo. 7s. 6d.
The Alpine Club Map of Switzerland. In Four Sheets. 42s.
Three in Norway. By Two of Them. Crown 8vo. Illustrations.
Weld's Sacred Palmlands. Crown 8vo. 10s. 6d.

WORKS OF FICTION.

Buried Alive, Ten Years of Penal Servitude in Siberia. Crown 8vo. 6s.
Cabinet Edition of Novels and Tales by the Right Hon. the Earl of Beaconsfield, K.G. 11 vols. crown 8vo. price 6s. each.
Cabinet Edition of Stories and Tales by Miss Sewell. Crown 8vo. cloth extra, gilt edges, price 3s. 6d. each :—

Amy Herbert. Cleve Hall.
The Earl's Daughter.
Experience of Life.
Gertrude. Ivors.
Katharine Ashton.
Laneton Parsonage.
Margaret Percival.
Ursula.

Novels and Tales by the Right Hon. the Earl of Beaconsfield, K.G. Hughenden Edition, with 2 Portraits engraved on Steel and 11 Vignettes engraved on Wood. 11 vols. crown 8vo. price £2. 2s.

Lothair. Coningsby.
Sybil. Tancred.
Venetia. Henrietta Temple.
Vivian Grey. Endymion.
Contarini Fleming.
Alroy, Ixion, &c.
The Young Duke, &c.

The Modern Novelist's Library. Each Work in crown 8vo. A Single Volume, complete in itself, price 2s. boards, or 2s. 6d. cloth :—

By the Earl of Beaconsfield, K.G.
Lothair.
Coningsby.
Sybil.
Tancred.
Venetia.
Henrietta Temple.
Contarini Fleming.
Alroy, Ixion, &c.
The Young Duke, &c.
Vivian Grey.
Endymion.
By Anthony Trollope.
Barchester Towers.
The Warden.
By the Author of 'the Rose Garden.'
Unawares.

By Major Whyte-Melville.
Digby Grand.
General Bounce.
Kate Coventry.
The Gladiators.
Good for Nothing.
Holmby House.
The Interpreter.
The Queen's Maries.
By the Author of 'the Atelier du Lys.'
Mademoiselle Mori.
The Atelier du Lys.
By Various Writers.
Atherstone Priory.
The Burgomaster's Family.
Elsa and her Vulture.
The Six Sisters of the Valleys.

Novels and Tales by the Right Hon. the Earl of Beaconsfield, K.G. Modern Novelist's Library Edition, complete in 11 vols. crown 8vo. price £1. 13s. cloth extra, with gilt edges.

Whispers from Fairy Land. By the Right Hon. Lord Brabourne. With Nine Illustrations. Crown 8vo. 3s. 6d.

Higgledy-Piggledy; or, Stories for Everybody and Everybody's Children. By the Right Hon. Lord Brabourne. With Nine Illustrations from Designs by R. Doyle. Crown 8vo. 3s. 6d.

POETRY & THE DRAMA.

Bailey's Festus, a Poem. Crown 8vo. 12s. 6d.
Bowdler's Family Shakspeare. Medium 8vo. 14s. 6 vols. fcp. 8vo. 21s.
Cayley's Iliad of Homer, Homometrically translated. 8vo. 12s. 6d.

London, LONGMANS & CO.

General Lists of New Works. 11

Conington's Æneid of Virgil, translated into English Verse. Crown 8vo. 9s.
Goethe's Faust, translated by Birds. Large crown 8vo. 12s. 6d.
— — translated by Webb. 8vo. 12s. 6d.
— — edited by Selss. Crown 8vo. 5s.
Ingelow's Poems. New Edition. 2 vols. fcp. 8vo. 12s.
Macaulay's Lays of Ancient Rome, with Ivry and the Armada. 16mo. 3s. 6d.
The same, Cheap Edition, fcp. 8vo. 1s. sewed, 1s. 6d. cloth.
Moore's Poetical Works, 1 vol. ruby type. Post 8vo. 6s.
Ormsby's Poem of the Cid. Translated. Post 8vo. 5s.
Southey's Poetical Works. Medium 8vo. 14s.

RURAL SPORTS, HORSE & CATTLE MANAGEMENT &c.

Blaine's Encyclopædia of Rural Sports. 8vo. 21s.
Fitzwygram's Horses and Stables. 8vo. 10s. 6d.
Francis's Treatise on Fishing in all its Branches. Post 8vo. 15s.
Horses and Roads. By Free-Lance. Crown 8vo. 6s.
Miles's Horse's Foot, and How to Keep it Sound. Imperial 8vo. 12s. 6d.
— Plain Treatise on Horse-Shoeing. Post 8vo. 2s. 6d.
— Stables and Stable-Fittings. Imperial 8vo. 15s.
— Remarks on Horses' Teeth. Post 8vo. 1s. 6d.
Milner's Country Pleasures. Crown 8vo. 6s.
Nevile's Horses and Riding. Crown 8vo. 6s.
Ronalds's Fly-Fisher's Entomology. 8vo. 14s.
Steel's Diseases of the Ox, being a Manual of Bovine Pathology. 8vo. 15s.
Stonehenge's Dog in Health and Disease. Square crown 8vo. 7s. 6d.
— Greyhound. Square crown 8vo. 15s.
Youatt's Work on the Dog. 8vo. 6s.
— — — Horse. 8vo. 7s. 6d.
Wilcocks's Sea-Fisherman. Post 8vo. 12s. 6d.

WORKS OF UTILITY & GENERAL INFORMATION.

Acton's Modern Cookery for Private Families. Fcp. 8vo. 6s.
Black's Practical Treatise on Brewing. 8vo. 10s. 6d.
Buckton's Food and Home Cookery. Crown 8vo. 2s.
Bull on the Maternal Management of Children. Fcp. 8vo. 2s. 6d.
Bull's Hints to Mothers on the Management of their Health during the Period of Pregnancy and in the Lying-in Room. Fcp. 8vo. 2s. 6d.
Campbell-Walker's Correct Card, or How to Play at Whist. Fcp. 8vo. 2s. 6d.
Edwards on the Ventilation of Dwelling-Houses. Royal 8vo. 10s. 6d.
Johnson's (W. & J. H.) Patentee's Manual. Fourth Edition. 8vo. 10s. 6d.
Johnston's Land Law Ireland Act. Crown 8vo. 1s.
Longman's Chess Openings. Fcp. 8vo. 2s. 6d.
Macleod's Economics for Beginners. Small crown 8vo. 2s. 6d.
— Elements of Economics. 2 vols. small crown 8vo. VOL. I. 7s. 6d.
— Theory and Practice of Banking. 2 vols. 8vo. 26s.
— Elements of Banking. Fourth Edition. Crown 8vo. 5s.
M'Culloch's Dictionary of Commerce and Commercial Navigation. 8vo. 63s.

London, LONGMANS & CO.

Maunder's Biographical Treasury. Fcp. 8vo. 6s.
— Historical Treasury. Fcp. 8vo. 6s.
— Scientific and Literary Treasury. Fcp. 8vo. 6s.
— Treasury of Bible Knowledge, edited by Ayre. Fcp. 8vo. 6s.
— Treasury of Botany, edited by Lindley & Moore. Two Parts, 12s.
— Treasury of Geography. Fcp. 8vo. 6s.
— Treasury of Knowledge and Library of Reference. Fcp. 8vo. 6s.
— Treasury of Natural History. Fcp. 8vo. 6s.
Pereira's Materia Medica, by Bentley and Redwood. 8vo. 25s.
Powtner's Comprehensive Specifier; Building-Artificers' Work. Crown 8vo. 6s.
Pole's Theory of the Modern Scientific Game of Whist. Fcp. 8vo. 2s. 6d.
Quain's Dictionary of Medicine. 1 vol. 8vo. *in the press.*
Reader's Time Tables. Third Edition. Crown 8vo. 7s. 6d.
Scott's Farm Valuer. Crown 8vo. 5s.
— Rents and Purchases. Crown 8vo. 6s.
Smith's Handbook for Midwives. Crown 8vo. 5s.
The Cabinet Lawyer, a Popular Digest of the Laws of England. Fcp. 8vo. 9s.
West on the Diseases of Infancy and Childhood. 8vo. 18s.
Willich's Popular Tables, by Marriott. Crown 8vo. 10s.
Wilson on Banking Reform. 8vo. 7s. 6d.
— on the Resources of Modern Countries 2 vols. 8vo. 24s.

MUSICAL WORKS BY JOHN HULLAH, LL.D.

Hullah's Method of Teaching Singing. Crown 8vo. 2s. 6d.
Exercises and Figures in the same. Crown 8vo. 1s. sewed, or 1s. 2d. limp cloth; or 2 Parts, 6d. each sewed, or 8d. each limp cloth.
Large Sheets, containing the 'Exercises and Figures in Hullah's Method,' in Two Parcels of Eight, price 6s. each.
Chromatic Scale, with the Inflected Syllables, on Large Sheet. 1s. 6d.
Card of Chromatic Scale. 1d.
Grammar of Musical Harmony. Royal 8vo. price 3s. sewed and 4s. 6d. cloth; or in 2 Parts, each 1s. 6d.
Exercises to Grammar of Musical Harmony. 1s.
Grammar of Counterpoint. Part I. super-royal 8vo. 2s. 6d.
Wilhem's Manual of Singing. Parts I. & II. 2s. 6d. or together, 5s.
Exercises and Figures contained in Parts I. and II. of Wilhem's Manual. Books I. & II. each 8d.
Large Sheets, Nos. 1 to 8, containing the Figures in Part I. of Wilhem's Manual, in a Parcel, 6s.
Large Sheets, Nos. 9 to 40, containing the Exercises in Part I. of Wilhem's Manual, in Four Parcels of Eight Nos. each, per Parcel, 6s.
Large Sheets, Nos. 41 to 52, containing the Figures in Part II. in a Parcel, 9s.
Hymns for the Young, set to Music. Royal 8vo. 8d. sewed, or 1s. 6d. cloth.
Infant School Songs. 6d.
Notation, the Musical Alphabet. Crown 8vo. 6d.
Old English Songs for Schools, Harmonised. 6d.
Rudiments of Musical Grammar. Royal 8vo. 3s.
School Songs for 2 and 3 Voices. 2 Books, 8vo. each 6d.
A Short Treatise on the Stave. 2s.
Lectures on the History of Modern Music. 8vo. 8s. 6d.
Lectures on the Transition Period of Musical History. 8vo. 10s. 6d.

London, LONGMANS & CO.

Spottiswoode & Co. Printers, New-street Square, London.

www.ingramcontent.com/pod-product-compliance
Lightning Source LLC
Chambersburg PA
CBHW020101020526
44112CB00032B/803